Danish Modern

Danish Modern

Between Art and Design

Mark Mussari

Bloomsbury Academic
An imprint of Bloomsbury Publishing Plc

B L O O M S B U R Y
LONDON • OXFORD • NEW YORK • NEW DELHI • SYDNEY

Bloomsbury Academic

An imprint of Bloomsbury Publishing Plc

50 Bedford Square	1385 Broadway
London	New York
WC1B 3DP	NY 10018
UK	USA

www.bloomsbury.com

BLOOMSBURY and the Diana logo are trademarks of Bloomsbury Publishing Plc

First published 2016

British Library Cataloguing-in-Publication Data
A catalogue record for this book is available from the British Library.

ISBN:	HB:	978-1-4742-2370-6
	PB:	978-1-4742-2372-0
	ePDF:	978-1-4742-2369-0
	ePub:	978-1-4742-2368-3

Library of Congress Cataloging-in-Publication Data
Mussari, Mark, author.
Danish modern : between art and design / Mark Mussari. – 1st [edition].
pages cm
ISBN 978-1-4742-2370-6 (hardback) — ISBN 978-1-4742-2372-0 (paperback)
1. Modernism (Aesthetics)—Denmark.   2. Design—Denmark—History—20th century.   I. Title.
BH301.M54M87 2016
745.409489'0904—dc23
2015035977

Cover image: Arne Jacobsen at Asbjøm Møbler: Aeg (Egg) Chair, June 1963.
Courtesy of www.danish-modern.co.uk

Typeset by RefineCatch Limited, Bungay, Suffolk

In memory of Anne and Knud Koefoed

Contents

Illustrations

Acknowledgements

I would like to thank Nils Frederiksen, Designmuseum Danmark, for his invaluable help and support throughout the writing of this book and Michael Sheridan for his help in obtaining certain visuals for the project. Thanks also to Jørgen Strüwing and Jan Helmer-Petersen for their generosity, and to Rina Troxler at Verner Panton Design and Katja Kejser Pedersen at PP Møbler. A special thank you to Marianne Wegner at Hans J Wegner's Design Studio for her help and input.

I am also grateful to David Brody, Parsons School of Design, for all his support, suggestions, and comments since this project's inception. Special thanks also goes to Marianne Stecher, the University of Washington, for her friendship and support throughout the years.

Two Danish books, one mammoth and one condensed, have been especially inspiring to my own research. Per H. Hansen's *Da danske møbler blev moderne* (*When Danish Furniture Became Modern*, 2006), which I had the fortune of translating, offers the most thorough history of the efforts to brand and market Danish design in the mid-twentieth century and of the Copenhagen Cabinetmakers Guild and their wrangling to maintain authority in that challenging time. Viggo Sten Møller's *Funktionalisme og brugskunst* (*Functionalism and Applied Arts*, 1973) is a compact book that takes a more pan-Nordic look at developments in Modern design while offering a rare selection of quotes from speeches and publications contributing to mid-century design developments throughout Scandinavia.

Thank you also to Jen Mussari and to my former design history students Cyrus Ahmadi, Sebastian Campos-Alvarez, Chelsea Chun, Amanda Taylor, and Brendan Rice for useful discussions and commentary on all matters involving design.

Finally, I could not have written this book without the love and support of Peter S. Dillard. Our ongoing discussions about art and philosophy, particularly over tea at Seven Cups, were a constant source of inspiration.

Mark Mussari

Note on translations

As a professional translator, I am acutely aware of the importance of using source material in its original language. Therefore, wherever possible I have used the original language sources for any quotations and, except where indicated with another translator's name in notes, supplied my own translations.

Introduction: Subject and Object

Danish Modern. Say the words and many people conjure up images of sleek teakwood furniture from the 1950s and 1960s. Maybe they think of the stylized offices in the AMC television series *Mad Men* (first set in 1959), where for the first few seasons a pair of teak and cane chairs (1953) by the Danish designers Peter Hvidt and Orla Mølgaard-Nielsen sat in Don Draper's fictitious advertising office. Symbols of the character's ascendance in the burgeoning American consumer culture of the 1950s, the chairs would be replaced after two seasons by more Op-art designs, including another Dane's work: Poul M. Volther's upholstered and chromium-steel Corona Chair (1964). Some might vaguely recall a magazine advertisement with a model (Christine Keeler) straddled on one of Arne Jacobsen's curvaceous Seven chairs (actually, a knockoff of his irrepressible design), or the images of his Swan and Egg chairs that continue to surface in advertisements, television shows, and films more than half a century after the designs' introduction.

Danish Modern is not simply an exercise in nostalgia, however. Countless websites, home magazines, upscale design stores, and auction houses continue to proffer images of Danish design 'classics' either still being produced, like the works of Jacobsen, or of vintage pieces that have become collector's items demanding astronomical prices. An original Chieftain Chair – designed by Finn Juhl in 1949 – sold in 2013 for £422,500 (about $669,000) at Philips auction house in London. In 2014, the centennial of Hans J. Wegner's birth resulted in new retrospective exhibitions and career-encompassing publications. Furnishings designed decades ago by Danes but long out of production, or only produced in prototypes, have gone into production recently, each one heralded as a return to form. Chairs designed more than forty years ago by Grete Jalk, Wegner, and Jacobsen are finally on the market. The pages of design publications such as *Wallpaper* and *Interior Design* are rife with contemporary variations on Wegner's Wishbone and Jacobsen's Egg. In 2014, *Wallpaper*'s annual Design Awards included one for the Metropolitan, a chair designed in 1959 by Ejner Larsen and Aksel Bender Madsen. Annual furniture fairs, like those held in Cologne, continue to showcase names etched into the annals of mid-twentieth-century Modernism: Eames, Henningsen, and Jacobsen. In Denmark, the weight of the legacy of these designers rests heavily on many contemporary Danish designers still struggling to get out from under the enormous burden of what the Danes call '*de tunge drenge*' (the big boys – and girls).

On this level, time has not diminished the relevance of Danish design, especially that created in the middle of the last century, but it has altered both articulation and reception of it. A 2014 article in the *New York Times* on streaming classical music featured an illustration of an effete-looking man – complete with pencil-thin moustache and top hat, looking like someone in the 1930s – holding a remote, facing a flat-screen television, and sitting in an Egg Chair.[1] Whereas the man's personal style and accoutrements look dated, the Egg Chair seems surprisingly at home with the flat-screen TV. People can still buy a brand new Finn Juhl 45-Chair, designed in 1945 and originally executed by the cabinetmaker Niels Vodder, but today it will cost them about $11,000 at Design Within Reach. The company has built its reputation on marketing designers, especially those from the mid-twentieth century, as icons: each store features a wall with pictures of Harry Bertoia, Florence Knoll, Mies van der Rohe, Greta Magnusson Grossman, Charles and Ray Eames, Le Corbusier – and all of those ubiquitous Danish *'tunge drenge.'*

Still, the trajectory of Danish Modern's success has been anything but consistent. Following its heyday on the international stage in the 1950s and 1960s, Danish home furnishings fell victim to changing global tastes, especially in Europe and the United States. The ebb and flow of advertising and the undeniably fickle nature of 'style' worked against the more normative efforts of Danish design. A number of concepts have attended Danish design for decades, among them the idea that the furniture would be 'healthier' to live with and that it was more 'democratic' in both intention and execution. Still, it is naïve to think that consumers worldwide were buying modern Danish furnishings because they thought these items were healthier for their lifestyle or more democratic. While these early modernist goals may have been catalysts to the creation of some Danish designs, just as they were catalysts to many modernist designs in other countries, they are not notions that ever drove most world citizens to purchase products of Danish design.

Instead, in time, the very idea of Danish Modern fit snugly into the booming post-war economy and more sophisticated and increasingly international sense among many people, mostly in the educated upper middle class, in the mid-twentieth century, especially in the United States where it was easy to market Danish design to these consumers. Whereas the social endeavours that attended much of early Modern design in Denmark (and elsewhere) never actually transferred to international sales, by the 1950s the American market had been aesthetically primed by public abstract art, popular domestic modernist furniture lines (such as those by Knoll and Herman Miller), and biomorphic shapes in textile designs and home furnishings. More importantly, however, visually Danish Modern represented a break with the traditional past: design-wise, Danish furnishings were often a rejection of Victorian, Colonial, and other historical influences, especially the pseudo-historical use of ornamentation. In comparison, Danish Modern was pared-down, smaller in scale, and uncluttered with unnecessary ornament: on this front, the movement shared qualities with the efforts of the Bauhaus designers who had embraced the Austrian Alfred Loos's vehement rejection of ornamentation. Yet, thanks in great part to an early emphasis on wood and a theoretical resistance to certain modernist currents by influential designers, the term Danish Modern has, over time, avoided associations with cold industrialization and machine aesthetics. Its early marketers were wise enough to seize upon that aspect and utilize it in constructing a useful and surprisingly enduring narrative, but can a marketing narrative constructed over half a century ago be the only source of any design's longevity? In 2004, the Museum of Modern Art in New York underwent a massive renovation that included replacing 95 per cent of its furnishings in public spaces with Danish furniture, glass, and utensils, mostly from mid-century designers, to the tune of $850,000. That may well constitute a zenith in the tautology between an institution with the agency to determine what constitutes 'good' design and designs comprising enough of an aesthetic achievement to reinforce the credibility of the same institution.

Danish Modern designs are mostly utilitarian objects and as such they can become consonant with users in ways no designer, cabinetmaker, or marketing executive ever envisioned. Within that consonance lie the various reasons for the endurance of certain designs (and the obsolescence of others). Designs represent a dialogue with the culture that surrounds them. Through myriad changes in styles and preferences, the various iterations of what has come to be called Danish Modern have managed to go on 'speaking' to consumers, collectors, and design aficionados – and most importantly to users – in rapidly changing cultures. As a popular home style, it went out of vogue in the 1970s and was pushed aside by the rise of postmodernist design and its affinity for ornament, playfulness, and historical reference. What place would woodsy Danish Modern have in the Crayola chromaticism of Ettore Sottsass's Memphis aesthetic in the 1980s? By the mid-1990s, however, Danish Modern experienced a renaissance within the design world, and interest – along with prices – has not abated since then.

Perhaps the most significant achievement of Danish designers, cabinetmakers, and craftspeople at the height of mid-twentieth-century modernist design was their ability to humanize what had been standardized – erasing the very dichotomy that had made other then-contemporary designs less appealing. This reaction was not superimposed on the development of Danish Modern design after the fact: as early as 1928, an exhibition of German Bauhaus furniture resulted in Poul Henningsen ridiculing it in the press for its machine-driven aesthetic and tubular steel expression, establishing an ideological resistance that would last for decades. Whereas it may have been difficult to get most world citizens to embrace the more machine-like approach of the Bauhaus designers – and blatantly rhetorical efforts were made in the mid-twentieth century by some American design mavens to resist it – many of the Danish designers' predilection for curvilinear shapes and certain woods proffered an alternative. Although the sharp, flat painted surfaces of a design like Gerrit Reitveld's Mondrian-like Red-Blue Chair (1923), however artistic, look anything but inviting, the warm wood and sinuous curves of Juhl's 45-Chair recall the bending of the human body. The difference remains pronounced, not because of the myriad associations each chair conveys but, rather, because people continue to sit and in the familiar act of sitting are drawn not only to what looks comfortable but also to what looks more organic. None of this implies that Danish designs were the only organic ones or that all mid-century Danish designs were organic – they were not.[2]

In this significant sense, Danish Modern allowed aesthetics to flow more naturally from design and the act of creation, rather than permitting aesthetics to be driven solely by concept (although concepts – ideologies – are always at play when designers take certain approaches to their work). Those searching for some monolithic structure of thought hiding behind the concept of Danish Modern will search in vain. Instead, much of the history of Danish design in the twentieth century is one of ideological oscillation. Whereas some European modernist architects and designers wanted a complete break from traditional approaches to materials and furniture, many of the early progenitors of Danish Modern design kept one foot in the historical woodworking tradition. Partially, they had no choice because of the influence wielded by the powerful Copenhagen Cabinetmakers Guild, founded in 1564. Yet, in time, Denmark's designers did not allow even this more historical bent to preclude invention or to limit them, and they moved freely into synthetic materials, plastics, moulds, steel, and laminates. Juhl's creations illustrate this duality: he worked knowledgeably with wood, yielding to its warmer chroma and textural nature, but he also lifted backs and seats off the supporting wooden structure – a structure not only exposed for what it is but sensual in form and inviting to the touch. Juhl designed objects out of traditional wood reconfigured in non-traditional ways.

The best examples of Danish Modern successfully conveyed that duality and they continue to do so. In this sense, no matter how expensive Danish design objects have become, no matter how many of them appear in museum collections, no matter how they are marketed to the elite, many of them remain examples of Modernism directed at everyday life. Their simplicity in idiom speaks of accessibility. They reflect various approaches to design, living, materials, objects, and sustainability, yet their purpose remains undeniably clear. They are still, and have always been, marketed objects, but the resilience of their trajectory indicates an appeal reaching beyond the marketing narrative once applied to them. People go on responding to them, perceiving them in a sometimes-shifting manner, and – most importantly – using them. Their continued visibility and popularity indicate that they are still prodding users about the role of certain artefacts in their lives and our relationship to them.

Over time, Danish Modern design produced in the last century has come to impart a sense of resistance to faddism. To use the German designer Gui Bonsiepe's bifurcation: its forms draw users back to the idea of design as intelligent problem-solving rather than vapid styling. That dichotomy should not be surprising – nor is it endemic to Denmark: diverse modernist theorists such as Anni Albers, George Nelson, and Max Bill wrote extensively on the theoretical chasm between task and style, and their writings are replete with efforts to separate modern design from transient fashion. Perhaps some of their rhetoric represented nothing more than wishful thinking. The endurance of these and other mid-century designs became even more apparent in the Museum of Modern Art's 2009 exhibit, 'What Was Good Design? MoMA's Message 1944–56.'[3] The message, it turns out, has remained somewhat consistent, though one should never lose sight of the historical context in which designs first appear.

Numerous books have approached the history of Danish design from varying angles, but this is not primarily a history book. The popularity of Danish Modern in the United States in the 1950s and 1960s has tended to make people think that these two decades are Danish Modern's time, yet the development of Danish Modern design far precedes the mid-twentieth century. In the first chapter that follows, I create a historical and ideological time frame by placing the development of Danish Modern design in its cultural context, both in Denmark and more broadly in Scandinavia, and by alluding to those concepts, thinkers, and publications that helped to shape design ideology in the twentieth century in the Nordic countries. This early history explains how material and ideological developments occurred in consortium – and how they laid the foundation for the efforts of the designers who followed them. Clive Dilnot has pointed out: 'Without the grounding that only historical study can give, prescriptions for design are incidental; they cannot be redeemed because they lack the necessary immersion in real historical complexity.'[4]

Also, while it would be foolish to ascribe the approach and accomplishments of designers in Denmark to some notion of innate national ability, I agree with Kjetil Fallan that design is 'a mesh of cultural, social, political, and economic configurations and codes,'[5] and that we can use those codes to draw national lines of demarcation. At times, Danes have been most guilty of defining themselves by supposed 'national' traits. For example, in his introduction to *Contemporary Danish Design* (1960), Arne Karlsen insists that the domestic 'heritage' of the Danes lies in their 'sober approach' to ideas from other countries and the 'sober manner' in which Danes adapt them.[6] His descriptions appear to reinforce stereotypes about Scandinavians being reserved and colourless in their reading of international currents, yet the designers who helped to craft what has come to be known as Danish Modern were anything but hesitant in many of their innovations. As chair designs go, Wegner's Peacock, Jalk's laminated GJ, and Juhl's Chieftain are anything but sober in appearance: their insistent forms fairly swagger with presence – even today, in a world far removed from their inception.

Cries of 'hagiography' are also often levelled against scholars discussing specific designers; this fear has grown ever since Nikolaus Pevsner published *Pioneers of Modern Design: From William Morris to Walter Gropius* in 1936.[7] To this day, a number of Modern designers are revered and their work alluded to as if it developed in a vacuum of personal creativity. Adrian Forty has pointed out the paradox of assigning designers responsibility: 'On the one hand, design is determined by ideas and material conditions over which designers have no control, yet, on the other hand, designs are the result of designers exercising their creative autonomy and originality.'[8] What designers do remains an act, whether they do it in consortium with others, bend to market forces, adapt to technological advances, consult manufacturers, or stand at a work desk and perform their task alone. Contingency and context do not nullify talent or personal endeavour.

Design is also a transitive verb, that is, it is something that designers do. Penny Sparke made this point quite pithily when she wrote: 'Both a noun and a verb, it is not just a feature of our surroundings; it is also the creative process that makes them possible.'[9] Ascribing specific accomplishments, decisions, influences, or efforts to a designer should not be confused with hagiography. When Wegner stood in his workshop struggling through the challenge of creating a top-rail that would still support a person comfortably, even allowing the sitter to slouch, he disclosed both his proficiency as a trained cabinetmaker who understood joinery and the innovative nature of many of his decisions. Jeffrey L. Meikle returns focus to the existence of three-dimensional objects when he writes: 'Perhaps it is too easy to focus on a philosophical or ideological forest of design definitions and commentaries and thereby miss the solid oaks and maples of the material world in all its randomly branching specificity.'[10] Thus, I believe it remains worthwhile to look at what specific designers do and have done, particularly as a way of understanding their reactions to the currents and demands surrounding them at any given time. The alternative is to delimit what they do in the name of contingency and determinism – and that is to deny that they worked.

I have chosen to focus on certain designers and their respective projects as representative of the interplay between design and culture, between ideology and execution, between designed object and articulation, between similitude and distinction, and between form and aesthetics, all of which have contributed to the construction of Danish Modern as a concept in mid-twentieth-century design. Following the initial chapter on the history of exchanging ideas, Chapter 2 focuses on Kaare Klint and Poul Henningsen as representative of both differing and similar design approaches in the early stages of Danish Modern's development. Never translated into English, Henningsen's writings, in particular, provide some of the finest expressions of the ideological foundation for modernist design developments in Denmark. Chapter 3 looks at the issue of Platonic readings and uses chairs and the idea of 'chairness' as a starting point for that discussion, focusing predominantly on Wegner and his efforts. Chapter 4 uses some of Juhl's designs and writings, especially those produced in the 1940s, to discuss attempts to articulate furniture designs as three-dimensional art, with a focus on sculptors Sonja Ferlov Mancoba and Erik Thommesen. Chapter 5 focuses on the Danish weavers, especially Lis Ahlmann and Vibeke Klint, in a discussion of materiality and structure and the abstraction of shape in modernist textiles. In Chapter 6, Arne Jacobsen's SAS Royal Hotel and his accompanying designs provide a springboard for a Hegelian reading of the *Gesamtkunstwerk* and community in modern design. Chapter 7 offers a look at Verner Panton's chromaticism and his Pop- and Op-art efforts to move 'modern' back into the realm of contemporary design. Chapter 8 questions the way that designs are sometimes contextualized as parts of art movements, particularly in the case of Poul Kjærholm and Minimal Art from the 1960s. In Chapter 9, the 'Arts of Denmark: Viking to Modern' exhibition from 1960 provides the basis for a discussion about thematizing design in catalogue copy within a nationalist context. Chapter 10 uses Nanna Ditzel's transitional innovations as a catalyst to a discussion of claims of timelessness in design and of the evolution of the changing articulation of Danish Modern design. Readers will find no emphasis on biography except when it relates directly to the discussion at hand, nor is there any attempt at a catalogue raisonné or thorough review of any designer's oeuvre. I have also made no effort to be all-inclusive, as in an encyclopaedic book, but rather to take a representative approach towards design issues in their historical and ideological context. Chair designs tend to dominate because they have had the broadest cultural influence on the construction of Danish Modern as a concept. Where texts are available, especially those written by the designers, I have struggled to bring them into the discussion and to use them as exemplary of specific approaches.

With this book, I shed some light on the continuing attraction of Danish Modern design by applying theoretical tools that are not limited to one lens. While looking at modernist theories, philosophical underpinnings, rhetorical devices, technological advancements, cultural articulations, and the tension between art and design, I hope to present a more productive method for explaining the legacy of Danish Modern design. In our acute time of sustainability and limited resources, the endurance of any designs for more than half a century seems well worth the investigation.

Notes

1. 'At Home with Renée and Placido,' *New York Times* (22 August 2014).
2. For some modernist thinkers, this dichotomy was not exclusive: the American architectural critic Lewis Mumford, for example, contended in 1934 that the only path to achieving the organic was to 'assimilate the machine' – but his goals were 'objectivity, impersonality, [and] neutrality.' See Mumford, *Technics and Civilization* (Chicago, IL: University of Chicago Press, 2010), 363.
3. Reviewing the exhibit in the *New York Times*, Roberta Smith commented that its message is that 'good design should never be more than it needs to be, and that notions of restraint, economy, and efficiency should be built into it.' Smith, 'The Ordinary as Object of Desire,' *New York Times* (4 June 2009).
4. Clive Dilnot, 'The State of Design History, Part II: Problems and Possibilities,' *Design Issues*, 1(2) (Autumn 1984), 20.
5. Kjetil Fallan, 'Introduction,' *Scandinavian Design: Alternative Histories*, ed. Fallan (Oxford: Berg, 2012), loc. 125.
6. Arne Karlsen, 'Introduction,' in *Contemporary Danish Design*, ed. Karlsen, Bent Salicath, and Mogens Utzon-Frank, trans. Birthe Andersen (Copenhagen: Danish Society of Arts and Crafts and Industrial Design, 1960), 5.
7. But see Dilnot, 'The State of Design History, Part I,' 9.
8. Adrian Forty, *Objects of Desire: Design & Society from Wedgwood to IBM* (New York: Pantheon Books, 1986), 242.
9. Penny Sparke, *The Genius of Design* (London: Quadrille Publishing, 2009), 10.
10. Jeffrey L. Meikle, 'Writing about Stuff: The Peril and Promise of Design History and Criticism,' *Writing Design: Words and Objects*, ed. Grace Lees-Maffei (Oxford: Berg, 2012), loc. 841.

1 A History of Ideas: Constructing Danish Modern

When any style of design becomes fashionable or influential, a tendency exists to perceive it as arriving abruptly and then instantaneously altering aesthetics and taste. Design eras are frequently presented and taught as self-contained developments appearing in a sequence: Art Nouveau, Art Deco, Modernism, Postmodernism, etc. Yet, periods often overlap, and elements from previous movements often surface in the next phase. The general view of Danish Modern furniture is that it appeared on the world stage in the 1950s and that its sleek lines and lighter woods immediately took the world by storm. This is a mostly American reading of Danish Modern's evolution, a reading rife with nostalgia for the mid-twentieth century, as well as a romanticized view of home furnishings from Denmark. Some of this undoubtedly stems from the marketing of not only Danish but, more broadly, Scandinavian design to Americans in the 1950s, especially in the Design in Scandinavia exhibit (1954–57), which was seen by some 600,000 people in North America. In the United States in the 1960s, the preponderance of furniture chains with names such as the Happy Viking and Dane Décor – selling mostly teak and rosewood furniture from such Danish manufacturers as Koefoed, Dyrlund, and Skovby – reinforced certain ideas about what 'Danish Modern' looked like for decades. In reality, the history of Danish Modern design's development far precedes the 1950s, and many of its roots lie in theoretical and aesthetic design and architectural changes beyond Denmark's shores.

Theories of Modernism

In Scandinavia, as elsewhere, especially in Europe and the United States, Modernism constitutes a broad term involving the influence of a number of movements in the early twentieth century: Expressionism, Fauvism, Cubism, Dadaism, Surrealism, Constructivism.[1] These movements had a profound effect not only on visual and literary art but also on the applied arts of design and architecture. The German Bauhaus, for example, began in a more expressionist mode (thanks to figures like Johannes Itten) before moving into an emphasis on machine aesthetics. In its own way, each movement represents a characteristic step away from mimetic representation in art and a rejection of excessive or undirected ornamentation in architecture and design. Journals, manifestos, and exhibitions helped to usher in each new mode of thinking and introduce its philosophical underpinnings to the broader culture. Many of the designers' names we now associate with Modernism were rhetoricians: Le Corbusier, Muthesius, Loos, Gropius, Mies van der Rohe. As an ideological movement, Modernism often seems to manifest itself even more in the representative writings of these early modernists than in any designed objects.

When Kjetil Fallan writes that Modernism can be viewed as 'a constant quest for modernity, or the wish to establish an anti-traditional tradition,' his description reflects the dominant approach of the above-mentioned modernist thinkers.[2] In early twentieth-century design, Modernism came to define the effort to exorcise fashion and contemporaneity for its own sake from being 'modern'; it reflects the paradoxical effort to conceive of and to construct a present in visual form that is not ultimately bound to the present in which it is constructed. Just as the responses to the ideological tenets of Modernism by figures such as Le Corbusier, Gropius, and Mies were variegated when put into practice, the same can be said for the ways in which Modernism manifested itself among the Danish architects and designers of the mid-twentieth century – particularly in their relationship to tradition.

Although it is frequently viewed narrowly as a European or American movement, developments in Modernism also often reflect a dialogue among different cultures. In Denmark, for example, many modern artists, including the expressionist mask-painter Egill Jacobsen, were influenced by Oceanic and African art, French Fauvism, and Soviet Constructivism. Nordic artists who studied with Matisse brought Fauvism and its subjective chromaticism back to Scandinavia in groundbreaking images garnering attention at exhibitions. Primitive arts – and the mediation of the same sources in abstract art – would also influence Danish designers and their often-sculptural forms. Finn Juhl, for example, collected sculptures by the Danish artist Sonja Ferlov Mancoba, who was heavily influenced by African art. Journals, both art-oriented and more broadly cultural, also helped to expose Danes to changes and theories in the art world. The journal *Klingen* (the Blade, 1917–20), founded by the painter, ceramicist, and graphic designer Axel Salto, helped to disseminate avant-garde European art movements and theory in Denmark, as did the pan-Nordic *Konkretion* (1935–36), founded by the Danish surrealist painter Vilhelm Bjerke Petersen and featuring articles by Herbert Read and images of Henry Moore's sculptures.

In design, the early modernists were determined to move away from historical styles they viewed as no longer appropriate to their time. Form became the dominant consideration to many European modernists; they strove for constructive certainty in design solutions, and standardization was viewed as a social necessity. In Denmark, when the lamp designer and theorist Poul Henningsen stated, 'Only art bearing the stamp of its time lives forever,' he expressed the central paradox of early twentieth-century Modernism: the belief that by addressing their own time and its needs and by rejecting styles and solutions from previous eras, modernists could find enduring solutions to modern living. Often abetted by advancements in technology, modernists in general tended to strive to find forms that would transcend fashion – to define design as something more than transient style – regardless of how successful they were in this endeavour. The dictum 'less is more,' often attributed to Mies van der Rohe (who once said he first heard it from the German architect and designer Peter Behrens), is frequently associated with the basic modernist approach to architecture and design – to the point of the American postmodern architect Robert Venturi ridiculing it with his own dictum: 'Less is a bore.'

For decades, discussions about Modernism in design focused predominantly on aesthetics. Machine-age aesthetics, in particular, served as the central subject of many design historians' narratives about the development of Modernism in the early twentieth century. The basic premise was the early modern designers' rejection of historical styles in favour of contemporary designs addressing not only the modern world but also the growing industrialization of designed objects. Yet, one cannot also deny the influence of developments in modern art. The English poet and literary and art critic Herbert Read, for example, wrote frequently about the industrial designer as an abstract artist, as he does in *Art and Industry* (1934). Addressing the then contentious issue of the aesthetic value of machine arts, Read compared the utilitarian arts to abstract art: 'the utilitarian arts . . . appeal to the aesthetic sensibility as *abstract art* . . . the form of objects in use is not simply a question of harmony and proportion in the geometric sense, but may be created and appreciated by intuitional modes of apprehension.'[3] Insisting that 'furniture, utensils, and vessels' have an 'aesthetic appeal,' Read dismisses the existence of consciously applied laws of perception and, instead, refers to them as 'intuitional forms.'[4] Read even cites Walter Gropius, German architect and founder of the Bauhaus, as an artist and proceeds to define the designer of steel or plywood furniture as a designer of abstract forms.

Much of this aesthetic assessment of Modernism rested on the early influence of the Austrian Alfred Loos's now infamous essay on ornamentation, 'Ornament and Crime' (first given as a lecture in 1910), in which he derided every form of non-essential ornamentation and decoration, from elaborate filigree to personal tattoos, as signs of depravity and an absence of civilization. 'The evolution of culture,' Loos claimed, 'is synonymous with the removal of ornament from objects of everyday use.'[5] The Swiss architect, painter, and designer Le Corbusier (Charles Édouard Jeanneret-Gris) built on Loos's dismissive attitude by emphasizing that ornamentation, design-wise, hides flaws. Instead, through mechanization, Le Corbusier hoped to achieve aesthetic beauty and cleanliness – even deriding style-driven designs such as ornate chandeliers as dirt catchers. Machine technology would provide harmony and organisms tending towards purity, particularly as defined in Le Corbusier's *Towards a New Architecture* (1923): 'Tail pieces and garlands, exquisite ovals where triangular doves preen themselves or one another, boudoirs embellished with "poufs" in gold and black velvet, are now no more than the intolerable witnesses to a dead spirit. These sanctuaries stifling with elegancies, or on the other hand with the follies of "Peasant Art," are an offence.'[6] To Le Corbusier, object-types would lead to a brighter, cleaner, and less aesthetically offensive future. As Le Corbusier observed, 'every kind of functional need is met'[7] in the white geometry of his machines for living, such as Villa Savoye (1928–31) in Poissy, France, with its open floor plan and rationalist built-ins. As Jonathan M. Woodham observes in *Twentieth-Century Design* (1997), members of the European and American avant-garde considered ornamentation 'detrimental' and 'out of touch with the *Zeitgeist*.'[8]

Politically, these early Modern designers were merging late-nineteenth-century concerns for social reform (Le Corbusier was obsessed with urban planning, as was Henningsen – who once accused Copenhagen's city planners of being a collection of Christmas gnomes) with developments in modern technology for the hopeful betterment of society. In Europe, this melding of interests finds its strongest expression in the German Bauhaus, which, under the auspices of Gropius, moved at first from an arts and crafts orientation, influenced by William Morris, to embracing a machine aesthetic that the designers and theorists hoped would create a universalist approach to design: no more borrowed styles or conventional decoration. Theatre productions at the Bauhaus featured performers dressed in costumes, designed by Oskar Schlemmer, as geometric shapes, sometimes wearing metal masks to reduce their individuality. This attempt at erasing nationalist and personal characteristics in favour of abstracted, machine-age modernist forms would set the Bauhaus up for the National Socialist backlash that developed under Hitler, resulting in the Bauhaus being closed in 1933.

Postmodernists have tended to read the early modernists' affection for innovation as a fetishizing of the new and/or different. Some critics of Modernism see this obsession with innovation as an effort by modernists to function outside of social and institutional determinants. As Gropius points out in *The New Architecture and the Bauhaus* (1925), however, the aims of the early modernists were 'not the personal whims of a handful of architects avid for innovation at all cost, but simply the inevitable logical product of the intellectual, social, and technical conditions of our age.'[9] In early Modern design, the creation of types was aimed specifically at addressing and erasing social inequalities. Gropius observed: 'In all great epochs of history the existence of standards that is the conscious adoption of type-forms has been the criterion of a polite and well-ordered society; for it is commonplace that repetition of the same things for the same purposes exercises a settling and civilizing influence on men's minds.'[10] This normative emphasis on repetition and the creation of types as best for society appears to reflect the hope that types would transcend both the influences of the past and the ephemeral demands of the present.[11] It is one of the most persistent tenets of early twentieth-century Modernism.

In Germany, this focus on types surfaced in 1914 when Hermann Muthesius and Henry van de Velde held their acrimonious debate in the Werkbund, with Muthesius opposing individualism and lauding the 'organic way' of types. In the Netherlands, De Stijl's founders – Theo van Doesburg, Piet Mondrian, Bart van der Leck, and Gerrit Reitveld – also opposed rampant individualism and took solace in geometric abstraction, which they viewed as universal. A belief in the power of the machine to balance any conflict between intuition and intellect drove van Doesburg, who claimed in his 1922 lecture 'The Will to Style': 'The needs of our age, both ideal and practical, demand constructive certainty.'[12] Yet, these stylistic endeavours also reflect the view of artists as agents of social change. In England, Read would echo these thoughts, lauding standardization and dismissing uniqueness as part of 'a bygone individualistic phase of civilization.'[13] In the United States, the Bauhaus-educated weaver and theorist Anni Albers (1899–1994) addressed the conflict between what was temporal and what was lasting in her 1947 lecture, 'Design: Anonymous and Timeless': 'The imprint of time is unavoidable. It will occur without our purposely fashioning it. And it will outlast fashions only if it embodies lasting, together with transitory, qualities.'[14] All of these ideas are present in the theoretical underpinnings of the development of Danish Modern design.

In Denmark, Henningsen provided the most prominent voice to theories of Modernism, but they were filtered through his own task-oriented reading. In fact, as discussed in the next chapter, Henningsen rejected modernist aesthetics for their own sake almost as much as he rejected the historical and neoclassical styles he found anachronistic and pointless in the modern world. This dual rejection reflects a mediation of specific design currents by some Danes in the first half of the twentieth century.

Modernist design developments in Scandinavia

In Scandinavia, modernist efforts in architecture and design date back to the late nineteenth century. In 1897, Pietro Krohn, the first Director for Denmark's Kunstindstrimuseum (the Museum of Decorative and Applied Arts, now known as Designmuseum Danmark, the Danish Museum of Art and Design), gave a lecture at the General Art and Industrial Exhibition in Stockholm about establishing some standards for new design: 'Consideration for use, consideration for utilization, consideration for material, that should be the first consideration, but it is not enough. No, beauty shall also be added.'[15] Almost twenty years before Gropius founded the Bauhaus, and more than thirty years before the highly influential Stockholm Exhibition, Krohn was already prompting his pan-Scandinavian audience to reject the historicizing tendencies of the late nineteenth century.

The first Nordic Exhibition of Industry, Agriculture, and Art had taken place in Copenhagen nine years earlier, in 1888.[16] The brainchild of the Danish industrialist Philip Schou, who was also the director of the Royal Copenhagen Factory, the exhibition offered a rich sampling of Denmark, Norway, and Sweden's leading manufacturers. The heavily detailed Swedish Villa, for example, showcased the wood products of the cabinetmaker Ekman. However, even a successful industrialist like Schou could not refrain – in a speech given also in 1888 – from referring to the Danish people's character as 'soft' (*bløq*) and their temperament as 'complacent' (*mageligt*), and thus not well suited to 'great industrial development.'[17] Long before the next century's cabinetmakers would stake their territory, or twentieth-century design historians would speak of a 'sober' Danish approach, Schou was already constructing a national character at odds with the advances of industrialism. In her article 'Scandinavianism – A Cultural Brand,' Mirjam Gelfer-Jørgensen points out that the

Nordic Exhibition 'is reckoned to be the first important indication of what Nordic decorative arts and industry could achieve.'[18] She also notes the rise of pan-Nordic efforts at the 1889 and 1900 World Fairs in Paris.

Art Nouveau would hold sway over many of the designs presented in late nineteenth- and early-twentieth-century exhibitions, particularly in textiles, ceramics, and metalwork. Yet, by 1909, the Århus Exhibition in Denmark would present a coda on Art Nouveau's strong influence among the Danes – although the Royal Copenhagen Factory would go on producing numerous wares influenced by Art Nouveau. In 1924, the architect and academic Anton Rosen, who built the Palads Hotel in Copenhagen and organized the Danish exhibit at the 1925 Exposition des Arts Décoratifs et Industriels Modernes in Paris, held a meeting at the Industriforeningen (Confederation of Danish Industry) and called for 'a cleansing, intended to reach into the very core of objects, excise all superfluous decoration, let the object whether a building or a piece of handicraft, appear in its simplest dress, in its most unadulterated and constructive form of use.'[19] Still, Neoclassicism in some Scandinavian designs would move to the forefront by the 1925 Paris Exposition, although Henningsen premiered his strikingly modernist lamps to the world at this very exhibition.

Already in 1926, when Norwegian architect Lars Backer designed Skansen restaurant, considered Norway's first purely functionalist building, he furnished it with contemporary lamps by Henningsen.[20] At a 1928 exhibition in Bergen, the Norwegian art historian and theorist Einar Lexow emphasized the dichotomy between individuality and practicality in utilitarian objects that are appropriate, a word that surfaces frequently in much early-modernist rhetoric – especially when applied to the use of materials. 'Either we require an actual work of art, free, individual, unfettered by all practical concerns, or we demand those good and solid everyday wares that have wonderfully little to do with art but that fill us with delight, because we feel that they are appropriate,' wrote Lexow.[21] This focus on what is 'appropriate' would become a frequent motif among the Nordic modernist designers. From 1932 to 1934, the journal Brukskunst (Arts and Crafts), produced by Foreningen Norsk Brukskunst (the Norwegian Applied Arts Society), provided a forum in Norway for discussions about the future of utilitarian objects.

In Sweden, the Svenska Slöjdföreningen (Swedish Society of Industrial Design) had been founded in 1845 and began publishing a journal of the same name in 1905. In 1899, the social theorist and feminist Ellen Key published a collection of essays, Skönhet för Alla (Beauty for Everyone); in her essay 'Skönhet for Hemmen' ('Beauty for the Home'), she argued for replacing unattractive and uncomfortable furnishings with beautiful everyday objects emphasizing function and simplicity for the purpose of social improvement. Many historians view Gregor Paulsson's 1919 publication Vackrare vardagsvara (More Beautiful Everyday Goods), written for the Svenska Slöjdföreningen's exhibition that same year at a trade fair in Göteborg, as a philosophical battle cry for improved design. Paulsson argued against imitating previous styles and for the characteristic forms of machine production in the hope of creating quality everyday items for a reasonable price. The cover describes Paulsson's work as the society's 'first propaganda publication.' Although its effect was limited, the phrase '*Vackrare vardagsvara*' became a slogan for early modernists in Sweden and the other Nordic countries – but the concept had not originated in Scandinavia. The German Werkbund (founded in 1907) had employed a similar slogan earlier in the century, a reflection of its struggles with the effects of industry and art on visual forms.

All of these early efforts indicate that broader Nordic endeavours towards Modernism in design laid the foundation for what would eventually become Danish Modern. More importantly, they point towards the development of a somewhat shared design philosophy not limited to Denmark, yet manifesting itself differently within the culture of each Nordic country. In Denmark, Landsforeningen Dansk Brugskunst og Design (the Danish Society of Arts and Crafts and Industrial Design) was formed in 1907; the Society and its governing board would become highly influential in the direction of modern Danish design by promoting cooperation between artists and industry and by organizing exhibitions. In addition to holding local exhibitions every spring and organizing important international exhibitions (such as the Arts of Denmark in 1960), the Society also published the journal *Dansk Kunsthaandværk*, starting in 1928.

Published from 1914 until 1927 by the Selskab for Dekorativ Kunst (Society for Decorative Art), the Danish periodical *Skønvirke*,[22] founded by the architect Caspar Leuning Borch, provided another national forum for discussions of design issues in this important transitional period. In 1918, Thor Bendz Keilland, the Norwegian art historian and director of the Norwegian Museum of Decorative Arts and Design, wrote an article entitled 'Til hvad? For hvem? Af hvad? Og hvorledes?' ('For what? For whom? By what? And how?') in *Skønvirke* in which he called for industry to work with the arts while simultaneously bemoaning industry's over-reaching influence. Keilland reinforced these concerns in his 1938 book *Den nye Verdensstil (The New World Style)* in which he lauded functionalism for having led to a new international style that was still 'healthy enough in theory and flexible enough in expression to offer latitude for all necessary national and local variations.'[23] Thus, the tension between industry and the arts, particularly the regional arts, was already well established and certainly well debated before the term Danish Modern came into vogue.

A somewhat hesitant step further into Modernism occurred in 1924 when Kaare Klint, an architect still enamoured of historical types, took over the Furniture School at the Danish Royal Academy of Fine Arts. Klint was obsessed with systematic measurement in design. His work is often referred to as anthropometric because he based most of his designs on involved studies of measurements – of the human body, of serving pieces, of anything contained or held by furniture. His followers, such as Børge Mogensen and Arne Karlsen, were ardent about pursuing his line of thinking. While the historical nature of many of Klint's designs appear blatantly at odds with the modernist project,[24] his almost Cartesian approach reflects the early modernists' adherence to objectivity (what the Germans referred to as *Die neue Sachlichkeit* – the New Objectivity). More importantly, his fealty to wood, even in the somewhat de-ornamented historical styles he worked within, reinforced the firm influence of that material on furniture design developments in twentieth-century Denmark. It is important to remember that Klint was establishing the thrust of the Royal Academy's Furniture School just as the Bauhaus was establishing its worldwide reputation.

Three years later, in 1927, the powerful Copenhagen Cabinetmakers Guild instituted its annual furniture exhibitions, a brilliant marketing tool that would give rise to a significant collaboration between the craftsmen and modern architects. These occurrences set up the overriding conflict in Denmark about the direction of furniture design – a conflict reflecting the tension between tradition and Modernism that would come to define much of Danish Modern design ideology in the first half of the twentieth century. The conflict would also provide fertile ground for Henningsen's myriad published musings on the subject, as we shall see in the next chapter.

These pan-Nordic efforts also illustrate the myopia of viewing Danish Modern as a product of the 1950s, or even as simply a part of mid-twentieth-century Modernism. They indicate, instead, that similar concerns about everyday wares, the effects of industrialization, the state of craftsmanship, the relationship between art and utilitarian objects, and the societal consequences of design had been driving Danish and Nordic design developments for decades before the 1950s. In addition, pan-Nordic efforts, including lectures and publications, illustrate that the notion of a broader 'Scandinavian' design was not simply a marketing construct of the 1950s, as has often been contended (mostly because of the Nordic countries' joint marketing entries in the Milan Triennales and the rhetoric surrounding the Design in Scandinavia exhibition of that decade). Instead, ideologically, Danes, Swedes, Norwegians – and especially Aalto from Finland – had been interacting and influencing each other on these issues since the late nineteenth century.

The Stockholm Exhibition

It was an international exhibition, though, that introduced a new approach to architecture and home wares into Scandinavia. In 1930, the Stockholm Exhibition brought Modernism – particularly in the form of functionalism – into Scandinavia in full force. Organized by the City of Stockholm and the Svenska Slöjdföreningen, the exhibition was mostly the brainchild of the art historian Gregor Paulsson (1889–1977) – the fair's catalyst – who had been influenced by witnessing a similar event in Stuttgart in 1927. Paulsson's first book of propaganda, *Den nya arkitekturen* (*The New Architecture*), appeared in Sweden in 1916 and was published in Denmark in 1920. He gave a lecture on 'Kunsthåndværkets stilling in Europa' ('The Place of Arts and Crafts in Europe') in Copenhagen in 1925 and then spoke there again in 1931 about the Stockholm Exhibition as a significant link in the development of a modern society. Throughout his life, Paulsson fought for improvements in the industrial arts that would generate better economic, social, and cultural conditions. Influenced by the German Werkbund, he also stressed the appearance of types and not exceptions.[25]

Initially, the exhibition met with some resistance: the more traditional press expressed a fear of industrially produced products usurping handicrafts and questioned Paulsson's leadership in the Svenska Slöjdföreningen. Socialist critics viewed the event as an exhibition of Swedish capitalism. A Swedish American even took a hotel room in the capital so that he could hand out pamphlets warning people not to attend. Still, the flat roofs, clean lines, curvilinear walls, predominance of white, and profusion of glass in Gunnar Asplund's arresting architecture, such as the exhibition's futuristic Paradise Restaurant (Fig. 1.1), proved irresistible to many Nordic modernists. Asplund's architecture had already influenced Aalto in Finland, Arne Korsmo in Norway, and Jacobsen in Denmark (after the event, Henningsen referred

Fig. 1.1 Gunnar Asplund's Paradise Restaurant at the 1930 Stockholm Exhibition. A number of Danish designers attended the event, including Arne Jacobsen, Poul Henningsen, and an eighteen-year-old Finn Juhl. Courtesy of Designmuseum Danmark/The Library

to Asplund as the hero of the exhibition). Some 400 exhibitors showed their designs, and a 278-page catalogue accompanied the exhibit. From Denmark, Jacobsen and Henningsen attended, as did an impressionable eighteen-year-old architect manqué, Finn Juhl. Reviewing the exhibit in *Nyt Tidsskrift for Kunstindustri* (*New Journal for Industrial Art*), Henningsen observed: 'I know no greater artistic experience than when task and solution come together, and it is the first time in the history of functionalism I have encountered it.'[26]

Before the exhibition closed in September, a group of prominent Swedish architects and design figures – Paulsson, Asplund, Uno Åhrén, Sven Markelius, Eskil Sundahl, and Wolter Gahn – began work on a publication called *acceptera* that would answer critics of the exhibition. First published in 1931 by Tiden, the publishing arm of Sweden's Social Democratic Party, *acceptera* called for the acceptance of the time's demand for functionalism[27] in architecture and everyday goods. The authorship was presented as collective, and the visuals came straight out of the Bauhaus playbook, complete with sans-serif typeface and diagonal print on the cover (some influences from Henningsen's visuals in *Kritisk Revy* are also evident in the Swedish publication). Like Henningsen's laments in his Danish journal, *acceptera*'s Swedish authors also bemoaned the use of historical styles in such utilitarian buildings as department stores and assembly halls, demanded an objectivity that reflected the current age, and rejected ostentation for its own sake.

Theoretically, *acceptera*'s authors discussed the dichotomy between the individual and the masses, the collective and the individual; their arguments are not a simple embrace of the collective at all costs but an admittance of the tension between these forces. Instead, the authors (to emphasize the importance of the collective effort, they never revealed exactly who wrote which chapter) argued for recognizing evolving cultural needs. 'Not truth,' read one subheading, 'but social adaptability makes a theory powerful.'[28] This battle cry reflects the utilitarian efforts that accompanied most early modernist endeavours. Swedish publications, such as Gustaf Näaström's *Svensk Funktionalism* (*Swedish Functionalism*, 1930) and Gotthard Johansson's *Funktionalismen i Verkligheten* (*Functionalism in Reality*, 1931), further enhanced this new wave of functionalism. Johansson had also carried out surveys on living conditions in Sweden.

Modernism in Danish design

In Denmark, no powerful embrace of machine aesthetics occurred in the first third of the twentieth century, although early Danish modern designers and theorists expressed many of the same concerns as their counterparts in the Bauhaus. Modernism in Danish design was often filtered through a Danish lens – and that meant, at least rhetorically, a rejection of machine aesthetics. This lens does not represent some innate national trait (whatever that might be): it is, instead, a confluence of historical and social events, especially the dilatory nature of industrialism's rise in Denmark, a powerful union of artisans determined to maintain their authority, the rapid rise of socialist policies in the early twentieth century, and a long history of resistance to excess motivated by lean times in the nation's development.

Through his highly influential journal *Kritisk Revy* (*Critical Review*, 1926–28), Henningsen gave the strongest voice to the Danish response to burgeoning modernist aesthetics. In the journal, some of Denmark's most prominent avant-garde figures (Edvard Heiberg, Hans Kirk, Otto Gelsted) fought for cultural reforms that would have social and pedagogical ramifications. Henningsen, who not only wrote numerous articles for the journal but also designed every aspect of the publication, down to the typeface and advertisements, wrote on a number of topics, from urban planning to Cubism to a defence of Josephine Baker's nude dancing in Copenhagen. His pointed claims about the industrial arts, however, had a profound effect on design developments, abetted by his own meticulous and forward-looking lamp designs. Theoretically, Henningsen could not support an aestheticism that abandoned social and human concerns or that subjugated those concerns to the confines of a specific visual paradigm. He focused, instead, on basing design on an inner necessity rather than a forced modernity. Throughout *Critical Review*, Henningsen's rhetoric points to the sometimes testy exchange of ideas with international currents occurring in Denmark as Modernism began to prevail.

In an ironic development, as Modernism – influenced by Soviet Constructivism and De Stijl abstractions – becomes more international and machine-driven in places like the German Bauhaus, it actually becomes less receptive to pure machine aesthetics in Denmark. Commenting on the motivation behind most early twentieth-century modernists, Paul Greenhalgh observes: 'The desire to escape the specifics of time and place, to simultaneously transform the ideological fabric and visual appearance of the world linked most radicals in the opening decades of our century.'[29] In Denmark, however, Modernism remains narrower in focus, almost provincial, as we see often in Henningsen's at times sardonic descriptions of the Danes' preferences in design. Hans Wegner once cited industrialization's slower evolution in Denmark as a contributing factor: 'one might dare to contend that the real reason for our success was that we were behind in industrial development. There was nothing technically new in things, no money for large technical experiments.'[30] Comments such as this one point to the ongoing dialogue that occurs between design and the culture that surrounds it, how design both reflects and affects that culture in which it is produced.

Thus, the Danish response was even more tempered than the Swedish one to the Stockholm Exhibition, and – throughout this period – the burgeoning Cabinetmakers Guild Exhibitions reinforced the correlation between designers and woodworkers. It is not a mythologizing of wood in Danish design by later critics, scholars, and historians, but rather the actual exhibitions and physical designs that gave preference to designs created mostly in wood in Denmark in the first half of the twentieth century (although even Henningsen tried his hand at a tubular steel chair, the Snake, in 1931). In retrospect, seeing Flemming Lassen's puffy sheepskin-upholstered armchair from 1938 borders on unnerving, in that it bears no resemblance to the pared-down forms and sculpted wooden frames we have come to associate with Danish Modern furniture. However, Juhl did some of his most sculptural work in upholstered designs, including furniture still in production, such as *Pelikanen* (the Pelican Chair, 1939).

A 1943 cartoon, 'An Architect Went through the Room,' by Carl Jensen, illustrates the ongoing tension between embedded ideas about taste and comfort and the demands of Modernism (Fig. 1.2). In the cartoon's first panel, an older Danish couple are relaxing in a cozy Biedermeier-style living room, complete with velvety upholstery and nineteenth-century rocking chair. A young architect is entering from the left with T-square and blueprints in hand. In the next panel, the same elderly couple struggle to get comfortable in their now de-cluttered, modernized living room – redecorated with PH-lamps, bare white walls, and low wood-frame furniture forcing them to sit forward. The young architect is exiting on the right-hand side, and the caption informs us that he 'decided with a heavy hand to beautify Danish homes.' The cartoon indicates that, culturally, even in Denmark, the move into modernist design was not always a smooth or easy one. By the 1950s and 1960s, all of this emphasis on wood would change, however, with the designs of Arne Jacobsen, Poul Kjærholm, and Verner Panton, yet they too would be folded into the larger history of Danish Modern.

SANERING

Unge Arkitekter har besluttet sig til med haard Haand at forskønne de danske Hjem.

— *Der gik en Arkitekt gennem Stuen!*

Fig. 1.2 Carl Jensen's 1943 cartoon, 'An architect went through the room,' offers a sardonic look at the supposed modernist discomfort superimposed on everyday Danes by contemporary designers. Courtesy of Designmuseum Danmark/The Library

The Cabinetmakers Guild Exhibitions

In the 1920s, as the Copenhagen Cabinetmakers Guild noticed increased competition emanating especially from the German furniture industry, they took steps to combat the perceived threat. As mentioned above, the guild began its annual furniture exhibitions in 1927, even adding a design competition that preceded each exhibition in 1933. Well attended by the public, these exhibitions offered concrete examples of the very debate that was occurring in the Danish press about the future of furniture design, a debate focusing on the tension between Modernism's aesthetic demands and traditional notions of taste and comfort. Early on, many of the cabinetmakers' workshops had been producing historical furniture; master cabinetmaker Rud. Rasmussen, for example, had been renowned for his oak furniture rendered in a Renaissance style.

A.J. Iversen (1888–1979),[31] a master cabinetmaker and tireless defender of wood, had seen the writing on the wall even before the guild's first exhibition. In 1925, the same year he participated in the International Exposition of Modern Industrial and Decorative Arts in Paris with furniture designed by Kaj Gottlob, Iversen wrote an article for the Danish periodical *The Architect* in which he addressed the ongoing conflict between democratic design and artistic innovation. Iversen perceived a dichotomy between artistic and social problems. More importantly, he stressed the necessity for architects and cabinetmakers to collaborate (some older cabinetmakers were resistant to any modernist developments); his rhetoric repeatedly reinforced the need for designers to be conscious of the cabinetmaker's craft. In his article for *The Architect*, Iversen wrote that architects, no matter how well trained, would not succeed without acquiring 'a more fundamental understanding of and affection for the cabinetmaker's craft and furniture design.'[32]

Aesthetically, Iversen argued for a tempered Modernism in design: clear forms without exaggeration, he contended, would endure the fickle nature of fashion. His approach was a pre-emptive mediation of the modernist currents he saw approaching, currents he viewed as extreme, before they could take root in Denmark. His lifelong efforts point to the construction of a history of the cabinetmakers' indispensable contribution to Danish Modern design running parallel to that of the architects and designers' efforts – architects and designers who were already receiving most of the notoriety. As Hansen points out, Iversen's argument 'was a clear reference to the moderate functionalism and simplicity that were about to establish themselves as the apparently special Danish contribution to modern furniture design.'[33]

Not surprisingly, Iversen became a staunch defender of craftsmanship and the cabinetmakers' participation in the development of Danish modern design. He was adroit at getting private and state funding to support annual exhibitions and at involving the two major Danish daily newspapers – *Politiken* and *Berlingske Tidende* – to the cabinetmaking tradition's advantage. His efforts, including writing copy for the Cabinetmakers Guild's anniversary publications and speaking in Oslo in 1939 to a gathering of architects and cabinetmakers, secured the craftsmen's place in the history of Danish design, but Iversen's efforts barely transferred abroad. Whereas many people still know the names of the Danish designers, few are familiar with the cabinetmakers who rendered their creations. Even in the renaissance of interest in Danish Modern furnishings in the past twenty years, people are much more inclined to know the names of Finn Juhl or Hans Wegner but not of their respective cabinetmakers Niels Vodder and Johannes Hansen. This dichotomy is interesting in light of Hansen's arguments for the cabinetmakers' involvement in the history of Danish Modern: 'Along with the story about Kaare Klint, the cabinetmaker narrative has determined or "framed" perceptions of modern Danish furniture design.'[34] Yet, beyond the notion that much of the furniture was handcrafted (even at times when it was not, all or partially), the cabinetmaker narrative never really 'travelled' abroad; it remains a more Danish component that in broader design history, especially in the United States, Japan, and Britain, is swallowed up in designer iconography.

Some design historians have argued that the efforts that began in Denmark in the 1930s to define a special Danish character in terms of simplicity (enkelhed) were part of a marketing narrative that helped to define Danish design both abroad and in Denmark. However, the history of the development of Modern design in general, and – as indicated above – especially in the exchange of ideas and approaches in the Nordic lands specifically in the late nineteenth and early twentieth century, is simply a movement into more pared down, less ornamented designs. The Danish silversmith and woodworker Kay Bojesen took up this issue in 1928 in an article entitled 'Hammerslag' ('Hammer Stroke') he wrote for Nyt Tidsskrift for Kunstindustri, in which he argued against the 'spurious' application of fake hammering on machine-manufactured silver. Abandoning the very Art-Nouveau-styling that had driven much of his own work in silver, Bojesen was embracing what he referred to as the 'honesty' of functionalism: 'It is obviously unjustifiable for industry . . . to attach a bogus appearance of handicrafts to its products.'[35] The tension between handicrafts and Modernism was also not endemic to Denmark. Widening the lens when observing these developments offers a more productive means of looking at design evolution than merely an attempt to construct a Danish national identity.[36] In fact, it seems almost inevitable, even natural, that the Cabinetmakers Guild would be resistant to International Modernism's machine-driven forms, as the craftsmen were not working in these idioms. What other reaction would cabinetmakers have to Mies van der Rohe's steel and upholstered Barcelona Chair (1929)? Also, these mostly imported currents were emanating predominantly from Germany, a country from which Denmark had suffered a number of military defeats and loss of territory. Thus, the resistance to International Modernism's burgeoning influence was not so much a narrative construction as it was an inevitable consequence of powerful factors at play.[37]

In 1930, the same year as the Stockholm Exhibition, the Cabinetmakers Guild's exhibition, with great effort and input from Iversen, along with government support, instituted the long-lasting collaboration between architects/designers and cabinetmakers. Young architects, many of them interested in social betterment, could partner with established cabinetmakers looking to ward off competition from industrially produced furniture. The collaboration offered fertile ground for the development of increasingly modern designs, though the Danish press was often decidedly mixed on the results. It was at this exhibition, in 1930, that Klint first exhibited his furnishings crafted by Rud. Rasmussen.

In the early 1930s, the notion of people owning sets of furniture that had to be bought all at once was also slowly being deconstructed.[38] Instead, people could choose from various furnishings designed specifically for rooms, adding them piecemeal when they wanted to or could afford them. A subtext of normative notions of taste attends much of these endeavours, taste merging with societal improvement (as it did in various early Modern design efforts) and economic concerns (affordable price points became another aim of the architects' designs). In 1932, the guild's exhibition's focus shifted to the furnishing of two-room apartments, a staple of Danish residences at that time; the architects Viggo Sten Møller and Hans Hansen had initiated this approach. 'Paradoxically enough, it was thus the hand-craftsmen and their designers – and not the furniture mass-producers – who set out to produce clean-lined and simple pieces for use in small [apartments],' wrote Karlsen and Tiedemann in 1961.[39] To this day, people are often surprised at how much smaller in scale many still-in-production Danish mid-twentieth-century designs appear, much of which is due to the early design of forms for apartment rooms.

Functionalism and *funkis*

In Denmark, the Stockholm Exhibition reinforced the sense that functionalism in Scandinavia emanated from Sweden. Henningsen viewed the exhibition as a breakthrough for modern architecture and design. Although he believed that, technically, the exhibition had offered very little, and though he had already referred wryly to functionalism as 'that infamous Swedish word,' he predicted it would serve as a major impulse for Nordic industrial arts and architecture. Henningsen responded positively to the exhibition as 'cubist, painterly architecture.'[40] In Henningsen's eyes, the event represented another major step away from the neoclassicism then exerting a tight grip on Nordic architecture. The exhibit appeared to validate many of his basic contentions, including an insistence that modern furniture should be produced with modern techniques and reflect both contemporary and future ideals. To Henningsen, this focus on the present seemed to illustrate his paradoxical contention that only art bearing the stamp of its time lives forever.

The Danish architect Kay Fisker (1893–1965), who had also worked for Asplund in Stockholm, once noted that functionalism was 'not a style but rather an ethic, a work ethic.'[41] This comment reflects a reactionary stance to the concept of the contemporary functionalist aesthetic emanating from Sweden and elsewhere in Europe. Fisker's remark also points to the dichotomy between function and style, the latter viewed as part of the time's problem, both socially and aesthetically. The term *funkis*, initially an abbreviated allusion to functionalism, became common in Denmark,

Sweden, and Norway: in time, it took on a pejorative connotation, implying that something was 'modern' in the worst way. Reviewing the Danish cultural critic Arne Sørensen's book *Funktionalisme og Samfund* (*Functionalism and Society*, 1933) in *Politiken* (27 December 1933), Henningsen observed that he had, since the time of *Critical Review* in the 1920s, fought 'the superficial funkis.'[42] Yet, he also contended that even the vacuous examples of *funkis* surrounding the Danes at the time, vestiges of which he claimed appeared in every decorator's window, were better than any return to past stylizations. While reinforcing the dichotomy, Henningsen's argument implied that functionalism had, on some level, won – at least enough to produce talentless imitations.

In 1954, on the 500th anniversary of the Copenhagen Cabinetmakers Guild, Iversen also reflected on the use of the word *funkis*: 'We viewed *funkis* as an insult, tantamount to degenerate, whereas we supported a healthy functionalism – in Danish: appropriateness.'[43] It is worth noting that Iversen used and made a point of drawing attention to a 'Danish' word (*hensigtsmæssighed*) to describe the cabinetmakers' intent, thus distancing the word *funkis* (and all that it entails) from something that was actually Danish. These observations by Fisker, Henningsen, and Iversen disclose a resistance to a complete embrace of modernist functionalism for its own sake. Their commentary also establishes appropriateness as the guiding force of functionalism in Denmark, another attempt at moving functional designs away from purely stylistic inventions while adding connotations of correctness to their designs. When the Danish cooperative FDB, Fællesforeningen for Danmarks Brugsforeninger (Danish Consumers Cooperative Society), instituted a line of Shaker-inspired mass-produced furniture in 1944 – driven by former Klint student Børge Mogensen and featuring textiles by his frequent cohort Lis Ahlmann – the organization accompanied the initial production with a brochure lauding this new 'appropriate furniture.' In 1945, FDB also produced a propaganda film, 'Og en lys og lykkelig fremtid' ('And a Bright and Happy Future'), featuring a young Danish couple being shown how to replace their large, inappropriate nineteenth-century-inspired furniture with new, modern FDB pieces and stressing that consumers can choose for themselves how to use, mix, and match the cooperative's functional designs (many of which were reintroduced to the Danish public in 2014).

The concept of 'Danish Design' as it developed internationally in the 1950s has often been tied to a more organic reading of international functionalism in which a number of designers and historians reinforced the dichotomy between the Danish response to functionalism and *funkis*. However, the Danes were not the only European designers wary of functionalism as its own end; in his 1958 essay 'Function and Gestalt,' Max Bill warned that functionalism '(like any other -ism) is prone to dissembling. It acts as if its aim is to fulfill all functions. In this respect it can be seen as either an offshoot of decorative art, saddled with the same deficiencies, or as a pseudo-solution reduced to the purely material functions.'[44] Mid-twentieth-century Danish design has often been framed as focusing more on aesthetic formalism than mere functionalism. As recently as 1994, in his monograph on Hans J. Wegner, Jens

Bernsen wrote that Danish design introduced a quality lacking in functionalism: 'Genuine interest in the interaction between users and their tools and a more organic understanding of form. Things were to be pure and simple . . .'[45]

Constructing Danish Modern (notions of craftsmanship)

All of these efforts, events, and responses led to the development and overarching approach of what came to be known as Danish Modern and, in particular, to the presentation of that approach by everyone from master cabinetmakers to marketers to government organizations. In the United States, a 1939 review in the *New York Times* of an exhibition, sponsored by the exhibition-showroom Den Permanente in Copenhagen, of 'modern Danish applied arts and crafts' at the department store Wanamaker's, already discloses now-familiar descriptions of Danish craftsmanship: 'contemporary simplicity,' 'high excellence,' 'no unnecessary wood,' 'modern sophistication.'[46] Even as late as 1961, this sense that craftsmanship attended all Danish designs surfaced in a comment on Arne Jacobsen's plywood Grand Prix Chair (1957), a chair recently put back into production. In *Hjemmets Brugskunst* (*A Treasury of Scandinavian Design*), Erik Zahle claims: 'Just like the rest of Arne Jacobsen's furniture, this piece is international in appearance but Danish in its fine finish and in the care with which it has been made. Although it is an industrial product, it has not been spit out of a machine; critical eyes follow its creation, from plywood to finished chair.'[47] Bifurcation abounds here: there is what is international and there is what is Danish; there is what is shoddily made and there is what is Danish; there is what is spit out of a machine and there is what is Danish. Still, designed objects exist and, as such, people respond to them: trained eyes and simple usage can help one to differentiate what is poorly made from what is well made.

One can detect similar efforts to maintain this crafts narrative in such commentary as the Danish architect Esbjørn Hiorth's claim – in an article that appeared in the 1960 catalogue for the travelling Arts of Denmark exhibition – that 'the borderline between hand work and industrial methods of production is very fluid. Even in the large industrial establishments a great part of the working process is carried out by hand.'[48] The dichotomy constructed by Zahle to describe Jacobsen's chair harkens back to the sense of craftsmanship stressed not only by Iversen's rhetoric and by design developments in Denmark's early Modern history, but also by the very designs in and of themselves. Designers and cabinetmakers spent much time on their designs and on producing them, as documents by Wegner, Vodder, and a host of others reveal; many of the architects' furniture designs challenged cabinetmakers, particularly in joinery. A craftsperson in any field knows that craftsmanship is not merely rhetoric but a learned skill that manifests itself in material culture.

Therefore, development of Danish Modern as both a style and an approach does not simply rest on the use of materials, a paring down of forms, or the marketing efforts of a network of players on the national or international stage. The theoretical considerations that drove most of Modernism, not solely in design but also in art, architecture, music, and film, played a significant role in the evolution of Danish Modern design in the twentieth century. Again, notions of a sudden break with tradition and an immediate embrace of the innovative as the thrust of Modernism reflect a narrow view of design developments – and not only in Denmark. As indicated before, even Gropius denied the mindless fetishizing of the innovative for its own sake in the Bauhaus endeavours; his early influences from William Morris's Arts and Crafts movement also disclose less avant-garde beginnings. In fact, it was the Grand Ducal-Saxon School of Arts and Crafts in Weimar that Gropius first took over in 1915 (replacing Henry van de Velde) and later transformed into the Bauhaus in 1919.

Danish designers and theorists had already shown an interest in the German Werkbund's early craft-driven work and its effects on style and taste: in 1916, Carl Brummer and Karl Larsen published the book, *Tyskernes Kamp mod den slette Smag: Der Deutsche Werkbund og dets Arbejde* (*The Germans' Battle against Bad Taste: The German Werkbund and its Work*). Thus, a tradition of craftsmanship lay at the very basis of the Bauhaus and *all* Modernist developments, no matter how experimental or machine-oriented its artists, craftspeople, and designers would eventually become. The refined metalwork of Bauhaus-er Marianne Brandt offers evidence of this meld of craftsmanship and industrialism. Fine craftsmanship is anything but a purely Danish tradition or solely a marketing construct crafted by protectionist Danish cabinetmakers. The embrace of craftsmanship by early modernists all over Europe grew initially out of the Arts and Crafts movement and was a reaction to the proliferation of poorly made, mass-produced products. The normative title of Brummer and Larsen's book also indicates how early European designers were viewing Modernism as a bulwark against mindless ideas about taste.

The Danes were more than aware of the juxtaposition between romanticized historical notions of craftsmanship born in an agrarian culture and modernist interpretations. A 1963 print advertisement by the furniture company Asbjørn-Møbler A/S presents an avocado-green Egg Chair (1958) by Arne Jacobsen in the yard of a colourless farm scene featuring half-timbering, grandmother's plates on a shelf, heavy metal pots, and a pair of hand-carved peasant chairs (see the cover image). 'Can the egg teach the chicken?,' the copy asks, quickly replying, 'Yes.' The copy goes on to read: 'Arne Jacobsen's "Egg" can teach peasant chairs a great deal about consummate design and thorough comfort.' The ad lauds a new reading of Danish craftsmanship in the futuristic shape of the upholstered Egg Chair while subverting the notion of Danish agrarian bliss. This is what Danish Modern looks like now, the ad seems to say, and it is not made of wood.

Notes

1. For a fine discussion of early modernist movements, see Richard Weston, *Modernism* (London: Phaidon, 1996).
2. Kjetil Fallan, 'Modern, Modernity, Modernism,' in *Design History: Understanding Theory and Method* (Oxford: Berg, 2010).

3. Herbert Read, *Art and Industry: The Principles of Industrial Design* (New York: Horizon Press, 1961), 36.

4. Ibid., 39.

5. Alfred Loos, 'Ornament and Crime,' in *The Industrial Design Reader*, ed. Carma Gorman. New York: Allworth, 2003), 76.

6. Le Corbusier, *Towards a New Architecture* (Thousand Oaks, CA: BN Publishing, 2008), 91.

7. Jean-Louis Cohen, *Le Corbusier* (Köln: Taschen, 2006), 47.

8. Jonathan Woodham, *Twentieth-Century Design* (Oxford: Oxford University Press, 1997), 33.

9. Walter Gropius, *The New Architecture and the Bauhaus* (Cambridge, MA: MIT Press, 1965), 20.

10. Ibid., 37.

11. Espen Johnsen refers to 'modernism's demand for anti-historicity'. 'Form Follows Emotion? Northern Minimalism and Neomodernism,' in *Scandinavian Design Beyond the Myth*, ed. Widar Halén and Kerstin Wickman (Stockholm: Arvinius/Form, 2003), 137.

12. Theo Van Doesburg, 'The Will to Style,' in *The Industrial Design Reader*, ed. Carma Gorman (New York: Allworth, 2003), 102.

13. Read, *Art and Industry*, 38.

14. Anni Albers, 'Anonymous and Timeless,' in *On Designing* (Middletown, CT: Wesleyan University Press, 1971), 7.

15. Viggo Sten Møller, *Funktionalisme og brugskunst siden 1920erne. Danmark. Norge. Sverige* (Copenhagen: Rhodos, 1978), 19.

16. There had been a Nordic Exhibition of Art and Industry in Copenhagen in 1872.

17. See: http://www.denstoredanske.dk/Dansk_Biografisk_Leksikon/Handel_og_industri/ Industridrivende/Philip_Schou.

18. Mirjam Gelfer-Jørgensen, in *Scandinavian Design Beyond the Myth*, ed. Wider Halén and Kerstin Wickman (Stockholm: Arvinius Forlag, 2003), 19.

19. Møller, *Funktionalisme og brugskunst siden 1920erne*, 42.

20. See Christian Norberg-Schulz: *Nightlands. Nordic Building* (Cambridge, MA: MIT Press, 1996), 155.

21. Quoted in Møller, *Funktionalisme og brugskunst siden 1920erne*, 35.

22. The Danish word *Skønvirke* refers to the Danish reading of *Jugendstil*, Art Nouveau, and the Arts and Crafts movement.

23. Møller, *Funktionalisme og brugskunst siden 1920erne*, 37.

24. In *Da danske møbler blev moderne* (*When Danish Furniture Became Modern*), Per H. Hansen (2006) does an excellent job of deconstructing the myth of Kaare Klint as the 'father' of Danish modern design.

25. See Møller, *Funktionalisme og brugskunst siden 1920erne*, 25.

26. Ibid., 29.

27. In *Modern Swedish Design: Three Founding Texts* (2011), Lucy Creagh refers to *acceptera* as the 'Manifesto of Swedish functionalism', 127.

28. Ibid., 148.

29. Paul Greenhalgh, ed. 'Introduction,' in *Modernism in Design* (London: Reaktion Books, 1910), 15.

30. Christian Holmsted Olesen, *Wegner: Just One Good Chair*, trans. Mark Mussari (Ostfildern, Germany: Hatje Cantz, 2014), 22.

31. As Hansen indicates in *Da danske møbler blev moderne*, as a youth, Iversen, who had been trained as both a fisherman and cabinetmaker, had to return to fishing until 1910 because of unemployment in the cabinetmaking trade (2006, 68).

32. Olesen, *Wegner: Just One Good Chair*, 23.

33. Hansen, *Da danske møbler blev moderne*, 73.

34. Ibid., 88.

35. Quoted in Lars Hedebo Olsen, *Kay Bojesen. Store danske designere* (Copenhagen: Lindhardt og Ringhof, 2008), 33.

36. See Hansen, *Da danske møbler blev moderne*: 'an attempt at a constant (re)construction of a Danish national identity', 98.

37. At the 1932 Cabinetmakers Guild Exhibition, the architects Arne Jacobsen and Flemming Lassen displayed furniture designs blatantly influenced by International Modernism; the boxy upholstered and lacquered forms meant for a gentleman's room were met with much resistance and derision. Though he went on to world-renown, Jacobsen never exhibited again at the guild's events.

38. Many of these heavily upholstered, period-piece furniture sets were pejoratively referred to as 'butcher sets' by the more modern-oriented Danes.

39. 'Karlsen and Tiedemann, 'Denmark,' in *A Treasury of Scandinavian Design,* ed. by Erik Zahle (New York: Golden Press, 1961): 12.

40. See Poul Henningsen. 'Kubismens politiske indhold,' *Kritisk Revy. En antologi af tekster og illustrationer fra tidsskriftets tre årgange,* ed. by Sven Møller Kristensen (Copenhagen: Gyldendal, 1963): 156–62.

41. 'Funktionalisme er ikke en stil, men snarere en moral. En arbejdsmoral!' Møller, 37.

42. Poul Henningsen. 'Funktionalisme og Samfund' ('Functionalism and Society'), *Kulturkritik I, 1918–33* (Copenhagen: Rhodos, 1973), 259.

43. *Møbler* (1954), 31(7), 37–39. Quoted in Hansen (2006), 101.

44. Max Bill, 'Function and Gestalt,' in *Form, Function, Beauty = Gestalt*, trans. Pamela Johnston (London: AA Publications, 2010), 111.

45. Jens Bernsen, *Hans J Wegner om Design* (Copenhagen: Dansk Design Center, 1994), 18.

46. Walter Rendell Storey, 'Home Decoration: Danish Crafts Rank High as Art,' *The New York Times* (8 October 1939), 63.

47. Erik Zahle, ed. *Hjemmets Brugskunst. Kunsthåndværk og Kunstindustri i Norden* (Copenhagen: Hassings, 1961), 91.

48. Esbjorn Hiorth, 'Trends in Contemporary Danish Design,' in *The Arts of Denmark: Viking to Modern*, ed. Erik Lassen (Copenhagen: Det Berlingske Bogtrykkeri, 1960), 122.

2 Tradition and/or Modernism: Kaare Klint and Poul Henningsen

The Danish National Pavilion at the 1929 International Exposition in Barcelona (La Exposición Internacional de Barcelona) was a building of reddish wood with a gabled roof, designed by the Danish architect Tyge Hvass (1885–1963). Photographs reveal that the pavilion's interior walls were decorated with landscape paintings and portraits of Danish girls in nature (Fig. 2.1). A curious tension exists, however, between the understated furnishings, especially the dining table and chairs, the latter rendered in Nigerian leather and a warm reddish-brown wood, and the chandeliers hanging from the celling beams. Whereas the chairs – their gently concaved seats and back in studded leather, and curving back legs and perpendicular front legs in Cuba mahogany – owe much to the English Chippendale chairs from the 1700s, the more modernist chandeliers seem almost anachronistic in their industrial aesthetic. Their

Fig. 2.1 The Danish Pavilion at Barcelona in 1929: Poul Henningsen's modernist chandelier seems like an intruder among the pavilion's more nationalist elements, including Kaare Klint's more historical Red Chair and tables in deep mahogany. Courtesy of Designmuseum Danmark/The Library

elegance is transmitted through metallic angular arms and inverted bowl-shaped glass shades. The table and chairs were designed by Kaare Klint and produced by cabinetmaker Rud. Rasmussen in 1927, and the lamps by Poul Henningsen in the same year.[1] In retrospect, their design approach seems decades removed.

The Danish Pavilion's overall décor recalls a nineteenth-century drawing room and even features a mannequin dressed in national peasant costume. Yet, the twin chandeliers seem to have been dropped from the future, their spider-like forms pointing not only upward but metaphorically forward as well. The entire room seems surprisingly open in its spatial sense, uncluttered and understated. Still, viewed in light of Mies van der Rohe's groundbreaking modernist pavilion, which he worked on with fellow designer Lily Reich, at the same exposition in Barcelona, the Danish Pavilion appears staid, grounded in tradition, and decidedly nationalistic.[2]

To refer to Mies's work as the 'German Pavilion' seems almost inappropriate; at the time it was referred to as the Pavilion of German Representation. Nothing about the meld of floor-to-ceiling glass, smoothly polished rectilinear surfaces (travertine, marble, and onyx doré), and steel and leather furniture seems redolent of anything particularly German in any historic, romantic, or nationalist sense.[3] Historians have, in fact, referred to Mies's blatantly modern structure as the Barcelona Pavilion for decades now.[4] The stainless steel and leather chair that he and Reich designed for the pavilion – now also known simply as the Barcelona Chair – is one of the most recognizable designs from the last century. Over the decades it has transmogrified into a symbol of Bauhaus Modernism; Tom Wolfe even mocked it as a fetishized 'Platonic ideal' in his satirical *From Bauhaus to Our House* (1981). Mies and Reich designed it originally for the Spanish king and queen to sit in at the opening of the German sections of the exposition (Mies referred to the chair's design as intentionally 'monumental'). Although Klint's pavilion chair seems much more rooted in history in comparison, Mies took inspiration from the ancient Roman folding curule seat (*Sella Curulis*) for his Barcelona design. Influence from the Roman folding chair also surfaces in Kint's Propeller Stool (1930), a design that began as an exercise by his students but did not make a public appearance until the Cabinetmakers Guild Exhibition in 1964. Even with the addition of the allegorical figurative statue *Der Morgen* (Morning) by Georg Kolbe, the entire Barcelona Pavilion functions in tandem, a medley of materials rendered in then ultra-modern rectilinear forms with enclosed and open spaces slipping easily in and out of each other. Aspects of it even presage regional interpretations of Modernism, as in those used in California homes in the mid-twentieth century. Curiously, Mies would use some of Henningsen's pendant lamps in his next major project, the Tugendhat House (1928–30) in Brno, Czechoslovakia.

Yet, despite the blatant nods to national identity and wistful landscape paintings gracing the walls in the Danish Pavilion, the furniture and lamps present two varied responses to modernist currents in the late 1920s. In 1929, Klint and Henningsen were apt designers to choose for the Danish Pavilion's furnishings. The Danish architect Kay Fisker's remark that functionalism was first and foremost a work ethic (*en arbejdsmoral*)[5] could serve as a legend over the life work of the two designers.

Both employed highly detailed studies resting on rationalist, 'scientific' notions to craft their designs.[6] However, the two architect-designers, though contemporaries, could not be further apart in their attitudes towards aesthetics. As the chandeliers in the Danish Pavilion illustrate, Henningsen's series of PH-lamps – many still in production almost a century after their inception – display a forward-looking, futuristic form, whereas Klint's furniture – some of his designs are also still in production – disclose a designer reinterpreting historical types as a guiding force.

Historicizing Klint

In 1924, Klint, educated as an architect, became a lecturer – and eventually professor – at the Furniture School of Det Kongelige Danske Kunstakademi (the Royal Danish Academy of Fine Arts).[7] He had already been teaching furniture design at Copenhagen's Tekniske Skole (Technical College), where he had emphasized the measurement of old furniture designs with his students since 1920. His *Faaborgstol* (Faaborg Chair), designed with his mentor Carl Petersen in 1914 for the Faaborg Museum of Art, is the only piece of Danish furniture still in production after 100 years. Gorm Harkær has determined the chair's meaning for the construction of a national design legacy: 'The Faaborg Chair is cleansed of unnecessary decoration. The simple construction is a kind of decoration in itself, in a way unlike any other chair in 1914. One could even say that the chair was a turning point, for with it the phenomenon of Danish design begins.'[8] During his tenure at the Royal Danish Academy (until 1954), Klint crafted an aesthetic approach to furniture design based on the involved study of historical types, materials, and ergonomics, the latter of which came to be known as anthropometrics, and the formal organization resulting from this study. In 1930, in his article 'Instruction in Furniture Design at the Royal Academy,' appearing in the Danish journal *Architektens Maanedshæfte* (*The Architect's Monthly*), Klint described the thrust of his elaborate studies: 'In teaching, I view this material as more valuable than a review of aesthetic refinements. On the basis of these dry facts, you can learn to construct a piece of furniture; everyone can then apply the changing artistic designs that suit him and the time.'[9] More importantly, Klint defines the Furniture School's main purpose as 'an ongoing analysis of common furniture types.'[10]

Thus, Klint and his students – especially Ole Wanscher, Børge Mogensen, Rigmor Andersen, and Mogens Koch – took a Cartesian approach to design, one resting heavily on elaborate measurements of the human body, utilitarian objects, and storage spaces. More than half of Klint's article in *The Architect's Monthly* consists of detailed drawings and measurements. Yet, despite this focus on usage, Klint derided the popular functionalism that had already lapsed in his eyes into *funkis*. In his approach we see two worlds colliding: the affinity for historical types seems to fly in the face of the modernist aesthetics emanating from the Bauhaus and from technological advancements in the use of new materials (such as tubular steel), whereas the notion of measuring oneself to the ultimate or 'perfect' design actually recalls the normative sense of appropriateness and rationality – the striving for objective solutions – that drove many early European modernists in their design endeavours (consider Le Corbusier's human measurements, based on Vitruvius and Leonardo, for his modular system). Even Klint admits to bowing to modern demands about 'order' and 'hygiene.'[11] This duality in Klint's teachings reveals how and, to some extent, why Danish designers in the mid-twentieth century (designers as diverse as Nanna Ditzel, Grete Jalk, Arne Jacobsen, and Poul Kjærholm studied with Klint or his students) mediated modernist currents by not completely abandoning all sense of tradition but, instead, often by creating a dialogue with it. Still, the forms of the various designers' responses were notably varied, and Klint's fealty to wood does not transfer into the works of such influential designers as Jacobsen and Kjærholm. Also, some of the most recognizable names from Danish Modern's heyday – Wegner and Juhl – did not attend Klint's Furniture School.[12]

The 1929 Danish Pavilion's Red Chair, one of Klint's most studied creations, offers a prime example of the design approach he both employed and established at the academy. Studying historical furniture types was a mainstay at the Furniture School, and the Red Chair reinterprets the eighteenth-century Chippendale by maintaining its lower structure (even to the point of the stretchers mimicking their exact position in the English prototype).[13] However, the Chippendale's elaborately carved backrest has been replaced by studded leather, matching the red-leather seat covering. Klint felt that the English chair's back 'in its ornamental beauty [was] inimitable' and 'higher than necessary for decorative reasons,'[14] and therefore inappropriate for modern society (he was also fond of American Shaker furniture, which eschewed ornament in its simplified forms). Instead, he and his students used a different, simpler chair from the same period as the prototype for the back (that chair model is faulted for having a Rococo bottom – though the use of studs on the leather transfer from this chair). Klint extended the more simplistic structure of the seat and legs into the Red Chair's back, turning it into a simple rectangular form covered in the same studded red leather as the seat. He wanted, as he explained in his article in *The Architect's Monthly* (1930), a chair that would 'answer to the demands of modern times, yet one that you can see comes from good old family.'[15] As Anne-Louise Sommer points out in her monograph on Klint (2008), Klint did not create the chair on his own: 'It was a product of the active re-appropriation of tradition, and it was a product of the students' and Klint's joint work with measuring old chair types, which became a significant part of education at the Royal Art Academy.'[16] In fact, Klint's students presented at least three variations on the reinterpreted design.

Aesthetically, though, the Red Chair does not at first glance seem connected to the concept of mid-twentieth-century Danish Modern. The chair's squared off legs bear no relation to the rounded, tapered legs of, say, Finn Juhl's most renowned designs or the abstracted animal-based forms of many of Wegner's chair designs. Yet, in its overall appearance, the Red Chair is of a piece – and this sense of oneness, of wholeness, may be one of its few shared characteristics with a number of later, more inventive designs. Speaking in England in 1947, the Danish architect Steen Eiler Rasmussen observed: 'Klint and his students made a point of creating a new chair, which had the virtues of the old, combined with the simplicity and comfort of the present.'[17] Whereas the original Chippendale Chair's ornamental back is purely decorative and definitely class-conscious, the Red Chair's form is continuous: the back appears to be just as intended for leaning against as the seat does for sitting. Historically, the Red Chair presents another step away from the European tradition of naming chairs first after monarchs (Louis XIV, Louis XVI) and then after designers (Chippendale, Sheraton) to a chair that is both historically allusive and yet anonymous at the same time.

Visually, however, the chair is not innovative; it feeds well into the historicized view of Klint as leading the charge against the Bauhaus while clinging to historical precedents. 'Instead of flirting with machine-age glamour,' wrote Douglas Brenner in the *New York Times* as late as 2005, 'Klint bows to Thomas Chippendale, but the discretion of his homage exudes self-confidence. And the chair is also comfortable, thanks to his study of human anatomy and movement.'[18] This remark reveals all the elements that have contributed, rightfully or not, to Klint's legacy: the antipathy towards machine aesthetics, the adherence to historical forms, the discretionary (read: sober, subtle, conservative, modest) nature of his readings, and the studied ergonomics leading to supposed universal comfort. From these we may extrapolate certain characteristics that were carried into later developments (and marketed as such) in Danish Modern: the furniture is handcrafted (even when it isn't); the furniture is subtle and not radically modern; the furniture is comfortable because of the attention to ergonomics.

The historicizing of Klint's approach – placing him on a line that appears to lead inevitably from previous styles through him to mid-century Danish Modernism – together with the narratives that have grown around it, has proven quite resilient. For example, Klint is frequently alluded to as the 'father of Danish modern design' or the 'grandfather of Danish Modern,' even though most world citizens who recognize Jacobsen's Egg Chair (1958) would have no idea who designed the Red Chair (or even some of Klint's other notable pieces, such as the Safari or Deck Chair). By 1961, Arne Karlsen and Anker Tiedemann could confidently write that Klint 'created the modern Danish tradition' and described his approach towards furniture design as 'a common inheritance that every Danish furniture designer . . . carries, consciously or unconsciously.'[19] That same year, Ulf Hård af Segerstad wrote that Klint's 'primary aim was to create truly functional furniture.'[20] In 1999, Charlotte and Peter Fiell asserted that Klint's teachings 'laid the foundations for the renewal of Danish design after the Second World War.'[21] Yet, considering that it was Juhl and Wegner – neither of whom studied under Klint – who first put Danish design on the international map after the Second World War, one can see how Klint is repeatedly rewoven into the history of Danish Modern's development (Juhl was actually antithetical to Klint's approach).

Still, the conventional sense that figures such as Kaare Klint and Mies van der Rohe were moving in opposite directions can be misleading. Certain parallels, for example, also surface in their use of materials. Klint chose Cuba mahogany for many of his chairs (like the Red Chair), often waxing it instead of lacquering it to emphasize the idiosyncrasies of the wood's grain; the use of optically vibrant ebony and travertine in Mies's projects reveals a similar approach – a sense of remaining 'true' to the material (a frequent tenet espoused by modernists). Klint's approach, however, rests so heavily on historical precedents that one can detect an overarching resistance to the threat of an encroaching industrialization.[22] Danish historians have repeatedly emphasized or exaggerated a split in design approach between the Bauhaus and the Danes. Sommer refers to the Central European currents as 'militant and socialistic' and the Nordic approach as 'humane, social-democratic, and reformative,' with Klint as evidence of the latter.[23] That juxtaposition would prove useful when marketing Nordic design to Americans in the mid-1950s. In their monograph on Arne Jacobsen for the Great Danish Designers series, Thau and Vindum observe that Danish modernists 'believed that the Germans in the Bauhaus replaced the detailed ornamentation of previous eras with a substance-less industrial style.'[24]

At the same time, Klint's preference for costly and exotic woods shows no signs of the social concerns driving many modernists (like Henningsen); Cuba mahogany and fine Nigerian leather were expensive materials for furniture and obviously not intended for the working class. One can also trace the commitment to solid wood as the preferred material from Kint's influential endeavours all the way to Grete Jalk's lament in 1973 that Scandinavian designers should still be working in wood: 'It would be gratifying if Scandinavians would return to wooden furniture and rely on this beautiful material, that employed correctly is the most living and variegated material for producing furniture.'[25] Similar concerns appear in a comment by contemporary Danish designer Jonas Bjerre-Poulsen about the thrust of his company, Norm. In a 2014 Design Within Reach catalogue, Bjerre-Poulsen stated that he and partner Kasper Rønn were 'working with Danish norms and standards refined over hundreds of years, rather than rejecting them in the endless search for the new.'[26] Those words echo many of the Klint Furniture School's sentiments, including a negative response to innovation for its own sake and the sense that a more tempered response is somehow 'Danish.' In 2015, at the Stockholm Furniture Fair, Klint's Red Chair was exhibited next to the Finn Yrjö Kukkapuro's Karuselli lounge chair (1964) in a separate display area defined as 'Inside Scandinavian Design.' Speaking about the two chairs, the English designer Ilse Crawford commented that Klint's chair 'is not flashy or spectacular but a beautiful, simple, useful solution to sitting that can fit anywhere.' Asked to define Scandinavia Design, she referred to 'a sensitive approach to materials and a rigorous approach to function' – determinants that fit snugly into the Klintian legacy.[27]

In retrospect, Klint's furniture – which many consider the foundation for Danish Modern as it would come to be known – seems more like a point of departure. For example, later designers such as Wegner and Juhl responded to Klint's English-inspired creations with more curvilinear, sculptural forms; Klint's cautious employment of Chinese chairs as prototypes turned into opportunities for pared-down abstraction in Wegner's series of Chinese chairs. As Hansen points out in *When Danish Furniture*

Became Modern (2006): 'Finn Juhl's and to a certain extent Hans J. Wegner's approach is and was a rejection of all the Klintian school with its theoretical meticulousness and desk-work on furniture types.'[28] In 1964, in the Danish newspaper *Politiken*, Wegner would even have a public debate with Klint's former student and devotee Børge Mogensen and the textile designer Lis Ahlman, both of whom argued for using only 'old, natural materials,' whereas Wegner was open to experimentation, even for its own sake. Mogensen also revealed something of his former mentor's demanding pedagogy in the following comment: 'From Klint we learned a method. At the same time, he ground us down, and we had enough difficulty breaking free afterwards. But we learned our limitation. You have to accept it.'[29] Wegner was much less sanguine, however, about Klint's legacy: 'At first, I wasn't in the least bit interested in Klint.'[30] Klint's historically driven, formalist endeavours were also antithetical to Poul Henningsen, his co-exhibitor at the Danish Pavilion.

PH – the conscience of Modernism

The leading voice of Denmark's avant-garde in the period between the two world wars, Poul Henningsen – known in Denmark simply as PH – maintained parallel careers as both a broad social commentator and the designer of lamps, some of which have remained in production for more than eighty years (Fig. 2.2). Many years of study on the directional diffusion of light led to his world-renowned series of hanging, wall, and table lamps. Henningsen employed a three-shade system of curves based on the shapes of plates, saucers, and cups. In 1925, one of his lamp designs – the first in his enduring PH-series – won a gold medal at the Exposition Internationale des Arts Décoratifs et Industriels Modernese in Paris. One of Henningsen's lamp designs in this series – Model PH5 (1957) – provides one of the most ubiquitous examples of Danish Modern ever produced: rendered in enamelled sheet-metal, which offers easy mass production, the lamp's five diffusers completely cover the light bulb, preventing glare and distributing light in varying degrees dictated by direction. The lamp's simple functionalism has combined with its relentlessly modernist look to make it a favoured and useful design, particularly in Denmark where it appears in homes, offices, stores, and businesses. Internationally, the lamp's striking silhouette has come to symbolize Danish Modern, thanks in great part to its somewhat 1950s' sci-fi aesthetic. Commenting on the cultural narratives attached to the PH-lampshade, the architect and glass designer Jacob E. Bang observed: 'Somehow it set free something within us, and there was a *religious* element to it in the joy and veneration which greeted its appearance. To hang it on one's lamp-fitting was to affirm that one was an intellectual and of the avant-garde.'[31]

Trained as an architect, though he left the Royal Danish Academy of Fine Arts Architecture School after only a couple of semesters, Henningsen began writing for the Danish daily newspaper *Politiken* in 1921 and soon became the paper's first architecture critic. His earliest articles reveal a firm commitment to the notion that aesthetics should not trump societal concerns, his voice becoming one of conscience for the cultural

Fig. 2.2 Henningsen works on one of his numerous lamps featuring his multi-shade diffusers. His PH-series of lamps have been in continuous production since the 1920s. Courtesy of Designmuseum Danmark/The Library

radicals of his time. As early as 1923, PH participated in the International City-Building Congress in Göteborg, Sweden, and he remained deeply concerned about the social ramifications of growth in the world's expanding cities. His journal *Kritisk Revy* (*Critical Review*, 1926–28) became the dominant organ for the avant-garde to express its views on myriad aspects of Danish life, from nature preservation and literature to religion and architecture. Henningsen's numerous articles offer a rare glimpse into the ideological forces, particularly in the late 1920s, driving early developments in Danish Modernism. At one point in his seminal article, 'Tradition and Modernism,'[32] appearing in *Critical*

Review in 1927, Henningsen turns his attention to the design of chairs, his thoughts reflecting the aesthetic dichotomy between Danish and Bauhaus interpretations of Modernism.[33] The article includes a photograph of Bauhaus designer Marcel Breuer's steel-and-leather B3 Chair (later known as the Wassily Chair). Because of its superimposed use of tubular steel and sharp leather straps of parallel lines, Henningsen derides the design as patently uncomfortable: 'Mostly, you fear getting your arm torn off at the shoulder if you sit in it.'[34] Disgruntled by attempts to contort furniture design into the paradigm of a specific artistic movement, Henningsen disparages what he calls 'violent' attempts to make Constructivist, Dadaist, Surrealist, or Cubist chairs (all of which he accuses of being 'bad to sit in').[35] He cites an absence of any connection to society as a flaw in such form-driven aesthetics. One senses in many of his essays that he was searching for a visual language that would address both social and aesthetic issues and merge them into an all-encompassing perspective without arbitrarily superimposing design demands.

As a functionalist, Henningsen preferred to remain a man without a country; he wanted to abandon the absolute demands of certain '-isms' and replace them with 'a functional context, one in which the principle is decisive for us.'[36] When he alludes to the steamed-bent-wood Vienna Chair, designed by the German-Austrian Michael Thonet (1796–1871), Henningsen reaffirms the still prevalent Danish preference for wood at this time and presages the ongoing attraction to Thonet's chair (a stalwart in myriad settings, the chair design has survived more than one and a half centuries of stylistic changes and remains popular). The allusion also ties design efforts Henningsen believes should be made in his own time to Thonet's ability to design a lasting form that reflected manufacturing advancements in the German-Austrian's time.[37] Henningsen closes this section by admitting that when designing chairs, wood would probably be the preferable material.

Henningsen uses the question of chair design, which he returns to towards the end of the article, to establish a third position on the question of the efficacy of traditionalist or modernist resolutions. He locates certain representative decisions that must be made about chair design and insists that designers must work in tandem with the dominant mode of thinking at a given time. This approach means addressing issues of economy, unpretentiousness, precision, and clarity. Henningsen proceeds to offer examples of furnaces and lamps with illustrations representing three approaches: Traditional, Realist, and Modern. These examples illustrate his belief that stylistic approaches should enable designers to make decisions in which form expresses function naturally: therefore, examples of traditionalism with their superficial historical filigree are deemed 'indecent,' whereas a forced Modernism appears irrational. This third approach that Henningsen stakes out reflects the organic functionalism that would come to define many Danish design efforts in the mid-twentieth century, continuing to delineate it – even in retrospect – from more industrial developments in the German Bauhaus.

In his introduction to *Kritisk Revy: En antologi af tekster og illustrationer fra tidsskriftets tre årgange* (*Critical Review: An Anthology of Texts and Illustrations from the Journal's Three Volumes*, 1963), Sven Møller Kristensen defines Henningsen's journal as a specifically Danish expression of International Modernism: 'it is worth emphasizing the word "Danish," because they were critical not only of the antiquated tradition but also of modernism as a concept.'[38] Kristensen's observation returns us to that confluence of social and historical forces that added to Denmark's resistance to a simple embrace of Modernism – a tension that manifests itself in much of twentieth-century Danish design. This dichotomy becomes evident in Henningsen's observation in his article 'Le Corbusier,' from *Kritisk Revy* (1926, no. 1): 'His great love for technology can lead him astray.'[39] Unlike the influential Swiss architect, who referred to his furniture designs with Charlotte Perriand as 'equipment,' Henningsen views aesthetic compromise as a duty that, when properly addressed, leads to better solutions, both socially and economically. He also attempts to define this approach as culturally Danish by insisting that, at this juncture in history, the Danes prefer the economic, the technical, the social, and, not least of all, what is actually practical and possible, over the aesthetic.

Henningsen's (and Kristensen's) words indicate how Danish designers and historians repeatedly constructed a dichotomy between international currents and the specifically Danish response. Both comments are rife with practicality and resistance to ideology; they recall the cabinetmaker A.J. Iversen's distinction between *funkis* and Danish 'appropriateness.' As Niels Peter Schou points out in '*Kunst og Politik*' (*Art and Politics*), Henningsen's goal is to stake out a position in relation to other international currents, such as Russian Constructivism, the Bauhaus, and Le Corbusier – a position critical of their efforts but sympathetic to their cause, resulting in an independent position.[40] The advantage with the polemical Henningsen is that he left so much writing on the topic that it provides a window into ideological and cultural issues at that time. A closer reading reflects the origins of a number of concepts driving the development of Danish Modern.

Whereas Kaare Klint was resistant to modernist aesthetics but willing to employ historical precedents, Henningsen was searching, theoretically, for the third rail. In 'Tradition and Modernism,' PH insists that not only the houses people live in but also the everyday objects they surround themselves with need to look completely different from how they looked before the revolution that has taken place both socially and technologically. New tasks, he affirms, will require new forms and, thus, a departure from known styles: 'This new form will create a new aesthetic culture, and we must certainly let the more decorative and indifferent objects . . . be characterized by this new perception of beauty, whereby a new style will emerge.'[41] In the contemporary use of steel and glass, for example, Henningsen cites the ability to create larger windows, permitting more light and creating a spatial revolution in hygiene – but he also sees a tension between form and content, between aesthetics and hygiene (partially because of cost). By 1930, in his article 'Fremtidsperspektiver' ('Perspectives on the Future'),[42] he would caution against placing too much weight on the use of new materials revealing his – and a number of the Danish designers' – complex relationship with Modernism. 'One should not underestimate the meaning of the propaganda Modernism promotes with respect to the use of modern materials,' Henningsen warns, 'but one must also not overstate it.'[43]

Henningsen's response to the Werkbund's travelling exhibition[44] at Designmuseum Danmark, in 1928, exemplifies his decidedly mixed feelings about the modernist currents emanating from Germany. In a bitingly satirical *Critical Review* piece, 'Die neue Sachlichkeit!' (1928, vol. 3), Henningsen accompanies a photo of the exhibition, featuring tubular steel furniture by Mies van der Rohe, with a long, scathing caption (in both Danish and German, no less). The entire room is described as a 'tin box,' and PH derides every aspect from a pendant's light ('hard as barbwire') to an industrial-looking floor lamp ('grates like sand against your teeth') to chairs useless for either work or lounging as a failed attempt at mixing 'hygiene' with 'comfort' transferred 'from the hospital to the living room.'[45] Henningsen acknowledges the common enemies he shares with the German modernists: artistic conservatives and traditionalists. However, he sees no sign of cultural progress in the glass and steel arrangement. He cites the overriding effort to express 'the new objectivity' (the German *'Die neue Sachlichkeit,'* in Danish, *'den nye saglighed'*) as the problem and accuses the German modernists of turning it into tubular steel 'ornament,' designed as yet another style to sell to a snobbish public as 'an objective look.' Other Nordic architects and designers shared his view. At a lecture ('Rationalism and Man') given to the Swedish Society of Arts and Crafts in 1935, Alvar Aalto remarked: 'A confrontation with the mass of the neue Sachlichkeit produced in recent times causes a person to take a skeptical attitude and makes one ready to pursue all criticism directed against it . . . Modernism has run amok with the new world of forms that has arisen through the analysis of materials, new working methods, new social conditions . . .'[46]

Long before any marketing efforts to delineate Danish furniture from Bauhaus endeavours, long before design historians would describe mid-century Danish designs as 'organic,' PH had already drawn an aesthetic line in the sand. In Germany, *die neue Sachlichkeit* at first represented a rationalist, conceptual response to the hyper-subjectivity of Expressionism. Although Henningsen rejects what he sees as a superimposed aesthetic, based on *die neue Sachlichkeit,* he acquiesces to sharing the same concerns as some of the Bauhaus designers. More importantly, even in Denmark, this sense of *den nye saglighed* – as in Klint's efforts to find objective, measurable solutions – reflects the burgeoning modernists' attempt to construct a bulwark against the shifting sands of style and rapid advancements in technology in an increasingly unstable world. Applying Herbert Simon's division between inner and outer environments in *The Sciences of the Artificial* (1996), one can see that designers often maintain some semblance of independence by attempting to insulate themselves from exterior influences: 'In one way or another the designer insulates the inner system from the environment, so that an invariant relation is maintained between inner system and goal . . .'[47] Henningsen's satirical rhetoric delineates his own design theories, as well as the efforts of a number of Danish designers at that time, from the German aesthetic based solely on *Sachlichkeit* to, once again, construct and maintain a Danish response to Modernism. In his 1930 article in *The Architect's Monthly*, Klint also responded to the German designers' rationalist efforts by pointing out that he had already been working towards that goal for years: 'with hopefully forgivable pride, I can point out that four years later in Germany they have done far less rigorous testing.'[48]

Aesthetics of Cubism

As mentioned earlier, developments in art often paved the way for modernist advancements in architecture and design. For Henningsen, Cubism offered the best template for finding an approach that would address its time without yielding to the demands of specific aesthetic paradigms. In his article 'Kubismens politiske Forhold' ('Cubism's Political Situation'), from *Politiken* (18 December 1930), Henningsen refers to Cubism as pure painting and cites the contributions of Picasso, Braque, Metzinger, and Gleizes. He also mocks the more traditionalist criticism that Cubism is merely an 'atelier art' that should have remained a private affair. The rhetorician in Henningsen is quick to pre-empt and deflate any objections. Whereas he derides conservatives for viewing Cubism as a meaningless and abandoned experiment, he also berates Communists for dismissing it as the last empty gesture of the bourgeoisie. And he warns his Marxist contemporaries that their affection for representational poster art will never change the way the average citizen looks at the world.

Socially and aesthetically, Henningsen insists that Cubism has already changed the daily language in the world of seeing. People, he claims, now live 'in the sign of cubism. It has created a new typography that pervades the newspaper every day, mostly in advertising.'[49] Henningsen also traces a line from Rococo and Empire movements in design towards current artistic idioms revealing clear, obviously cubist effects – effects he even observes in fabric designs. Stylistic movements in applied art and architecture also disclose the influence of Cubism. In the pure forms of Cubism, Henningsen sees art's strongest value for people and, perhaps more importantly, a weapon directed at conservatism: 'Everything indicates that cubism, in its very idea of pure painting, can free us from habits and get us to look freshly and sincerely at the visual world surrounding us.'[50] Design will not abandon its class-conscious endeavours, PH insists, until people begin to see differently. Parallels to this aesthetic approach exist in Wegner's work with the chair's top-rail, each new design revealing a paring down of the form into more abstract shapes.

Finally, PH cites three areas in which cubist approaches bring viewers back to reality: form, texture, and colour. Before Cubism's influence, form had been arrested in snobbishness about style and ornamentation; the sense for materials stifled in silk, velvet, gilding, and marble; colours had been dictated by class-driven notions that fine colours should appear stuffy as they appear in the fashionable furniture stores of his time. PH views Cubism as a liberation from these restrictions: 'The cubists investigated these questions anew, from scratch, thereby tearing off all the exterior, costly, and ornamental drapery of beauty.'[51] Henningsen predicts a paradoxical development for the exorcising effects of Cubism, which will ultimately end in a Keatsian fulfilment of artistic negative capability: Cubism will erase itself, PH claims, as a good artist who erases her personality in her work to achieve the universally applicable. Henningsen argues that, despite some superficial styles inspired by Cubism's effect, once the cubist approach achieves full clarification, people will no longer need to call it Cubism – they will simply refer to it as 'modern spirit.'

In architecture, Henningsen finds parallels to Cubism's positive effects, and here he strikes an anti-nationalist chord: he derides the public's continued affection for the 'Danish-ness' of tile roofs, the venerability of brick, and the nobility of plaster. He would replace them with cement, asphalt roofing, and steel-framed windows. Once these materials achieve their worth aesthetically, he suggests thanking Cubism. Even in addressing the Stockholm Exhibit of 1930, Henningsen viewed its architecture as cubist specifically for its capacity to compel people to think outside the limits of previous styles. In PH's eyes, the event represented another major step away from the neoclassicism then exerting a tight grip on Nordic architecture. The exhibit appeared to validate many of his basic contentions, including an insistence that modern furnishings should be produced with modern techniques and reflect both contemporary and future ideals. This focus on the present illustrated Henningsen's paradoxical contention that art truly characterized by its time will live forever.

Henningsen believed that a cubist aesthetic would also have a socially levelling effect, another frequent modernist effort; it could function as the foundation on which to build a new architecture and a new industrial art, especially by creating residences for the average person, returning us to the positive notion of removing formalist trappings to achieve greater societal equality. He writes in another article, 'Motivets Betydning' ('Motif's Meaning'), that '. . . today, we are closer than ever before to objects themselves: the pure architecture, the pure design of objects based upon their use . . . cubism has landed in fortuitous economic soil, hence its political meaning.'[52] In this mostly hopeful remark, PH relates a cubist approach to current demands for functionalism: addressing use by creating utilitarian objects sans motif will help to create a stronger worker culture.

Henningsen's commentary and theories have application to the broader picture of the development of Danish Modern design. Because PH contends that it is better to base design on an inner necessity than a forced modernity, or any superimposed style, Cubism appears to offer the inner 'form' or shape hiding behind the trappings of style, allusiveness, and historicism – what the aesthetician Clive Bell had already referred to in 1914 as 'ostentatious cunning.' Henningsen excoriated his contemporary craftsmen for failing to create useful 'tumblers, plates, water-sets, spoons, knives or forks, while richer homes are flooded with trash and rubbish at fantastical prices . . . Down with artistic pretentiousness!'[53] In this lament, Henningsen recalls Alfred Loos's piece on 'Plumbers' (1898), in which the Austrian ridiculed the affection for Rococo flush valves, Rococo taps, and even Rococo washstands. PH took his inspiration for this cubist de-classing of object shapes from Vilhelm Lundstrøm's collages (known as packing-crate pictures because of their use of pieces of wood from crates). Because the materials of a cubist collage function only as themselves, understood solely as real objects, Henningsen finds broad application in this revolutionary visual development (at times transferring the cubist visual effect to *Critical Review*). People needed to see the wood in Lundstrøm's collages as 'material' and the pieces of it as 'form' – what Henningsen referred to as 'the objective beauty about things.'[54] Henningsen is building on the distinction made by the French cubist theorist Pierre Reverdy between artistic reality and bland realism; to Henningsen, achieving this standard in the utilitarian arts can only lead to a better world.

Another intersection may be found between Henningsen's desire for pared-down cubist shapes and Klint's affection for Shaker furniture. When Klint saw his first Shaker Chair – an armed ladder-back rocker with a cushioned seat[55] – he was so taken with the simplistic design that he ordered measurements of it for teaching purposes (although at the time he did not know the chair was Shaker and designed in Mount Lebanon, New York). A replica was ordered for Designmuseum Danmark. Once Deming and Faith Andrews' book *Shaker Furniture: The Craftsmanship of an American Communal Sect* (Yale University Press, 1937) became available in Denmark, Danish designers and scholars became aware of the Shakers and their egalitarian furnishings. Klint was, as Sommer points out, especially fond of this book, its passages 'in many ways could represent his credo.'[56] The overriding sense that utility should dictate design and that beauty emerged solely from usefulness held great attraction and application for Klint. Like Henningsen's belief in cubist shapes, de-ornamented Shaker designs also provided a way for Klint to absorb functionalism without a superimposed modernist aesthetic. Although Shaker furniture is historical, so much of what determines temporal style has been exorcised from these egalitarian designs that it is difficult to pin down any historical reference (all historical references, to Henningsen, are 'characterized by class'). The sparse Shaker designs also seem to fly in the face of class distinction – the same quality PH lauds in Thonet's ubiquitous Chair No. 14. This sense of indeterminacy, of being outside of time yet in it, was the very element that attracted many of the twentieth-century Danish designers and architects to the simplicity of Shaker furnishings. More broadly, Shaker influences continue to be woven into the narrative of modern design development. At the 2015 European Fine Art Fair in Maastricht, the Netherlands, Françoise Laffanour, the director of a Parisian gallery, said he recreated a series of nineteenth-century Shaker interiors to illustrate the origins of modern design: 'Shaker is the perfect illustration of design corresponding with lifestyle and intention. All the decorative detail has been stripped away.'[57]

Both Klint and Henningsen, in their respective attractions to Shaker designs and Cubism, are struggling to establish what both designers delineate as a 'Danish' reading of Modernism. For PH, the goal became creating types – typical objects – of lasting worth (although by the 1930s he already felt that modernists had failed at this task). In this endeavour, he wanted to retrieve what is of value in tradition, a point he emphasizes in 'Tradition and Modernism': 'The serious side of tradition involves the creation of types. Once generation after generation has solved the same task (with the same content), the result will necessarily become more and more harmonious and outstanding: a type will emerge.'[58] In this rhetorical stance, Henningsen sounds an awful lot like Klint, who comments on the German Bauhaus towards the end of his 1930 article on education in the furniture arts: 'Our efforts coincide to a certain extent with those abroad, especially Germany's, but we feel that they are working on a more primitive basis in use as well as in design. Apparently, they have thrown all tradition overboard . . .'[59] To return to Simon's notion of designers maintaining their inner environment, this attraction to some form of tradition served as another way for the Danes to achieve a sense of invariance in design approach. In the broader sense, as modernists, Henningsen is struggling to establish an anti-traditionalist tradition, whereas Klint is attempting to transfer traditional types into modern readings.[60]

Ironically, the most 'cubist' of Henningsen's creations may well by his 1958 lamp, *Koglen* (the Pine Cone – usually referred to in English as the Artichoke). The large lamp consists of layers of curved rectilinear diffusers imparting the overall impression of a sphere breaking into segments seen from different angles at the same time, a cubist concept, the pieces recalling Lundstrøm's swatches of packing-crate material. Yet, any striving for egalitarianism ends there. Designed for the restaurant in Langelinie's Pavilion in Copenhagen (where they still hang), the Artichoke is not classless in any meaning of the word. It is an ultra-expensive designer creation, a striking accomplishment, but worlds removed from Henningsen's social design contentions in 'Tradition and Modernism.' Still, it *functions*, distributing softly diffused light while hiding the bulb, connecting it to PH's original designs and studies in appropriate lighting. Stripped now of the societal concerns that drove so much of Henningsen's polemical writings, his designs have endured more than half a century of use. His entertaining and revelatory essays, however, have never been translated into English, a sad loss for design historians who cannot read Danish.

While the typical bifurcation between cold, impersonal Bauhaus modernism and warm, human Danish or Nordic modernism has served historians well for more than half a century, Klint's and Henningsen's approaches disclose the actual variegation of responses and developments in Danish design at this time. Tradition is both embraced and rejected, even by the avant-garde Henningsen; historicism is only partially rejected by Klint, who still reinterprets historical precedents, at times with Shaker-influenced simplification; objectivity is rejected as a superimposed aesthetic by both designers yet employed by both in measurements and, to some extent, in execution, however 'scientific' that may actually be; functionalism is reinterpreted by both Klint and Henningsen into a notion less absolute and more fluid in execution; ornament for its own sake is mostly exorcised by both men, yet not entirely. Both men struggled to separate design from fashion, reflecting the efforts of many European modernists to establish invariance in the face of temporal style. Modernism in design arises in Denmark within this dance between forces in a plurality of responses. Just as Klint's teaching at the Furniture School helped to disseminate his Cartesian approach and cautious, tradition-infused reading of Modernism, Henningsen's provocative publications both articulated and influenced design developments for decades.

Notes

1. In his 1930 article, Klint attributes the table's design to his student Rigmor Andersen (1903–1995), who also worked with Henningsen on lamp designs. Andersen went on to become an accomplished furniture designer, a teacher at the Furniture School, and the author of a monograph on Klint (1979).
2. For a fine discussion of design and national identity, see Woodham (1997), 87–109.
3. That same year, 1929, the National Socialist Alfred Rosenberg founded the Militant League for German Culture (Kampfbund für Deutsche Kultur), a group that supported the crafts and denigrated avant-garde culture as 'degenerate.'
4. Torn down after the exposition, the pavilion was painstakingly rebuilt in 1986.
5. Cf. Klint's detailed drawings of the human form and furniture and Henningsen's elaborate drawings of light diffusion for his PH series of lamps. See also Møller (1978), 37.
6. The modernists' desire to find objective or rational answers to design problems often led to pseudo-scientific notions of rationalizing one's way to final, verifiable solutions.
7. Klint studied at the Technical University of Denmark (Tekniske højskole) and Independent Art School (Kunsternes Frie Studieskole) and with furniture maker Johan Rohde.
8. Quoted in 'Dansk møbelkunsts puritanske førstemand,' *Politiken* (24 June 2014) [http://politiken.dk/magasinet/portraetter/ECE2324384/dansk-moebelkunsts-puritanske-foerstemand/; accessed: 20 March 2015].
9. Klint, 'Undervisning i Møbeltegning ved Kunstakadamiet,' in *Architektens Maanedshæfte* (October 1930), 200.
10. Ibid., 193.
11. Ibid.
12. Though Wegner studied under Orla Mølgaard Nielsen, one of Klint's most prominent students, at the Copenhagen School of Arts and Crafts.
13. The use of English antecedents has a long history among Danish cabinetmakers. In 1777, the Danish Furniture Store (Det kgl. Meubel-Magazin) was founded by the government to advise and educate the carpentry profession. The institution's designers were cabinetmakers and architects who had studied in England.
14. Klint 'Undervisning i Møbeltegning ved Kunstakadamiet,' 194.
15. Ibid.
16. Ann-Louise Sommer, *Kaare Klint*, in *Store Danske Designere*, ed. Tøjner and Vindum (Copenhagen: Lindhardt og Ringhof, 2008), 116.
17. Steen Eiler Rasmussen, 'Modern Danish Design,' *Journal of the Royal Society of the Arts*, 96(4761) (1948), 141–42.
18. 'The Remix: The Other Danish Modern,' *New York Times* (3 April 2005).
19. Karlsen and Tiedemann, 'Denmark,' in *A Treasury of Scandinavian Design*, ed. Zahle (New York: Golden Press, 1961), 10.
20. Ulf Hård af Segerstad, *Scandinavian Design* (New York: Lyle Stuart, 1961), 97.
21. Charlotte and Peter Fiell, *Design of the 20th Century* (Köln: Taschen, 1999), 385.
22. In a 2003 review of an exhibition in New York of the furniture of one of Klint's most successful students, Ole Wanscher, Roberta Smith mentions the 'living delicacy of

wood' and the 'echoes of the furniture of Egypt, Rome, Viennese Secession, and Biedermeier era' (*New York Times*, 3 October 2003).

23. Sommer, *Kaare Klint*, 141.
24. Carsten Thau and Kjeld Vindum, 'Arne Jacobsen,' in *Store Danske Designere*, ed. Tøjner and Vindum (Copenhagen: Lindhardt og Ringhof, 2008), 254.
25. Quoted in Kristine Irminger Sonne, 'Træets kvindelige mester,' *Berlingske Tidende* (12 October 2008) [www.fri.dk/livstil/traeets-kvindelige-mester; accessed 12 November 2009].
26. Design Within Reach catalogue (April 2014), 7.
27. Crawford quotes taken from Katie Treggiden, 'Inside Scandinavian Design at the Stockholm Furniture Fair,' *Design Milk* (25 February 2015) [http://design-milk.com/inside-scandinavian-design/; accessed 25 February 2015].
28. Hansen, *Da danske møbler blev moderne. Historien om dansk møbeldesigns storhedstid* (Odense: Syddansk Universitetsforlag/Copenhagen: Aschehoug, 2006), 61.
29. Jørgen Hartmann-Petersen, 'Om at begrænse sig. Rullebords-samtale mellem tre af pionererne i dansk kunst håndværk,' *Politiken* (29 March 1964), 29.
30. Ibid.
31. Quoted in Karlsen and Tiedemann (1961), 15.
32. Henningsen wrote 'Tradition og Modernisme' ('Tradition and Modernism') partially in response to an earlier *Kritisk Revy* article (appearing in 1926) by the Swede Uno Åhrén, who would become one of the premiere designers for the housing section of the 1930 Stockholm Exhibit.
33. Parts of this section appeared in the article, 'Poul Henningsen: Cubism and the Conscience of Modernism,' *Scandinavian Studies*, 85(1) (2013), 79–98.
34. 'Tradition og Modernisme,' in *Kritisk Revy*, 3 (1927), 31.
35. Ibid., 43.
36. Ibid.
37. See Jørn Guldberg, 'Den nye tids former: PH om den kunstneriske produktions historiske karakter,' in *Tradition og Modernisme: Indfaldsvinkler til PH* (Odense: Syddansk Universitetsforlag, 2008), 98–124.
38. Sven Møller Kristensen, ed., *Kritisk Revy: En antologi af tekster og illustrationer fra tidsskriftets tre årgange* (Copenhagen: Gyldendal, 1963), 11.
39. Henningsen, 'Le Corbusier,' *Kritisk Revy* 1 (1926): 52.
40. See 'Kunst og Politik,' in *Tradition og Modernisme: infaldsvinkler til PH*, ed. Bay and Jensen (Odense: Syddansk Universitetsforlag, 2008).
41. 'Tradition og Modernisme', 30.
42. Appearing in *Politiken* (22 July 1930).
43. Quoted in Neel Pørn, *PHs Arkitekturkritik* (Copenhagen: Arkitektens Forlag, 1994), 110.
44. The original 'Die Wohnung' ('The Housing') exhibition (1927) featured designs by Le Corbusier, Mies van der Rohe, and Gropius. Mies introduced his cantilevered chair (*Freischwinger*) there.
45. Henningsen, 'Die neue Sachlichkeit!,' in *Kritisk Revy*, 3 (1928), 5.
46. Quoted in *alvar aalto furniture*, ed. Juhani Pallasmaa (Cambridge, MA: MIT Press, 1985), 115.

47. Herbert Simon, *The Sciences of the Artificial* (3rd edn.) (Cambridge, MA: MIT Press, 1996), 8.

48. Klint, 'Undervisning i Møbeltegning ved Kunstakadamiet,' 197.

49. Henningsen, 'Kubismens politiske Indhold,' in *Kulturkritik I*, ed. Bay and Harsløf (Copenhagen: Rhodos, 1973): 170.

50. Ibid., 171.

51. Ibid., 174.

52. Henningsen, 'Motivets Betydning,' in *Kulturkritik I* (1973), 183

53. Quoted in Karlsen and Tiedemann, 'Danmark,' *Hjemmets brugskunst*, 10.

54. 'Kubismens politiske Indhold,' 174.

55. In an illustration in Klint's 1930 article in *The Architect,* the Shaker rocker is mistakenly identified as 'an American Colonial rocking chair.'

56. Sommer, *Kaare Klint*, 150.

57. Quoted in Scott Reyburn, 'European Fine Art Fair Showcases Shaker Furniture,' *New York Times* (12 March 2015) [http://www.nytimes.com/2015/03/13/arts/design/european-fine-art-fair-showcases-shaker-furniture.html?ref=topics&_r=0; accessed 16 March 2015].

58. 'Tradition og Modernisme,' 33.

59. Klint, 'Undervisning i Møbeltegning ved Kunstakadamiet,' 203.

60. For a good discussion of this aspect of Modernism, see Fallan, 'Modern, Modernity, Modern,' in *Design History: Understanding Theory and Method* (Oxford: Berg, 2010).

3 On Chairness: Platonics and Tectonics

In 1965, the American conceptual artist Joseph Kosuth (b. 1945) premiered his installation *One and Three Chairs*, a work presenting three versions of a chair: an actual chair, a photograph of the same chair, and the definition of the word 'chair' (or, in some of its foreign appearances, the translation of the English word 'chair'). Since its premiere, the installation has been repeated in numerous locales with different chairs; the work has garnered a lot of attention from art historians and prompted much debate. Is it a philosophical musing masquerading as a work of art? A semiotic exercise in signifier and sign? A commentary on the very nature of conceptual art? A playful work of art employing object, picture, and words? Kosuth once observed: 'All I make are models. The actual work of art are ideas.'[1] Because Kosuth employs an actual chair in his installation, he opens the door to issues concerning design theory (the installation itself is an exercise in design, particularly in the manner in which it is laid out). Does placing a chair – an object designed for use but inherently visual – in an installation and calling it a work of art in any way alter the function of the chair for the viewer? As Justin Clements suggests: 'It's a work of art, but you can still sit in it (if you can avoid the museum guards).'[2] Some critics have seen the three elements as a humorous commentary on Platonic notions of 'chairness': a physical representation of a chair is surrounded by an image of that chair and the definition of 'chair.' The concept is grasped in pure thought, encapsulated in the definition, instantiated in the chair, and represented by the photo of the chair.

'Chairness' resides in the definition of what constitutes a chair; an actual chair exists in three dimensions; and the image of a chair appears in the photograph. The notion that Kosuth has abstracted the idea of a chair from the chair to make art simply calls the viewer back to a chair's design and purpose, and to the act of designing and the fact that it is a designed object. In the perceived absence of anyone sitting in it, the empty chair speaks of presence or, phenomenologically, the presence of the sitter – whose absence seems further emphasized in each installation's specific setting.

If any designed object has come to define Danish Modern in the eyes of the public, it is the chair. Much of this continued fame owes not only to a well-marketed belief in Danish craftsmanship but also to a progressive sense of innovation. This latter characteristic surfaced in early modernist designs: a simple structure such as Klint's *Propeltaburet* (Propeller Stool, 1930) reveals that each pair of twisted legs has been cut from one piece of turned wood, resulting in adjoining ornament when the legs are folded together. In his collapsible *Safaristol* (Safari Chair, 1933), Klint designed Europe's first piece of knockdown furniture, also aiding in the reduction of shipping costs. Klint's students Mogens Koch, Ole Wanscher (both of whom were design historians, as well), and Poul Kjærholm also designed folding stools and chairs: variations on the form include Koch's simplistic beech and canvas folding chair from 1933, Wanscher's elegant reinterpretation of Klint's stool in deep rosewood (1957), and Kjærholm's minimalist reading of the stool in brushed stainless steel with twisted legs (1961). As late as 1968, Erik Magnussen was still reinterpreting the basic folding chair structure in chrome and canvas in his highly industrialized chair, Z. This repetition of one simple chair type indicates the evolution of types by Danish designers over decades of development – a process continuing to this day. Cecilie Manz's Miniscule (2012), a thinly upholstered, simple shell chair, builds on Jacobsen's *Gryden* (the Pot, 1958), replacing that chair's thin metal frame with a more contemporary reinforced grey plastic nylon.

A number of mid-twentieth-century Danish chair designs have remained in production since their inception, achieving world renown, reinterpreted by myriad designers, and inspiring countless imitations, among them Jacobsen's Ant (1952), Seven (1955), and Egg and Swan (both c. 1958); Wegner's Wishbone (1950); and Finn Juhl's Chair No. 45 (1945) and Chieftain (1949). All of these chair designs share an organic quality in their form, overall shapes, or arms and legs that bend or curve – void of any right angles – and there may well be something in this recurrence of curvilinear elements that unites much (though not all) of mid-century Danish Modern chair design. In the case of the Egg Chair, the ovoid shape encompasses the sitter, compelling her to sit *in* not on the chair. Its enveloping form has another visual side effect: it moves closer to the human form. The bending Seven Chair proffers a similar aspect: one form, like the human body, bending (to return to Nelson's description of the standard chair design, not something glued or riveted together). The Canadian sculptor and furniture maker Gord Peteran has observed: 'Furniture is our first sculptural encounter, after the body of the mother and slightly before the interior spatial volumes of architecture.'[3] The relation of body to both architectural space and furniture appears to be a dynamic one. In *On Architecture,* Fred Rush indicates that conscious perception is influenced 'by more implicit and perhaps in some sense un- or pre-conscious states having to do with motion and body equilibrium that are also responsive to being ensconced in architectural space.'[4] Whereas Rush emphasizes the experience of architecture as 'bound up' with the experience of the body, the same could be said of our responses to furniture, to which the body remains even closer. By emphasizing curvilinear, sinuous, and organic shapes, the Danish modernists were able to establish a persistent visual relationship to the human body, one at least less dependent on shifting styles and design movements, if only because of the superimposed restrictions of form.

When Wegner's *Den runde stol* (the Round Chair, 1950) made its broadcast debut in the first televised US presidential debate between candidates John F. Kennedy and Richard Nixon in 1960, the world became aware of a chair design in a theretofore unheard of way (Fig. 3.1). The Round Chair (known simply as 'The Chair' in the United States) was surprisingly minimalist. Its four legs are simply continuous turned wood, narrowing at the ends; its top-rail, consisting of three pieces of wood with barely discernible serrated joinery and resting on those four posts, curves subtly into armrests. Originally, Wegner had wrapped the centre of the top-rail in cane to hide the necessary joinery until he devised a method for turning construction into acceptable design. A thickening in the middle piece of the top-rail serves as the chair's only back support. Its minimal design elements seemed perfectly suited to the younger, more handsome Kennedy and his forward-looking message of progress for the United States. Chosen by the station's art director, the Round Chair's presence helped to articulate the image Kennedy – the first true television president – was attempting to convey. Reviewing a comprehensive exhibition of Wegner's work in 1965 at the Georg Jensen store (then on Fifth Avenue) in New York, Rita Reif wrote that the Round Chair exemplified Wegner's ability to turn wood into 'something that is lasting decorative art.'[5] Still, Wegner remained, throughout his life, resistant to the notion of having designed *the* chair. 'All that talk about "the chair" – it's nonsense,' he commented in 1992. 'Because the chair isn't there . . . You can't make something definitive. Only people who don't understand what it's all about think so.'[6]

Wegner's remark is revealing, philosophically, as the tendency has existed among design historians to talk of Neo-Platonist endeavours by many modernist designers. Vincent Scully, for example, once said of Mies van der Rohe's Barcelona Chair: 'It is

Fig. 3.1 While preparing for the 1960 presidential debate in the United States, held in Chicago, John F. Kennedy sits in one of Wegner's Round Chairs (1949), known simply as 'The Chair' in North America – although the designer eschewed the use of that name. Photo by CBS via Getty Images

not just, as some would say, the greatest chair of the twentieth century; it is the great Platonic image of chair itself.'[7] Much of this rhetoric rests on the graphic outline chair designs provide; no one ever makes such presumptuous claims about jewellery or dinnerware designed in the Modern era. Modernism's lasting chair designs – such as the Eames Lounge (1956) or Marcel Breuer's Wassily Chair (1927–28) – have strong profiles that are easily recognizable from their repeated reproduction in design histories and their ongoing appearance in advertisements and in movies and television shows. Within this narrative, Danish designers such as Wegner and Jacobsen are considered Neo-Platonists because they were supposedly struggling to create 'ideal' forms, that is, forms that would be ultimate. The Platonic subtext looming beneath this claim, however, implies that the sought-after form already exists; this approach appears to lean on an abstract idea or metaphysical notion of 'chairness' (as in Scully's remark).

In a Platonic context, that form would be something designers would then discover, or it might involve an elusive perfect chair (if such a thing were possible).[8] While notions of geometric abstraction as an aesthetic goal may have driven many of the De Stijl, Purist, and Bauhaus designers in a Platonic search for ultimate form, one is hard-pressed to find such a motivation among mid-twentieth-century Danish designers. For them, the effort to find the best form, the good form, or the form without precedence was not necessarily a struggle to discover any pre-existing form, nor did it rest on essentialist or utopian notions about geometry. A designer concerned with producing the best possible chair – if one were to assume that is his or her goal – has to think about much more than the idea of a chair. Particularly for designers trained as cabinetmakers, chair design must involve more than an intellectual pursuit. For designers, chair design always involves use; the potential that exists in designing any chair lies more in the human form than in any abstract notion of chairness. The Neo-Platonic reading, especially of the Danish modernist designers, seems to smuggle a metaphysical aspect into the design process; such a reading runs the risk of over-intellectualizing the process, whereas the human body is the most relevant form determining the physical design of a chair.

For certain mid-twentieth-century Danish designers, both the idea and design of the chair became more prominent in their use of sculptural and pared-down forms exposing construction. This effect is especially evident in the chair designs of Wegner who, unlike many of the other mid-twentieth-century Danish designers, was not educated as an architect but trained as a cabinetmaker. His development as a designer was, therefore, based on his familiarity with wood, his early apprenticeship to a master carpenter, and his thorough knowledge of materials and tools (he left a three-year programme of study in furniture building and design at the Kunsthåndværkerskole – the School of Arts and Crafts – after only two years because of his proficiency). Whereas Juhl and Jacobsen had been trained as architects, enabling them to view chairs as part of a larger spatial relationship (chair/room/house), Wegner's designs focused even more closely on the capacities of wood (he also worked in steel and, like Juhl and Jacobsen, in upholstery) and, early in his career, the developments of types to answer specific tasks: armchair, lounge chair, wingchair.

Continuity and change

Addressing his time, Wegner altered these types, reflecting the Swiss designer and theorist Max Bill's concept of continuity and change as twin elements in the development of a design Gestalt. In his 1953 talk, 'Continuity and Change,' Bill observed: 'with objects, we relate continuity and change to the life-span of the thing itself, in other words we judge a chair, for example, not only in terms of its individual qualities but also as a representation of a type – chairs as a whole over a longer time-span.'[9] Trained as a silversmith and educated at the Bauhaus, Bill views this ongoing design dialectic between continuity and change as anti-styling, because he believes it constitutes a struggle to find what is valid and constant. He applies the scientific concept of morphology to the designed object as a means to find connections 'between all its elements and all its functions, its technical properties, and ultimately also its appearance.'[10] Continuity is then transferred, functionally, to purpose; formal quality, to Bill, becomes the evidence that an object is functional in every aspect. This rhetorical stance sounds like a reflection of the hackneyed notion of form equalling function, often applied myopically to Danish Modern design, but Bill – like a number of the Danish modernists – views this formal quality as 'variable.' Its form is also sometimes dictated by technology, which is ever-changing and which Bill contends can only achieve so much at any given time. This tension echoes Wegner's perception of designing chairs as an ongoing process rather than one of achieving any perfect or ultimate form (which he sees as impossible and illusory, as in his comment about the nonsensical idea of *the chair*). At one point in his essay, Bill derides the earlier Bauhaus's Neo-Platonic fealty to geometry as true form and, sounding like Henningsen, claims that such an effort only resulted in a new style substituting for an old one. To Bill – and to many of the mid-century Danish modernists – there is no discovery of already existing ultimate form; there is only the progress towards trying to achieve better form in standard objects.

Bill's arguments provide a fine reflection of the efforts of a designer such as Wegner. For example, Wegner once questioned the form-follows-function dictum and altered it to form following the specific object's production process. Throughout his career, Wegner designed chairs and other furniture that maintained their types while mutating, sometimes slowly over many years, into new and different forms. Like many of the Danish modernists, he transferred his study of historical types into new readings with sculptural qualities. More importantly, he viewed construction as the incarnation of idea, once observing that a successful construction expresses the idea dwelling inside a design: 'Telling a story through a construction has to do with making clear what it is one wants to emphasize, with making clear what the point of the matter is in the construction.'[11] Decisions about joinery, to Wegner, could serve as

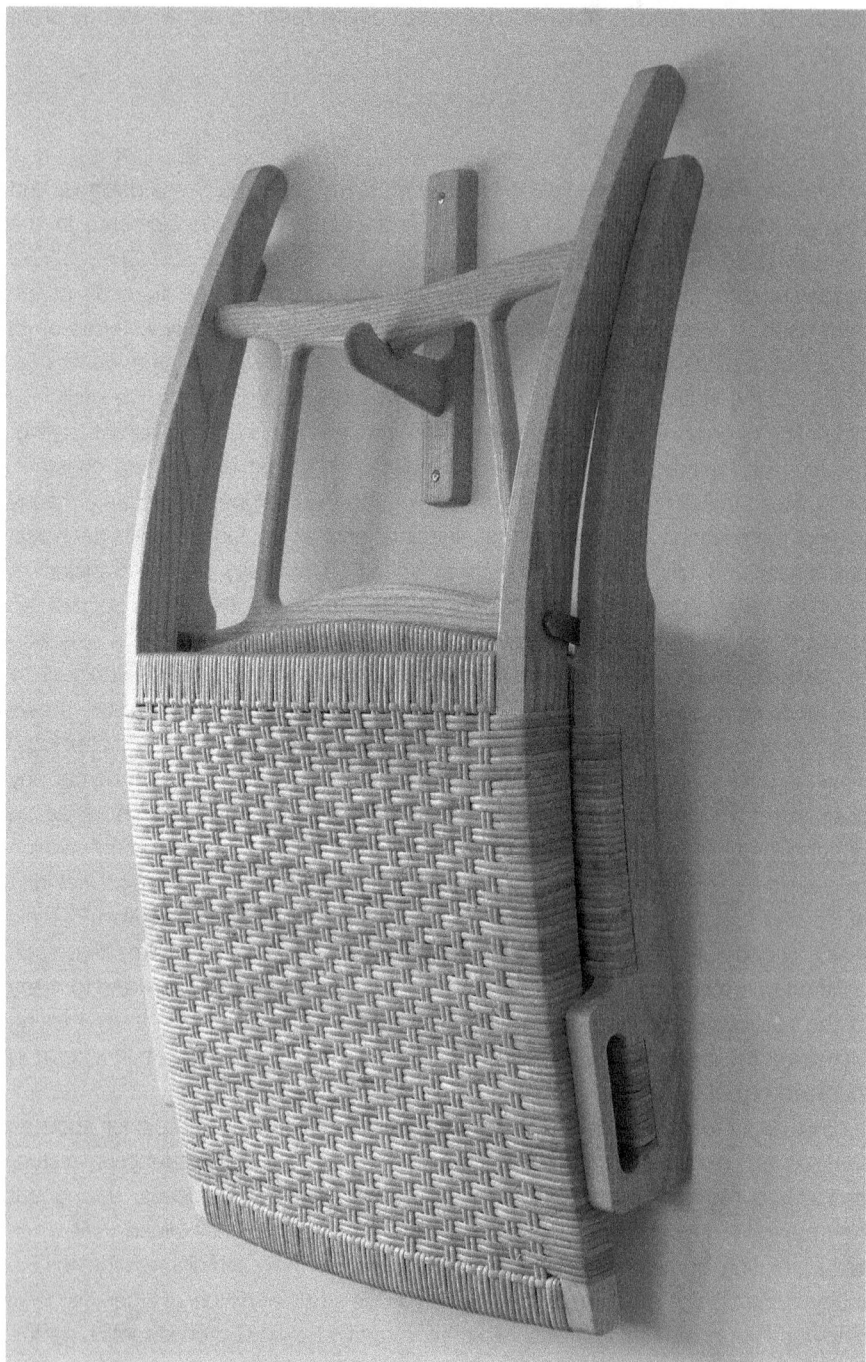

Fig. 3.2 Wegner's Folding Chair, designed in 1949, has Shaker antecedents in its ability to fold up and be hung on a wall. Courtesy of PP Møbler

the manifestation of the specific idea embodied in the design of that chair; materiality was never simply an element of the aesthetics of form.

Wegner's *Foldestolen* (Folding Chair, 1949) offers a prime example of this idea-driven effect: the designer answered the task of designing a lounge chair that could not only be folded up but also hung on the wall (a style inspired by the Shakers, who also crafted chairs that could be hung on walls to save room) (Fig. 3.2). Wegner attempted to explain the subliminal in the chair's visual effect:

> Or look at the folding chair with back and seat in woven cane. If you were to explain why it looks like this it would be complicated, because there is so much to take into account. But it is a thoroughly logical construction, and many of the details contributing to the chair's character are there of technical necessity. The crosses in the woven seat, for example, allow space for the handles at the side of the frame. Yet the finished chair must never be more complicated than necessary, even though it is not always so simple to explain why it is what it is.[12]

Wegner's design, particularly the appearance of handles carved into the front two edges of the seat, speaks immediately of its use. It draws the eye, and thus the use of one's hands, to the purpose of the handles, the folding upward; the effect is reinforced by the mirroring curves of the chair's two sections.[13] Use (for sitting) and idea (create a chair that can also be folded up) have merged in design, the only way utilitarian, functional design can operate. In a Wittgensteinian sense, the only way to 'know' the chair is to sit in it and, in this case, to fold it up. In *Philosophical Investigations I*, Wittgenstein posits how it is that people know what to do when they come to a sign-post: 'I have been trained to react to this sign in a particular way, and now I do so react to it.'[14] It is not a disembodied idea of 'chairness' that enables us to know it is a chair but, rather, a lifetime of sitting in and using chairs. The necessity for use is emphasized by Jens Bernsen's comment that Danish design introduced something that functionalism lacked: 'genuine interest in the interaction between users and their tools and a more organic understanding of form.'[15] While the notion of organic design has been stereotyped – even mythicized – in the ongoing narrative about Danish Modern, the preponderance of wood in curvilinear shapes in much mid-twentieth-century Danish design indicates a resistance to styles and materials not conducive to everyday use. In addition, Wegner's Folding Chair shares qualities with a folding deck-chair predecessor by Klint from 1933; Wegner's reading illustrates how the twin qualities of continuity and change helped over time to establish a 'Danish Modern' style through both repetition and alteration. In his Dolphin Chair (1950), Wegner added a hanging pillow and arms, rendered in a surprisingly playful boomerang-shape, to the folding chair, the type continuing its metamorphosis.

At first, many twentieth-century Danish chair designers turned to historical and cultural styles for inspiration. For example, Wegner worked from Chinese antecedents to design four versions of one Chair: his distillation process of this design, particularly in his work with the Chinese chair's expressive top-rail, reflects the development of most of his oeuvre. Two of those chair designs are still in production: model 4283

(1944), produced by Fritz Hansen, hews closer to the eighteenth-century Chinese Chair Wegner had studied and is more formal in nature, whereas model PP66 (1945), produced by PP Møbler, presents a more casual appearance, particularly in its Shaker-inspired base. In Wegner's hands, the original Chinese curved top-rail – which he had studied closely during his studies in the 1930s at the Kunsthåndværkerskole (School of Arts and Crafts)[16] – slowly morphed into a minimalist shape functioning as both back rest and armrest. It is, however, still a shape, a form, not merely an idea: the original idea could only drive the form's reduction into a more minimalist shape. That shape would reach an apex of minimalism in his *Y-Stolen* (the Wishbone Chair, 1950), a variant of Wegner's process in the four different versions of his Chinese Chair. In the Wishbone, the elbow rests have been reduced to the shortest possible length extending from the top-rail in one continuous curved piece, and the back legs bend forward from the seat upward. The standard one-piece solid back splat of the Chinese antecedent has been reduced to a slender Y-shaped support. Through its reduced construction, the idea of the Chinese Chair has been transformed into a modernist reading. Still in production and especially popular in Japan, Sweden, and the United States, the Wishbone illustrates the enduring tendencies of de-historicizing style, along with a material symbiosis between Bill's concepts of continuity and change.

In time, referents to the world outside the designers' own chairs were, for the most part, banished: no period-driven qualities attach their chairs to other historical determinants (perhaps presaging Postmodernism, in his 1957 version of Klint's simple stool, Wanscher would take the style back to its ancient Egyptian antecedent). Wegner's work with the Windsor Chair, a style first produced in England in the 1700s, illustrates this evolution; he was drawn to the Windsor-type chair because he felt it was 'a remarkable design precisely because it expresses so naturally what it is.'[17] The Windsor Chair from the mid-1800s that Wegner studied as a student at the School of Arts and Crafts had curvaceous cabriole legs, a bulge in the middle of its stretchers, and an arm rail that intersected the spindles in the high comb-back (with its ornamental top piece). In his own version of a Windsor Chair from 1949, Wegner deleted any armrest and reduced the spindles in the back to three thin pieces imparting a strikingly minimalist appearance. A rocking chair designed in 1944 (Model J16) follows simplistic Shaker precedents but adds spindles from the Windsor prototype. In each model, Wegner is altering and de-historicizing the Windsor Chair into a modernist reading.

By the time he introduced the more imposing Peacock Chair (1947), with the massive arc of its bowed top-rail extending to the seat, Wegner had taken the humble Windsor Chair into a more dramatic reading (Fig. 3.3). In the armrests, sometimes referred to as 'flippers,' Wegner reflects the angular biomorphic shapes that would become popular in the 1950s, as in the fins on automobiles. Also, as he will two years later in the Folding Chair, Wegner wraps a section of the paper-cord seating around the front ends of the seat. He also chooses ash for the chair (although initially it had teak armrests, partially to match a table and partially because teak is more resistant than ash to grease and dirt from hands); the light wood – soap-treated rather than stained – imparts a more informal, modernist appearance to the massive chair. Compared with the original nineteenth-century Windsor Chair he had studied, Wegner had expanded the historical type into a lighter yet larger and more open reading. Its subtle geometry is best indicated by a pair of armrest supports intersecting the seat. In the back rest, the fan of spindles that lend the chair its name (a name first christened by Finn Juhl) flatten where the back leans against the chair for comfort,

Fig. 3.3 The Peacock (1947), Wegner's showy variant on the Windsor Chair, provides a counterpoint to the notion of 'sober' Danish Modern design. Courtesy of PP Møbler

turning function into a decorative element. Thus, the chair's back support illustrates his belief in construction reflecting purpose. Wegner, who viewed this as a process of purification rather than obeisance to normative modernist notions, once observed that he wanted ultimately to pare a chair down to four legs, a seat, a top-rail, and an armrest.[18] In *Hans J. Wegner*, Christian Holmsted Olesen notes: 'But it is his enormous inventiveness and his sculptural sense of form that are able to move the somewhat dry functionalist carpentry trade beyond its own limits and create a groundbreaking new poetry that made a name for itself outside Denmark in the 1950s as a new style, a new variant of Modernism.'[19]

Seats of power

Cultural factors are, naturally, always at play in the designs produced during the heyday of Danish Modernism. In his essay 'The Seat of the Soul: Three Chairs' (1987), Arthur C. Danto focuses initially on the act of sitting and its cultural and symbolic significance. Viewing the furnishings in a room as a system of signs, Danto sees sitting as 'less a matter of taking weight off our feet than of declaring where we are and how we fit in the larger scheme of things.'[20] From Danto's perspective, the noted modernist chair designs separate from basic everyday chairs by conveying significance beyond their specific visual message: 'To suppose the Barcelona Chair or the Wassily Chair is simply an exemplar of fine design is to display a certain blindness to what it means to sit.'[21] The seated position already implies stability and solidity; therefore, Danto sees furniture arrangements as representative of structures of power. Whereas Mies van der Rohe's Barcelona Chair or Marcel Breuer's Wassily Chair seems built for those power structures, for the act of sitting as self-determined choice, Wegner – like a number of Danish designers in the twentieth century – was more determined to reduce associations of power from many of his designs. He endeavoured, instead, to craft chairs that would open the sitter up to various positions, including lounging, which he viewed as an important option. Tracing the evolution of Wegner's Chinese chairs, for example, Olesen presents this process as one of moving the chair from being a 'throne' to an everyday object of use. Thus, the costly nature of these chairs today strikes one as incongruous with any original notions about democratic or economically accessible designs, while their current price point moves them into the world of luxury items.

When Danto discusses the woven-rush seat in Vincent van Gogh's painting of his modest chair (Chair with Pipe, 1888), he perceives it as a symbol of abasement because of the rusticity associated with peasant furniture. Danto then relegates the woven-seat chair to the kitchen, a secondary location that he feels van Gogh uses to express his conspicuous humility. Wegner, however, designed a number of chairs with woven seats in cane and paper cord, elevating the rustic element to contemporary design – even to a level of elegance – but elegance without ostentation. Danto sees sitting as more than 'merely sitting,' and to that end views design relevant to purpose as not serving as the 'criterion to goodness.'[22] In this sense, he sounds like Kosuth:

concept (or idea of power) trumps utilitarian form. A designer like Wegner, trained as a cabinetmaker, does not have the luxury of delimiting the role of purpose in his chairs. Yet, his aim was not totally function-driven: form did not simply follow function in his designs, which ran the gamut from minimalist (the Round Chair) to playful (the Ox Chair) to majestic (the Peacock).

Danto's argument for the symbolic power of sitting expressed in chair designs rests on the notion of confidence. 'The great chairs of the modern era,' he contends, 'the chairs of stunning design, conveyed a confidence in human power where, in our shining chromium, profoundly industrial sitting pieces, we convey our confidence of the future.'[23] In a postmodernist reading, Danto wants to view this sense of human power imparted through modernist design reflectively, perhaps even nostalgically, as passé, the shining chromium functioning metonymically as a representative of belief in a failed futuristic machine age. He finds the more current (then late 1980s) approach to the symbolic nature of the chair lacking in the blatant confidence expressed by the Barcelona or Eames Chair – viewing the chair instead as a 'plaything.' As pointed out earlier, Wegner was a designer who, for the most part, avoided the blatantly industrial and who, therefore, designed chairs that could resist the time-specific concept of 'power' Danto wants to attach to Bauhaus-inspired chairs. While Wegner designed a number of pieces in steel (such as the Flag Halyard Chair with its casual throw of sheepskin to juxtapose its metallic frame), his work in wood transformed the more Bauhaus-like sense of industrial power into the more human tradition of woodworking (as Aalto had done earlier). Employing craftsman principles, such as kerfs, to many of his wooden designs, Wegner was able to create more modernist idioms without converting solely to metal frames.[24] His work does not necessitate a postmodern reading of any absence of power – what Danto calls 'an attack on the concept of power, rank, submission, domination, subservience' – to convey playfulness. A number of his designs take their power from their recognizable shapes, chairs with such playful names such as the Ox, the Papa Bear, the Dolphin, and the Bull.

Also, in his efforts to create chairs providing open seating positions, Wegner replaced the welded, static Modernism of Mies's Barcelona Chair with an open and dynamic approach. A design such as Wegner's *Cirkelstolen* (Circle Chair, 1986, but first designed in the late 1960s) illustrates how Wegner was able to create chairs with presence long past the heyday of Danish Modern. Originally, Wegner had designed the massive circle that encompasses the sitter in steel, but the master-cabinetmaker Ejnar Pedersen insisted that it be constructed of wood – even devising a new tool for laminating eleven pieces of wood to comprise the circle. The surprisingly geometric chair fairly exudes the confidence that Danto bemoans as missing in later chair designs. In many ways, the Circle is a radical reinterpretation of the Windsor type, spindles replaced with an intricate and open netting to support the back, further evidence of the ongoing mutation of types in Wegner's designs.

In *Designing Engineers* (1994), Louis Bucciarelli places design in what he calls the 'object world,' focusing specifically on how an object works. He insists that for the different participants in the execution of a design, the object they work with remains primary in patterning their thought and practice. In his discussion 'How a Chair Works – One Perspective,' Bucciarelli includes 'the craft knowledge' of chair-object-worlds. Within that definition, he mentions 'how to join the legs to the back and the seat, whether it is preferable to make the back an extension of the rear two legs.'[25] In this sense, he reminds us that design involves decisions about construction, a natural concern for designers of furniture. A chair, whatever else is done with it, has been designed for sitting. However, Bucciarelli sees certain chairs functioning not only as chairs but also as art, fashion, and symbols of power and prestige – and he names Reitveld's Red-Blue Chair and Le Corbusier's lounge as examples. Bucciarelli defines these designs as 'art' because they are uncommon: 'Each has its own special identity . . . Our object-world definition of a chair is meaningful only if we are talking about an anonymous chair.'[26] He argues that a chair's anonymity coincides with our generic and abstract response to its function. To Bucciarelli, there must be more of an idea behind Reitveld's chair and Le Corbusier's lounge than in the average chair.

This reading may partially explain the ongoing attraction of certain Modern chair designs: applying Bucciarelli's (and Danto's) distinctions, those that impart more of an idea have been able to endure, thus turning them into art and fashion.[27] Bucciarelli argues that a chair's inner constitution is not the first thing that comes to mind – but Wegner has turned the chair inside out, using its inner constitution as form reflecting process. Thus, the chair's construction narrates its idea. Danish modernists such as Wegner and Juhl would not make a distinction between aesthetics and functions; their desire to make chairs work from every angle indicates their ongoing attention to visual effect while pushing the boundaries of joinery. Form is not simply following function; it is emerging, instead, from the process of designing. Even if we were to view Wegner's designs solely as products, his aesthetic/functionalist efforts had profound economic effects as well. In *Kloge hænder – et forsvar for håndværk og faglighed* (*Wise Hands – A Defence of Craftsmanship and Professionalism*, 2013), the Danish mason and political activist Mattias Tesfaye notes that Wegner's artisanal decisions 'formed the basis for . . . a number of other Danish designers' international success.'[28] Wegner often combined his aesthetic choices (pieces of wood used decoratively in the back rest) with functional advantage (the wood inlay hiding areas for strengthened joints) directed at construction. Commenting on his design process, Wegner once explained:

> I never say to myself: Now I'm going to make a piece of art. I tell myself that now I want to make a good chair. And it always starts with an idea. You are just not sure that it's the right idea. Therefore, you test it, along with many other ideas. My experience is that often you end up with the original idea.[29]

An idea in design, though, cannot remain dismembered unless the design is never realized. In fact, the concept behind a design is often tacit; users are usually not aware of the idea behind a designed object because they are too busy using it in some capacity. For a chair, that means sitting in it.

In their organic chair forms, designers such as Wegner, Juhl, and Jacobsen drew further attention to use – to the very idea of chairness in what the Platonic term can

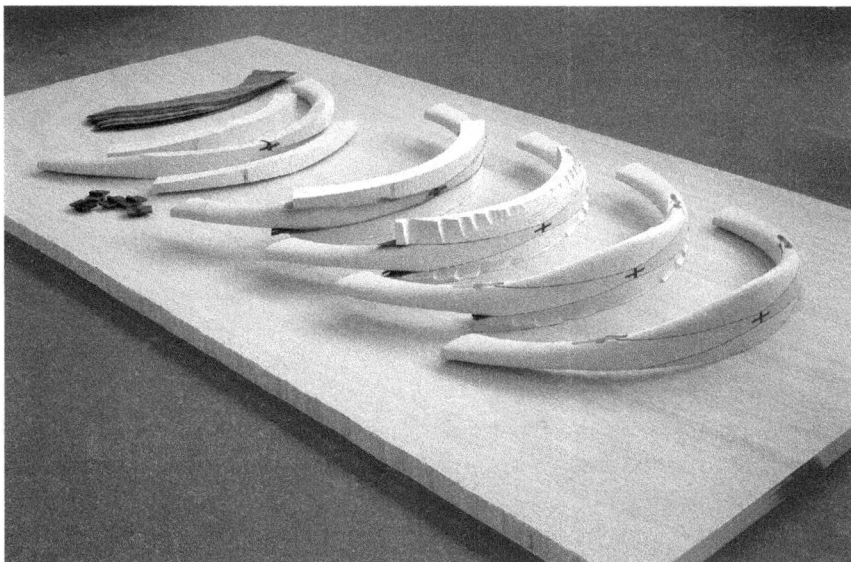

Fig. 3.4 The stages of joinery to construct a top-rail (this one for Wegner's Chair PP701). The photo illustrates the materials, technology, and craft involved in cabinetmaking. Courtesy of PP Møbler

only mean in a human way: not a spectral, metaphysical concept of 'chairness,' not solely the idea of a chair, but rather the object in which we sit. In *Objects of Desire*, Adrian Forty discusses how an emphasis on design as art has removed design from the function not only of making profits but also of transmitting ideas.[30] Forty writes: 'Every product, to be successful, must incorporate the ideas that will make it marketable, and the particular task of design is to bring about the conjunction between such ideas and the available means of production.'[31] Alluding to Barthes' *Mythologies*, Forty sees myths about the world driving many of these ideas. These ideas take precedence to Forty, who does not view creativity and imagination as the driving forces in design – only a drive to make products profitable. Ideologically, Forty believes that manufacturers' ideas and societal concerns take precedence over the ideas of the individual designer/artist.

Coming at it from the perspective of a designer and trained cabinetmaker, Wegner saw the creation of a chair in terms of work (Fig. 3.4). Facing design challenges he once observed that he often returned, both mentally and physically, to the moment when he was standing in his workshop with the material in his hand. Nothing was definitive or complete; he could only move on to the next design, only try to make a better chair.

Notes

1. Quoted in Justin Clemens, 'Neon Statements. Joseph Kosuth and Conceptual Art,' *The Monthly*, 52 (December 2009/January 2010) [https://www.themonthly.com.au/

art-justin-clemens-neon-statements-justin-clemens-joseph-kosuth-and-conceptual-art-2174; accessed 14 April 2015].

2. Ibid.
3. Quoted in Ken Johnson, 'Close Encounters with Tableness and Chairness,' *New York Times* (11 June 2009).
4. Fred Rush, *On Architecture* (New York: Routledge, 2009), 3.
5. Rita Reif, 'Modern Danish Furniture Inspired by a Chinese Copy,' *New York Times,* May 5, 1965: 40.
6. Quoted in Christian Holmsted Olesen, *Wegner: Just One Good Chair,* trans. Mark Mussari (Ostfildern: Hatje Cantz, 2014), 7.
7. Quoted in Galen Cranz, *The Chair: Rethinking Culture, Body and Design* (New York: W.W. Norton, 1998), 140.
8. Some of this reading stems from the influence of the De Stijl followers' beliefs in ideal geometric forms; however, no utopian belief in geometry ever drove much modernist Danish design.
9. Max Bill, 'Continuity and Change,' in *Form, Function, Beauty = Gestalt,* trans. Pamela Johnson (London: AA Publications, 2010), 71.
10. Ibid., 75.
11. Quoted in Nicolai de Gier and Stine Liv Buur, *Chairs' Tectonics* (Copenhagen: Royal Danish Academy of Fine Arts School of Architecture Publications, 2009), 58.
12. Jens Bernsen, *Hans J Wegner om Design* (Copenhagen: Dansk Design Center, 1994), 94.
13. The basic 'X' shape of the folding chair is a design dating back to ancient Egypt; the Romans used folding chairs solely for nobility. Wegner was aware of this: 'Five thousand years ago the Egyptians made folding chairs and thrones in almost the same way as we do now – simply because it's the right way to do it' (quoted in Bernsen, 1994, 94).
14. Ludwig Wittgenstein, *Philosophical Investigations* (3rd edn.), trans. G.E.M. Anscombe (New York: Macmillan, 1992), 80.
15. Ibid., 18.
16. Now Designmuseum Danmark. The School of Arts and Crafts offered an alternative to Klint's Furniture School at the Royal Academy of Fine Arts.
17. Bernsen, *Hans J Wegner om Design*, 94.
18. 'It was rather a continuous process of purification, and for me, of simplification . . . to cut down a chair to the simplest possible elements . . . four legs, a seat and then combine it with a top-rail and an arm rest.' See Barbara Berger, 'Hans J Wegner- Master of Wood,' *Design Directions* [www.dzinedirections.com/hans-wegner-interview; accessed 12 August 2013].
19. Christian Holmsted Olesen, *Hans J. Wegner* in *Store Danske Designere,* ed. Tøjner and Vindum (Copenhagen: Lindhardt og Ringhof, 2008), 482.
20. Arthur C. Danto, 'The Seat of the Soul: Three Chairs,' *Philosophizing Art: Selected Essays* (Berkeley, CA: University of California Press, 1999), 149.
21. Ibid., 157.
22. Ibid., 156.

23. Ibid., 163.
24. For a good discussion of these constructive principles, see de Gier and Buur (2009), 42–44.
25. Louis Bucciarelli, *Designing Engineers* (Cambridge, MA: MIT Press, 1994), 6.
26. Ibid., 10.
27. These ideas were used as fodder for commentary questioning the tenets of Modernism in the art exhibited in the MetaModern Exhibition of 2015 (discussed in the Conclusion).
28. Mathias Tesfaye, *Kloge hænder – et forsvar for håndværk og faglighed* (Copenhagen: Gyldendal, 2013), 127.
29. Bernsen, *Hans J Wegner om Design*, 49.
30. See Richard Buchanan, 'Rhetoric, Humanism, and Design' in *Discovering Design. Explorations in Design Studies* (Chicago, IL: University of Chicago Press, 1995), 23–66.
31. Forty, *Objects of Desire*, 9.

4

Sculpting Articulations: Finn Juhl in 1949

For the Cabinetmakers Guild Exhibition of 1949, Finn Juhl (1912–1989) designed much more than furniture. Throughout his career, Juhl participated in twenty-four of the Guild's exhibitions and won prizes sixteen times for his often-expressive designs. In 1949, he also executed a pen-and-ink and watercolour drawing of his exhibition booth at Kunstindustrimuseet (today Designmusem Danmark), accompanied by some of the designer's thoughts on the contextual place of furniture regarding aesthetics and construction. Juhl designed some of his most striking furniture pieces for the 1949 exhibition, including *Høvdingestolen* (the Chieftain Chair) and *Ægypterstolen* (the Egyptian Chair). Yet, the previous year, 1948, had not been a banner year for the cabinetmakers' exhibition or the designers' creations; the Museum of Modern Art in New York had sent Edgar Kaufmann, Jr., then director of the institution's industrial design department, to peruse the selection – and apparently he left Denmark less than impressed. The Danish press was also critical of recent designs; the influential Danish architect Svend Erik Møller blamed their tepid response on an absence of initiative, and the cabinetmakers feared the Golden Age of Danish design had ended. On 14 January 1949, Juhl responded to these growing concerns with a talk, 'Fortid-nutid-fremtid' ('Past Present Future'), held at the Danish Society of Arts and Crafts; his lecture was also published in the society's journal, *Dansk kunsthaandværk* (no. 4, 1949). Altogether, Juhl's designs, his delicate watercolour with its pointed commentary, and his insightful and at times scathing lecture provide an ideological portrait of Danish Modern developments, along with some telling reflections of artistic movements, particularly in sculpture. Juhl's observations unite him especially with two contemporary sculptors whose work he collected and sometimes exhibited with his own designs: Sonja Ferlov Mancoba (1911–1984) and Erik Thommesen (1916–2008).

That Juhl's is one of the names most associated with the concept of Danish Modern is not surprising. In addition to being one of the first Danish designers (with Hans Wegner) to achieve international fame in the 1950s, his work reveals an easily discernible tension with more rationalist strains of furniture design, especially those emanating from Klint's Furniture School at the Royal Danish Academy. The use of the word 'sober' to describe Danish design from the mid-twentieth century seems all but inapplicable to Juhl's highly expressive, sculptural, and at times blatantly sophisticated designs. Juhl – who had been trained as an architect under Kay Fisker at the Kunstakademiets Arkitektskole – initially wanted to pursue a career in art history and produced a number of deft illustrations, including those of his designs for the UN's Trusteeship Council Chamber (1950–52) and for the offices and terminals of SAS Airways (1956–61). Like Arne Jacobsen, who rendered numerous watercolours of his furnishings, textile designs, and botanical studies, Juhl transferred a strong artistic bent into his designs and their ideological underpinnings.

In his 1949 talk at the Society of Arts and Crafts, Juhl indulges in some clever rhetoric, constructing a dichotomy between an aesthetics determined totally by rationality or objectivity and one admitting the artistic and imaginative. As his talk progresses, Juhl deconstructs the notion of design that is somehow both rational yet tied to historical idioms: 'You cannot, by desire, hold historical modes of expression back in a 150–200-year-old state and yet simultaneously be correct in claiming that you're working rationally.'[1] In this polemical statement, Juhl sounds notably like Henningsen and the lamp designer and theoretician's admonishments about dependence on historical styles. At first, Juhl lauds Klint and his students (Mogens Koch and Ole Wanscher) for maintaining order in the Danish aesthetic empire and for returning to English and Chinese antecedents as an antidote to Art Nouveau's excesses – even noting that his fellow Danes' endeavours have led to a greater sense of quality in Danish design. Yet, these compliments are a set up in which Juhl eventually berates Klint's über-rationalist method of measuring to a perfect form merely to dress the results up in British and Chinese styling. Juhl insists that a piece of furniture is more than simply methods of joinery and focuses, instead, on the tension between static and constructive qualities. Juhl's arguments are leading to a defence of artistry in design; like Henningsen, Juhl suggests solving the functional task, but he departs in a more direct plea for liberation in artistic expression.

By presenting a somewhat self-deprecating assessment of his own chairs, Juhl draws attention to the formal nature of his designs, especially in their emphasis on the bearing and borne parts of the chair's construction. Pointing to an accentuation of rounded joinery and what he calls a 'false homogeneity' in his use of material, Juhl cites 'a stronger analyzing of the chair's individual parts and functions' as part of this effect.[2] Chair FJ45 (1945), a design that has received a plethora of attention for its elevation of upholstered seating off its frame, illustrates some of Juhl's observations. Careful joinery at the exact points of tension results in the back legs looking as if they have grown out of the curve in the armrests, as well as the front legs extending down from the front of the armrests (all points of connection). The chair was originally handcrafted by master cabinetmaker Niels Vodder (1918–), with whom Juhl worked for decades (Hansen points out that Vodder farmed out production of the challenging chair to a factory on the Danish island of Falster[3]). This sophisticated chair design, which reflects no effort at 'democratic' furniture for the masses, proffers a skeletal study in force: the rounded diagonal back legs, thickening where they join to the side frame (à la Wegner), push upward, while the armrests curve like human arms onto the support of the front legs, creating the illusion of one sinuous line. Further upward force is indicated by the angular stretchers extending from the brace beneath the chair and down towards the bottoms of the rounded front legs. Henrik Wivel views the emphasis on dividing the bearing and the borne as a strategy by Juhl to alleviate gravity: 'he wanted to make his furniture free from weight.' Yet, it is the chair's interplay between weight and space that comprises its strongest effect. The solid plane of the curved upholstered seat may seem to float, but it floats on a frame with lines, albeit slender, anchoring it to the ground.[4]

In his talk, Juhl indicates that he fears that design education in Denmark has left no room for personal expression or liberation and has led to a kind of stagnation. This absence is what drew Juhl to his contemporary sculptors, Ferlov Mancoba and Thommesen; their expressiveness in abstract form reflects movement and plasticity (Fig. 4.1). To Juhl, everything else in life involves movement, but he finds that quality absent in Danish modern design. Juhl then turns to sculpture in various forms as a model for design efforts: his article includes illustrations of a torso (1920) by Aristide Maillol, another of a torso in abstract form (1933) by Jean Arp, an ancient Greek torso of Apollo, the picture of a huge barrow stone resting on a trio of smaller stones from Bretagne, and a pair of ovoid marble forms (1935) by Barbara Hepworth. Juhl argues that designers can take something useful from these variegated sculptural approaches. From Arp, Juhl extracts the idea of total form – an inner organic context – not a reliance on bits and pieces (presaging Jacobsen's designs for the SAS Hotel). Even the fragment of Apollo's torso emphasizes form and surface in Juhl's context. Hepworth's egg shapes reflect a tension, one being static in positioning (on its side) and one in motion. Juhl, who cites a movement away from naturalism as the unifying force, adds that sculpture has worked both experimentally and analytically 'partly to show how earlier culture's achievements reveal quite related efforts, partly . . . to indicate what is important in this context, that such a study of form is good for any work in design.'[5] Juhl wants to extract these basic elements from three-dimensional art and apply them to furniture design – not by copying what has been done in the past but by creating something appropriate to his own time. Juhl builds to images of movement to illustrate the purpose of his arguments. His sculptural examples provide a picture of a moment, the sense of arrested movement. Movement, Juhl claims, compels viewers to become active participants in design (as in art). He is, at once, both justifying and conveying the intended effect of his furniture designs.

Illustrating design

Juhl's hand-coloured illustration of his 1949 booth for the Cabinetmakers Guild Furniture Exhibition depicts two views: at top, a wall and doorway with a dining room set consisting of three of his Egyptian chairs, a table, and a silverware sideboard (1949), an abstract painting by Ben Nicholson, a pendant lamp by Gino Sarfatti, along with a Chieftain Chair and a sculpture by Thommesen, *Pige med fletning* (Girl with Braids, 1949). The illustration below depicts a view looking down on the table, chairs, and sideboard, as well as a Chieftain sofa and a three-legged sofa table with hanging flap (also 1949). It is the captions, though, that disclose the artistic basis of

Fig. 4.1 One of Finn Juhl's stands at the Cabinetmakers Guild Exhibition of 1949: a rare Chieftain Sofa (1949) and a drop-leaf coffee table (1949) with some sculptures by Erik Thommesen, including *Girl with Braid* (1949), on the left. Courtesy of Designmuseum Danmark/The Library

Juhl's aesthetic approach. In the text below the first illustration, Juhl writes: 'A branch that is washed round, clean, and white at the seashore has the fine mixture of structure's clear composition in growth, treatment and surface, which must be the goal for furniture. In addition, the strength, the construction, the fulfillment of the functional requirement.'[6] In this statement Juhl, the artist and collector of art – including a number of paintings by Vilhelm Lundstrøm, whose cubist collages had influenced Henningsen's theoretical musings on Cubism's application to architecture and design – focuses attention on the sculptural aspect of his furniture by relating it to artistic concerns. Rhetorically, he places functional endeavours at the end of the list, thus prioritizing compositional and structural goals. Below the second illustration, Juhl states how the exhibition booth should function artistically; he insists that, although its primary purpose is to display the furniture, the booth should present furnishings in a context that explains and emphasizes forms in a 'unity with other artistic phenomena and with natural occurrences that appeal to the fantasy . . . the joy in shapes, lines, colors, materials.'[7] He adds that the back wall should be covered with striped fabric designed by the contemporary textile artist, Marie Gudme Leth (1895–1997), who had helped to introduce printed fabric to Danish textiles.

Contextually, Juhl struggles to unite his furniture with art and sculpture – including found art: at the end of the first caption, he lists a snail's shell, a branch, a gourd, a painting, a sculpture, and a piece of furniture (in that order) as needing to fulfill their respective functions: '. . . but fantasy and mode of expression are also functions,' insists Juhl. 'Mathematics is an excellent tool, but not a goal.'[8] In these words, Juhl distances himself and his designs from the rationalist obsession with measuring one's way to the perfect or ultimate form, an approach fostered by the Klint Furniture School. Instead, Juhl, flying in the face of any notions about purely democratic designs, opens up modernist design to playful, organic forms that are more artistic in nature. The art historian Sigurd Schultz, writing about the Cabinetmakers Guild's 400th anniversary exhibition in 1954, mentioned the influence of Thommesen on some of the designers and related this approach towards furniture design 'to modern abstract wooden sculpture . . . there is hardly any doubt that such abstract plasticity has been the initial experiments of this method.'[9] At one point in Juhl's article, however, he derides designers for designing solely for the museum (where, ironically, a number of his designs have landed in permanent exhibitions); this argument would be turned against him in the early 1960s by Klint's influential former students Børge Mogensen and Arne Karlsen, who found Juhl too focused on artistic renewal and fashion (a pejorative term for most modernists).[10]

Sonja Ferlov Mancoba

Juhl's first description of the sea-washed branch recalls the early sculptures of Sonja Ferlov Mancoba, the Danish sculptor who introduced African art (via her interest in the ethnographic collections of her parents' friend, Carl Kjersmeier) to the first Danish abstract painters in the 1930s. In the mid-1930s, Mancoba joined with the Danish artists Ejler Bille (1910–2004) and Richard Mortensen (1910–1993) to spend a summer on the island of Bornholm, where they collected found objects, discussed the subconscious (Bille was an avowed surrealist), and produced varied artworks. Constructed at that time, Mancoba's sculpture *Levende grene* (Living Branches, 1935) displays six pieces of washed driftwood in an abstract arrangement that still recalls something figurative (a piece on the left resembles an abstracted bird) as well as a sense of arrested movement. These simple, elemental *objets trouvés*, similar in approach to the Dada-esque sculptures of Hans (Jean) Arp and Kurt Schwitters, would appear in much of her work. 'I didn't tell any stories about them directly,' she once explained of her driftwood and branch sculptures, 'but afterwards I could clearly see how they sprang out of my life.'[11] Mancoba had also begun her career as a painter but was soon drawn to exploring form. A visit with Alberto Giacometti in Paris in 1937 further inspired her; she would end up spending most of her adult life in Paris, where she lived with her husband Ernest Mancoba, the South-African modernist artist. She had expected to find pure abstraction in Giacometti's sculptures but instead came to the realization that he was struggling to reveal the human form in an abstract language. In 1967, she told the art historian Gunnar Jespersen: 'some time went by before we understood that [Giacometti] was trying in his work to get closer to what was human, without abandoning abstraction's freedom for that reason.'[12] Her sculptural work took two paths: her study of ethnographic and tribal arts led to her use of the mask motif, a motif that would become essential to the abstract paintings of CoBrA co-founder Egill Jacobsen, and her attraction to human and animal forms led to abstract, organic figures. Mancoba's bronze sculpture *L'accord* (1967) (Fig. 4.2) still sits on a shelf in Juhl's house in Ordrup. The bronze sculpture depicts a circle of abstracted figures, bordering on anthropomorphic, connected at the 'face' and the 'arms,' forming a ring of energy conveyed in both curved and angular forms resting on four cylindrical shapes, emphasized by the spaces between them. These simple, elemental forms became a constant artistic language in all her work.

Mancoba's description of her realization about Giacometti's efforts, her thoughts on capturing the 'human' in the abstraction, and the influence of her sculptures – from her early found-object pieces to her later mask and anthropomorphic forms – have bearing on Juhl's designs. What makes Chair 45 so attractive even to contemporary viewers is not simply an emphasis on the bearing and borne parts but, more importantly, its human forms in abstracted shapes, especially the slender, curving armrests. A similar effect occurs in the top-rail of Juhl's more compact armchair from 1944 (a chair Hansen refers to as 'one of Juhl's masterpieces . . . one of Juhl's most difficult chairs to produce'[13]). The chair's top-rail, consisting of three pieces of solid wood, curves and thickens three-dimensionally; its four legs follow suit, straight lines on a slight inward diagonal from floor to seat – and then curving out, both in front and in back, to join the strong shape of the encircling top-rail. The chair has no apron, adding to the seat's floating effect; instead, its highly placed front stretcher curves in towards the centre beneath the seat, where two diagonal stretchers join to the back legs. Juhl and Vodder exhibited the chair – along with a

Fig. 4.2 Juhl owned Sonja Ferlov Mancoba's bronze sculpture *L'Accord* (1967), which still sits on a shelf in his home in Ordrupgaard. Photo: Ole Haupt. Courtesy Gallerie Mikael Andersen

dining table, wall cabinet, and a warming table – at the Cabinetmakers Guild Exhibition of 1944; on the wall hung a painting by the Danish abstract colourist Egon Mathiesen (1907–1976), whose work, like Lundtsrøm's, also appeared at different times on the walls of Juhl's home.

The energy-laden circle of Mancoba's *L'accord* shares reflective qualities with Chair FJ44's highly sculptural, expanding and contracting top-rail; the sculpture and

Fig. 4.3 Juhl's Chair NV-44 (1944): the chair was extremely difficult to produce because of its demanding joinery. This photo shows the re-launched chair (2011) from Onecollection and sold by Brun Rasmussen auction house to benefit the Finn Juhl Institute. Photo: ©Brun Rasmussen Auctioneers

chair reveal a similar abstraction of force and tension, one heavily dependent on the spaces surrounding connecting forms (Fig. 4.3). The chair's bony-like curves (it is sometimes referred to as the 'Bone Chair') and strong profile capture the same condensed energy as Mancoba's sculpture. Writing about Sonja Ferlov Mancoba's approach in 1979, the Danish art historian Troels Andersen noted two forces at work in a comment that could just as easily be applied to Juhl's wooden constructions: 'One is the analytical, constructive structure of space and figure, practically purged of associations. The other is a perception of form . . . filled with associations to the human body.'[14] Ultimately, organic form permeates structure; thus, claims of organic Danish furniture design are not simply marketing tools, particularly in the case of Juhl. The organic nature of many of his designs reflects the conscious artistic and sculptural approach he delineates in his 1949 lecture, an approach echoed in the sculptures of artists he both knew and collected.

Juhl and Thommesen

Among these artists, Erik Thommesen was the sculptor whose work Juhl most frequently exhibited with his designs. Throughout his professional life, Juhl owned seven to nine of Thommesen's sculptures, and two remain in the Juhl house in Ordrup.[15] *Pige med fletninger* (Girl with Braids, 1949), the Thommesen wood sculpture that appears in Juhl's coloured illustration for 1949, was one example of a theme the sculptor had worked with since 1941 (a wall relief of this motif appeared with a Chieftain sofa when Juhl's house opened as part of Ordrupgaard Museum in 2008). The series reflected Thommesen's development of a form of abstraction that gradually became increasingly organic and less detailed; curiously, it is the human form that informs most of Thommesen's wood sculptures, but the form has been reduced to an abstraction that manages to remain, however, more expressive than constructive. During his time (1945–49) exhibiting at 'Høstudstillingen' ('Harvest Exhibition') with other young, revolutionary abstract artists, Thommesen, who believed that content created shape and that forms can therefore not be solely objective, developed an anthropomorphic language lending his abstractions a natural sense of growth. By the time he joined other artists in 'Martsudstillingen' ('March Exhibition'), where he exhibited from 1951 to 1981, they were moving away from avant-garde notions of what art had to be. The human body remained, as it did for Mancoba, the driving force in Thommesen's sculptures, but their predominant visual effect is one of tension between mass and space. The same elemental force that drew Mancoba to her African influences manifests itself in Thommesen's sculptures – though at times Thommesen also imparts something architectonic in his work. Energy has either been contracted into a thick form (as in many of the more compact sculptures named simply *Woman* or *Man*) or extracted into extended and often parallel shapes stressing verticality, as in the Woman/Girl with Braids series. Still, the organic always dominates – and Thommesen remained resistant to superimposed artistic formalism.

Looking at Thommesen's sculptures, one can readily see why Juhl was drawn to them and how they inspired him in his furniture designs. The sculptures' highly organic wooden shapes lend themselves well to reinterpretation as chair frames (and cabinet frames, as in the case of a silverware cabinet, also from 1949, consisting of a rectangular sideboard encased in a Thommesen-like frame). In *Det menneskelige og det personlige* (The Human and the Personal), Henning Jørgensen points out that Juhl was one of the first of only a few collectors who appreciated the sculptor's work (Arne Jacobsen also owned some sculptures by Thommesen and even sold one to Juhl).[16] Many of Thommesen's wooden figures, rendered mostly in oak, combine a strong staff-like form – often the abstracted braid – with a swelling, figurative mass capturing a human essence. They impart a primitive aspect without direct reference, similar to the abstracting of Oceanic and other native arts by the early modernist painters and sculptors. The wood's natural grain adds a textural element enhancing the visual reference to nature. The wooden lines bearing the sculpture's weight, especially, must have captured Juhl's attention, and it is no accident that he chose *Pige med fletninger* to exhibit with the Chieftain Chair in 1949. Another study in an elevation of an upholstered seat and back from wooden frame, the Chieftain was presented at that year's guild exhibition with a backdrop of prehistoric objects in a poster display, thus creating triangulation between the chair, the ancient artefacts (including busts, weapons, and tools), and Thommesen's elongated wooden sculpture. The sculptural references and artistic context Juhl pleaded for in his lecture earlier that year had been given not only form but also setting, compelling viewers to experience the furniture as part of both a historical and an artistic tradition. In Juhl's designs, expressiveness trumped objectivity, just as it did in Thommesen's sculptural abstractions. In his exhibition booths, Juhl had illustrated the arguments in his lecture and article, particularly in the articulation of the Chieftain.

While the Chieftain Chair – an imposing design heavily dependent on the exchange between carefully determined frame and curved flattened abstract shapes – has a front apron with slight curves on its top ends, just below the far ends of the seat front, diagonal stretchers have replaced both the side and back apron (and they too curve up where they meet the seat in the back). The shield-like upholstered back is often cited as the reason for the chair's name, but it was an offhand remark by Juhl (who apparently only referred to the design as the 'Big Chair') that gave the design its name. Asked whom the imposing chair was for when it was first brought into the Cabinetmakers' exhibition of 1949, Juhl jokingly responded that it was 'for one or another African chief.' While it does somewhat resemble a shield, the back of the chair, along with its flipper-like armrests, also recalls many of the shapes (both faces and other abstracted forms) in the mask paintings of Egill Jacobsen (1910–1998). In countless paintings, Jacobsen abstracted masks into colourful curved and/or triangular shapes emphasizing upward movement, a positive visual effect enhanced by a vivid chromaticism and counterpointed by strong diagonal lines (Fig. 4.4). Once again flying in the face of any conventional notions about sober or simplistic design, Juhl designed a chair that fulfils his lecture's plea for personal and artistic expression: 'The strong and traditionally oriented education that handicrafts get in this country doesn't leave much room for personal efforts at liberation.'[17]

Early in his lecture, Juhl blames this absence on the Danish designers' proclivity towards *soberheden* (soberness). Juhl views these repeated efforts at soberness,

Fig. 4.4 Juhl contemplates a mask painting by Egill Jacobsen: Jacobsen's playfully abstract curves and angles disclose similarities to the shapes in Juhl's more organic designs. Courtesy of Designmuseum Danmark/The Aage Strüwing Collection

along with the myopic notion of measuring one's way to the perfect form, as restrictive. Through both his arguments and his furniture, Juhl has constructed a dichotomy between expressive and non-expressive designs. The Constructivism that had permeated many Bauhaus designs was, in Juhl's hands, being diluted into a more expressive form of abstraction. While many of Denmark's abstract artists in the first half of the twentieth century were taken with Constructivism, as time went on a number of them found this form of abstraction too restrictive. In his essay 'Saglighed og Mystik' ('Objectivity and Mystery'), from the avant-garde journal *Helhesten* (*The Hel-Horse*, April, 1941), Egill Jacobsen, whose mask paintings in the 1930s changed the face of Danish abstract art, noted that Lundstrøm's more painterly content enabled him to 'liberate himself from the restrictive speculations of Constructivism.'[18] Just as Juhl bemoans the restrictive way formalism has taken over design in 'Fortid-nutid-fremtid,' Jacobsen derides Constructivism for ultimately denying any sense of fantasy.

At one point in his lecture, Juhl bemoans the loss of upholstered furniture from previous exhibitions; he claims that these designs represented the last *en masse* attempt to create something new in a contemporary idiom, and he mentions Arne Jacobsen and Flemming Lassen among those who created inventive designs in upholstered furniture in the 1930s. During this earlier stage of designing, Juhl exhibited his upholstered designs with sculptures by the Icelandic artist Sigurjón

Ólafsson (1908–1982). In the 1940 Cabinetmakers Guild Exhibition, Juhl used Ólafsson's *Children at Play* (1938), a plaster relief featuring abstracted shapes of children, to reflect the biomorphic form of *Pelikanen* (the Pelican Chair), which took its name from its thick, forward-curving, wing-like arms. Even more abstracted forms are featured in Ólafsson's *Desire* (1940), which Juhl exhibited with *Poeten* (the Poet Sofa) in 1941. That year Juhl also exhibited furniture with Ólafsson's *Man and Woman* (1941) at 'Thirteen Artists in a Tent', an exhibition of avant-garde artists designed by Juhl and held on fairgrounds near Bellevue. These chunky, upholstered furniture designs established the ongoing dialogue Juhl was willing to pursue with sculptural art throughout his career. Wivel sees these early designs as human bodies translated into furniture 'in which the individual parts comprise an organic whole.' In his lecture, though, Juhl stresses that his references to sculptural examples revolve around movement – what he calls a 'snapshot' – and he hopes this sense of arrested movement will inspire more imaginative designs. In 2015, the Sigurjón Ólafsson Museum in Reykjavik, Iceland, held an exhibition entitled Interplay, dealing specifically with the relationship between art and design in Ólafsson's sculptures and Juhl's furniture in the 1940s.

Turning to American design towards the end of his 1949 lecture, Juhl cites the chairs of Eero Saarinen and Charles Eames as examples of designers working in new materials (Saarinen in plastics and Eames in moulded plywood) in an approach Juhl finds both analytical and liberating: 'They have made use of experimentation in abstract art, just as architecture benefitted from cubism.'[19] Juhl goes on to insist that he does not want to be misunderstood – that furniture is furniture – utilitarian – and not sculpture. Yet, he has spent the majority of his lecture explaining the advantage of looking at efforts in sculpture and applying them to furniture design; ultimately he calls it 'unnatural' for designers to ignore the correlation among the different efforts in all cultural areas. He would reinforce this correlation in his article 'Mellem to stole' ('Between Two Chairs'), appearing in *Dansk Kunsthaandværk* in 1952: 'Furniture should not imitate modern art, but it must be designed from similar points of view: honesty in use, materials, construction, in human and artistic understanding. We view aesthetics as another function.'[20] At the end of his 1949 lecture, Juhl, sounding very much like Henningsen, returns to the concept of time and suggests that designers have a choice: they can either continue to misunderstand past ideas and try to copy them, or they can contextualize those ideas as part of the past and try to create something appropriate for their own time's conditions.

In 'Writing about Stuff: The Peril and Promise of Design History and Criticism,' Jeffrey L. Miekle indicates most modernists' predilection for writing about designing to the point of, ironically, prioritizing words over objects, and he defines these efforts as writing 'ideologically engaged social criticism.'[21] Miekle sees many of these modernist theorists as subordinating material design concerns to abstract issues. Yet, one searches in vain for any rhetoric involving social improvement in Juhl's lectures and articles; Juhl was an unabashed boulevardier whose elegant designs seemed ill-suited (and often too costly) to fit into any social programme, although he also designed a number of furnishings for mass production – some even variants of his cabinetmaker designs. His arguments constitute, instead, pleas for an aesthetic approach with artistic precedents as a guideline. Miekle writes that 'modernists celebrated artificiality as the key to a rational machine civilization'[22] – and this certainly applies to Le Corbusier and other Bauhaus thinkers and their arguments for universalist geometric abstraction as a guiding force. One could even argue that some of Klint's and his acolytes' more Cartesian endeavours offered a hyper-rationalist parallel to this approach in Denmark. Juhl, however, aligned himself with an expressionist form of abstraction, one based on physical (i.e. material) sculptures. It is three-dimensional objects – sculptures and other artefacts – that Juhl builds his arguments on, not words. Trying to impart presence in furniture through a sense of arrested movement, à la Barbara Hepworth or Alexander Calder, holds no social impact other than possibly improving the visual environment.

Juhl's sculptural approach transferred well to the American market; his expressive aesthetic fit into the rhetoric surrounding the arrival and popularity of Danish Modern in the 1950s. In 1952, the Georg Jensen store – then on Fifth Avenue – became the first venue to offer Juhl's designs to American customers. Words like 'sculptural manipulation of wood' and 'artistic playfulness,' employed by the editors to describe Scandinavian Modern in the American magazine *House Beautiful* (July 1959), seemed well suited to his designs. More importantly, his involved designs helped to establish the heavily marketed notion of Danish Modern being more sophisticated or more carefully crafted than those designs emanating from other parts of the world. In his book *Chairs* (1953), George Nelson observed of Juhl's FJ46 (1946) chair, a variant on FJ45: 'For grace and elegance, neither Juhl nor his colleagues in Denmark have provided a better chair than the piece at the right.'[23] By the time Danish Modern came back into fashion in the 1990s, Juhl's designs were some of the first to go back into production – and to fetch some of the highest prices at auction for original examples (Hansen cites a 1982 retrospective exhibit of Juhl's work at Designmuseum Danmark as the inception of his renaissance in Denmark). In 1953, Juhl told Nelson: 'I was never trained to design anything but houses, which seems to have influenced me, so that I look at any piece of furniture as a construction based on the natural character of the material, more than a collection of cabinet-maker's joints, as many furniture designers are apt to do.'[24] This method of using construction to emphasize materials became part of the narrative about Danish Modern and the Danes' purported efforts at being 'true' to materials. In reality, it reflects an artistic approach towards using materials, especially wood, by emphasizing and matching grains and by employing more organic forms, often recalling the human body (particularly in chair designs).

Juhl's lectures and articles in 1949 held little promise of helping to make the social landscape more egalitarian or less class-conscious; his rhetoric served, instead, as a way of framing and articulating his own sophisticated furniture designs – of justifying their artistic nature in the face of socially motivated design and the ongoing expectation that modern designs be sober and objective. Juhl's arguments were, predominantly, aesthetic. As he emphasized in his 1952 article 'Mellem to stole': 'Chairs are, aesthetically, like everything else, part of an artistic environment.'[25] Informed by his broad interest in painting and sculpture, Juhl designed in dialogue with modern Danish art and viewed design mostly within this context.

Notes

1. Finn Juhl, 'Fortid-nutid-fremtid,' *Dansk kunsthåndværk*, 22(4) (1949), 58.
2. Ibid.
3. Per H. Hansen, *Finn Juhl and His House*, trans. Mark Mussari (Copenhagen: Strandberg Publishing, 2014), 85–86.
4. Hansen points out: 'The 45-Chair definitively established Juhl's status as an icon.' Ibid., 34.
5. Ibid., 59.
6. Henrik Wivel, *Finn Juhl*, in *Store Danske Designere*, ed. Tøjner and Frovin (Copenhagen: Lindhardt og Ringhof, 2008), 333.
7. Ibid.
8. Ibid.
9. Sigurd Schulz, 'The Jubilee Exhibition of Danish Cabinet-Makers,' *Dansk kunsthaandværk*, 27(10/11) (1954), 150–53.
10. For a fine discussion of this rhetorical battle, see Hansen, *Finn Juhl and His House*, 128–37.
11. Hans Edvard Nørregaard-Nielsen, *Dansk Kunst 1* (Copenhagen: Gyldendal, 1983), 419.
12. Quoted in Gunnar Jespersen, *De abstrakte. Linien. Helhesten. Høstudstillingen. Cobra* (Copenhagen, Berlingske Forlag, 1967), 40–41.
13. Hansen, *Finn Juhl and His House*, 27.
14. Troels Andersen, *Sonja Ferlov Mancoba* (Copenhagen: Borgen, 1979), 61.
15. Interview with Birgit Lyngbye Pedersen, Curator, Finn Juhl House (17 November 2014).
16. Jørgensen, 'Det menneskelige og det personlige,' in *Billedhuggeren Erik Thommesen* (Holstebro: Holstebro Kunstmuseum, 2001), 14–53.
17. Juhl, 'Fortid-nutid-fremtid,' 58.
18. Egill Jacobsen, 'Salighed og Mystik,' in Per Hovdenakk, *Dansk kunst 1930–50* (Copenhagen: Borgen, 1999), 138–44.
19. Juhl, 'Fortid-nutid-fremtid,' 60.
20. Juhl, 'Mellem to stole,' *Dansk kunsthaandværk*, 25(7) (1952), 5–10.
21. Jeffrey L. Miekle, 'Writing about Stuff: The Peril and Promise of Design History and Criticism,' in *Writing Design: Words and Objects,* ed. Grace Lees-Maffei (Oxford: Berg, 2012), 27.
22. Ibid.
23. George Nelson, *Chairs*, Interiors Library 2 (New York: Whitney Publications, 1957), 98.
24. Quoted in Nelson, *Chairs*, 100.
25. Juhl, 'Mellem to stole,' 10.

5

Weaving Abstractions: Vibeke Klint and Lis Ahlmann

In her seminal lecture 'Designing as Visual Organization,' given at Yale University in 1958, the German-born, Bauhaus-educated weaver and design theorist Anni Albers (1899–1994) defined the visual articulation of weaving as 'the manner in which interdependent thread units are connected to form a cohesive and flexible whole.'[1] Like many modernists, Albers focused on fealty to materials as a driving force; she viewed this as an 'attentive passiveness' on the part of the weaver guiding all design choices in textiles. Recalling *die neue Sachlichkeit* at the Bauhaus (known as *den nye saglighed* in Denmark), Albers pleaded for the artist to get out of the way of the designed object: 'For the less he himself, his subjectivity, stands in the way of the object that is to take form, the more it will have "objective" qualities and thereby will also take on a more lasting character than it otherwise could.'[2] Appealing to the modernist dichotomy between contemporary styling and lasting design, and the association of 'objective' with enduring, Albers privileges materials to achieve what she believes is a more honest design. Subjectivity, to Albers, could only get in the way of what she viewed as the inherent nature of materials. Her Bauhaus training also manifests itself in her insistence, as a weaver, on the primacy of geometric forms: 'But when the matter of usefulness is involved, we plainly and without qualification use our characteristics: forms that, however far they may deviate in their final development, are intrinsically geometric.'[3] Designing, for Albers, involves clarity, lucidity, and reduction to what is easily comprehensible.

In *Bauhaus Weaving Theory: From Feminine Craft to Mode of Design*, T'ai Smith delineates the attitudes towards the various schools of design that resulted in the feminization of certain crafts, especially weaving, at the German institution. Smith observes that weaving's practices and materials 'were considered subordinate to the more fundamental practices of form and color theory . . . or the functionalistic logic of architecture.'[4] This attitude resulted in a secondary status for the weavers at the Bauhaus – a status resulting, Smith argues, from the prioritizing of art and architecture over craft: 'This feminization happened through actual policies that created a hierarchy between art and craft and moreover aligned a certain workshop with a certain gender.'[5] Thus, the Bauhaus weavers had to justify their existence at the school by also producing texts about their medium – another nod to the broad modernist proclivity for writing philosophical texts about design matters. Albers' writing cut a wide swath; she wrote not only on weaving but also on numerous aspects of design, and she disseminated her theories especially during her tenure (1933–49) at Black

Mountain College in Asheville, North Carolina. Still, her pointed thoughts on weaving, and design in general, have special resonance among the modernist textile artists, including those in Scandinavia. In articles such as 'Design: Anonymous and Timeless' (1947) and 'Constructing Textiles' (1946), Albers pleaded for less individuality and more balance in form; she focused repeatedly on an object's purpose to dictate choice of materials and derided the notion of designing as simply imparting an outer appearance to utilitarian objects.

While some of her arguments sound typically modernist, ideologically Albers saw a paradoxical quality to a designed object's capacity for timelessness: 'The imprint of time is unavoidable. It will occur without our purposely fashioning it. And it will outlast fashions only if it embodies lasting, together with transitory, qualities.'[6] This tension, which dogged the Danish Modern furniture designers and theorists for decades, was possibly an easier one for textile artists to address, as the structure of their weaving remained relatively constant. Albers also spoke frequently about the freedom of the weaver, whom she viewed as the modern incarnation of the craftsperson; she felt that craftspeople had been swept aside by specialization and fragmentation, and she insisted that modern weavers be involved in newer production methods.

In Denmark, during the rise of twentieth-century modernist design, it is actually craftsmanship driving development; as mentioned earlier, the architects who began to design modern furniture in the 1920s and 1930s did so by aligning themselves with cabinetmakers, with designs exhibited at their guild events. As Hansen has pointed out, the entire craftsmanship narrative developed to market Danish design in the mid-twentieth century rests on this crafts-based collaboration. In addition to exhibiting rugs, the Danish textile artists, predominantly women, worked closely with architects on fabric designs for furniture; in time, these weavers also exhibited in various other venues, including international exhibitions that were both Danish and pan-Scandinavian. Textile design was never a course of study at the Royal Danish Academy, however; it was sent, instead, to the Kusthåndværkerskole (School of Arts and Crafts), where it remains. The architect and design historian Bent Salicath has argued that, whereas in Sweden and Norway weaving developed in a direct line tracing back to ancient peasant cultures, textile art had to be 're-created' in Denmark in the early twentieth century. Salicath felt that modern Danish weavers were not resting on any continuous folk-art tradition as in the other Nordic countries.[7] The subtext in Salicath's argument is that the opportunity to re-establish a weaving tradition opened up the Danish weavers to modernist currents in design sans the pull of long-lasting tradition. In many of the textiles the Danish modern weavers designed, especially for furniture, one can see simple 'peasant' patterns – stripes, checks – abstracted into more geometric forms. Albers' observation that textile forms are 'intrinsically geometric' evinces itself well in much of the Danish Modern textile art that accompanied furniture design, especially following the Second World War. Much of the simplicity in these textiles belies a conscious effort to express simplified geometric forms in highly textural structures. Whereas geometrics for their own sake seemed at odds with many of the Danish furniture designers' projects, a patterned geometric approach found a more comfortable home with many of the Danish textile designers. On furniture, these textiles could provide juxtaposition with more organic frames.

The early Danish modern architects were not as inclined to use printed fabrics in their interior designs. This exclusion was a painful one for a figure such as Marie Gudme Leth (1895–1997), Denmark's first teacher in the subject of textile printing. A three-year stay (1921–24) in Java had a profound effect on the artistic Leth, who became familiar with the technique of printing on fabrics. Interest in printed textiles grew in Denmark in the 1920s, but no school for learning the skill existed. Therefore, Leth trained at the Kunstgewerbeschule in Frankfurt am Main, Germany, and then led the textile-printing department at Denmark's School of Arts and Crafts in Copenhagen. In 1940, she founded her own studio for hand-printed fabrics. Although she worked initially in woodblock and then silkscreen printing, creating careful floral patterns (often in two colours) and involved village scenes in silhouettes, in the 1950s Leth's designs became more abstract and geometric, including patterns that were produced. Her printed textile designs appeared frequently at Den Permanente showroom, right beside the cabinetmaker furniture and other Danish crafts, and in exhibitions and promotional tours for Danish arts and crafts. As early as 1939, a *New York Times* reporter, Walter Rendell Storey, reviewing a selection of Danish crafts at the department store Wanamaker's, mentioned Leth's brightly coloured printed fabrics.[8] That same year she won a Gold Medal at the World Exposition in Paris, and in 1951 she won another Gold Medal at the Milan Triennale. In 1948, Harry Booth, writing in the *Journal of the Royal Society of Arts*, commented in a travel article about Denmark: 'Of the textile designers exhibiting there [Den Permanente], Marie Gudme Leth appears to be not only the most popular but also the most prolific. Her work typifies the prevailing spirit with regard to color, which is fresh, cool and shows a preference for green and yellows. The printed fabrics rely for their effect upon a narrow color range based upon the greens of Danish plant life.'[9]

In her more modernist prints, Leth employed simplified shapes (spades, ovals, hearts) in smaller patterns and bold colour combinations. In *Bølger* (Waves), a silkscreened pattern on cotton from 1955, Leth abstracts the rhythmic effect of waves into a stacked, diagonal blue and green pattern, thus using both chroma and repetition of shape to impart movement and an aqueous effect in an extremely modernist colour combination. These designs are worlds removed from the flora- and fauna-driven silhouettes of her earlier work. If anything, Leth's later, smaller patterns recall those of the English textile artists Jacqueline Groag (1903–1986, b. Czechoslovakia) and Lucienne Day (1917–2010), whose abstract patterns, such as Groag's roller-printed Pebbles (1952) and Day's Miró-influenced Calyx (1951), have come to represent another biomorphic element in standard mid-twentieth-century design.[10] As the 1950s progressed, colour increasingly became Leth's primary tool of expression: 'Modena' (1958), for example, features a brown and violet combination, whereas 'Mariatti' (1958) was offered in either a green, brown, and grey combination or a turquoise, green, and violet one. Further effects are garnered by printing one colour on top of another – as in the muted red, orange, and yellow stripes and blocks of the silkscreened 'Beirut' (1958) – allowing various shades to emerge from the printing process in different combinations. In 1961, Zahle commented that Leth's more modernist textile designs 'work ideally with modern architecture's clear spaces and large, clearly defined window- and wall-surfaces.'[11] Still, Leth once lamented the early modernist architects' predilection for using woven instead of printed fabrics in their designs: 'There was an architectural domain that did not allow for multi-colored patterns. The architects could not stand them.'[12] In the 1960–61 travelling exhibition 'The Arts of Denmark: Viking to Modern,' two of Leth's hand-printed designs were included: 'Jungle' (1934) and the softer, more geometric 'Beirut' (a pattern often reproduced industrially).

Vibeke Klint

In 2012, the Danish furniture company BoConcept celebrated its sixtieth anniversary with a line of sofas and chairs called Istra and fabrics designed by Vibeke Klint (1927–), a designer long associated with Danish Modern woven textiles. Founded in 1952, BoConcept was obviously attempting to impart a mid-century element to its anniversary design by using textiles that Klint (she was Kaare Klint's daughter-in-law) had designed in the 1950s (and by calling the fabric line 'Klint'). The company's in-house magazine captioned a picture of the Klint-designed fabrics on a sofa and chair: 'The jubilee fabric designed by Vibeke Klint back in the 1950s underlines the Danish design roots and the unique story of Urban Danish Design since 1952.'[13] Fabrics for the Istra line were offered in two mixed-pattern colourways, green and grey, each exhibiting horizontal and vertical stripes, with an emphasis on the vertical in contrasting colours to the predominant grey or green ground. The upholstered sofa and chair frames were rendered in a solid colour, whereas cushions revealed two patterns of stripes, one more spaced out and bolder than the other. While the grey cushion fabrics were offset with black and white lines, the green colourway featured both a white and a thin contrasting red line. In both the contrast between the solid background and patterned cushions and in the striped patterns themselves, it was the fabric – not the furniture designs – that seemed redolent of mid-century Modernism. In particular, the use of a solid-coloured ground behind coordinating fabrics recalled the effect used on some of Finn Juhl's chairs and sofas in the 1940s and 1950s (as on the two-toned upholstery on his chair No. 45, for example, with fabric originally designed by Vibeke Klint). This look, though resurrected every so often since then, is still used often to impart a retro style to upholstered furniture.

Klint was an apt choice for the Danish furniture company to turn to for mid-century fabric design. Her textiles helped to establish the 'look' of what came to be known as Danish Modern, particularly in her participation in three of the most significant touring exhibitions: 'Neue Form aus Dänemark' ('New Form from Denmark') in Germany (1956–57), 'Formes Scandinaves' ('Scandinavian Designs') at the Louvre in Paris (1958), and The Arts of Denmark: Viking to Modern in the United States (1960–61). Klint showed four works at the latter exhibition: a silk shawl (1954), a hand-woven cotton tablecloth (1955), a hand-knotted rya rug (1958), and hand-woven silk fabric (1959). Like many of the other mid-century designers and craftspeople, Klint attended the School of Arts and Crafts in Copenhagen. The school's textile department – then run by Gerda Henning (1891–1951), a mentor with whom Klint maintained a close relationship – was located in part of the building housing the Kunstindustrimuseum (now Designmuseum Danmark). No dichotomy existed between artist weavings and utilitarian weaving; the development into two separate lines of study to pursue came much later in the School of Arts and Crafts: 'at that time, the school just taught students how to weave,' Klint recalled in 1983, 'and then the students had to go out on their own.'[14]

One of Klint's first assignments after graduating in 1949, and brought to her by Henning, was to work on test samples for mammoth tapestries that would hang in the Danish Parliamentary Hall (Christiansborg) in Copenhagen. Henning even procured funding to send Klint to school in Aubousson, France, in 1951, where she studied with Jean Lurcat and Pierre Wemaere. Henning died suddenly, however, requiring Klint to return to Denmark, where she took over her mentor's weaving workshop. Although the Parliamentary tapestries project was abandoned, Klint used what she had learned in France for tapestries (designed by William Scharff) woven for the Egmont H. Petersen College in Copenhagen. Henning had worked closely with Danish architects, including Kaare Klint, for whom she designed and produced rugs for Thorvaldsen's Museum (1925) and both rugs and curtains for the Wedding Hall in Copenhagen's City Hall (1931–33). She passed this collaborative approach on to her student; even before graduating from Henning's weaving school, Vibeke Klint had already exhibited two rugs at the Cabinetmakers Guild Exhibition in 1950. Her first architect-designed textile work was for Mogens Koch (1898–1992), an architect and furniture designer famous for his 1928 bookshelf system who also worked on the interiors of churches. Klint and Koch designed and produced rugs for the Danish Church in London and, in Denmark, for Saint Jørgensbjerg Church in Roskilde and Holbæk Church.

From Henning, whom she once referred to as a 'true Bohemian,' Klint had also learned to apply all of her skills to finding the simplest solution: the elder artist told Klint repeatedly that the simplest solution to any design challenge was the most beautiful.[15] This approach, one frequently expressed by various modernist designers, manifested itself in the highly geometric patterns of most of her work – patterns bordering, as time went on, on minimalism. As Inge Alifrangis points out: 'The patterns, often extremely simple, form a natural part of the creation of the textile. Stripes and squares, rhombus and the zig-zag effect of the forked lightning now form the basis for the distribution of colors'[16] (Fig. 5.1). This focus on geometric forms and, especially, the use of a limited palette of stripes and checks conveyed a deceptive simplicity in Klint's textile designs, especially for home furnishings. The casual interplay between furniture and textile designer becomes apparent in the work she did with Hans J. Wegner: for example, a sofa-bed (GE-258) Wegner designed for Getama in 1954 reveals a two-tone red fabric with a strong casual appearance well-suited to the simple teak and teak-veneer sofa, whose upholstered back folds up to create room

Fig. 5.1 Vibeke Klint frequently abstracted Native American zigzag patterns in her rugs, as in this carpet in shades of red (1953). Ethnic patterns became colour-field chevrons. Courtesy of Designmuseum Danmark/The Library

for a daybed. That the textile artists were woven into the myriad designs that would become Danish Modern is evident not only in their constant exhibition at the annual Cabinetmakers Guild events but also in a 1956 exhibition at Designmuseum Danmark featuring the works of five contemporary utilitarian artists: Ruth Hill (textile printer), Wegner (furniture), Axel Knudsen (bookbinder), Gretrud Vasegaard (ceramist), and Klint (textiles).

Klint's designs, particularly in her mid-century rugs, rely often on sharp contrasts between blocks of solid colour and geometric patterns, frequently taking inspiration and chroma from Indian and Native American sources (as in much abstract art, modernist designers also tended to turn to what they referred to as 'primitive' arts for inspiration). 'I am influenced by American Indian works, by East Indian things, by Japanese designs,' Klint once observed. 'I think that in many native cultures in many countries, there are similar basic designs and colors because the native artists have so few materials to work with, and so few colors.'[17] In her process, Klint abstracted these borrowed patterns into simpler, more geometric forms; in many of her flat-woven rugs, a repeating scroll pattern, for example, receives a more rectilinear reading, functioning like a symbol for movement across the warp. A hand-knotted rya rug from 1957, consisting of wool on a flax warp, exemplifies Klint's design approach in the 1950s. The thick-piled red wool encompassing most of the rectangular surface of the rug (140 × 210 cm) is offset by a narrow frame of stripes, in black and white, quite thin on the warp peripheries and featuring an arrowhead pattern repeating twice on the latitudinal top and bottom (creating a margin, as on a sheet of paper). Along with stripes, Klint frequently employed a zigzag pattern to convey a strong abstract effect:

a 1953 rug in two close shades of red in a thick, bold zigzag pattern (an example of which sits on the floor in Finn Juhl's house in Ordrup) is offset by the black pointed ends of zigzags staggered up the sides, each point bleeding a thin black horizontal line a third of the way into the overall surface. Two thin black lines extend completely across the latitudinal top and bottom, finishing for the eye what the shorter lines imply visually.[18] These patterns seem to presage the strong chevrons of later Colour Field painters such as Kenneth Noland. In a comment that could be applied to the partial motifs of Klint's rug patterns, Diane Waldman observes that Nolan's chevrons 'are so thoroughly integrated with the square or rectangle of the support they always remain two-dimensional motifs on flat surfaces.'[19] For a 1958 carpet in two shades of deep blue, designed for the industrially produced Cotil Collection, Klint employed an elongated (along the warp) diamond pattern shifting between the two saturated blues (striped fabric she designed for the Cotil collection reveals the same two shades of blue) (Fig. 5.2). The diamond pattern would re-emerge, this time in grey and deep tan, in a thick rya rug (1958) shown at the Arts of Denmark Exhibition in 1960.

In Klint's visual articulation, materials, patterns, and colours work together to fulfil her designs without any one element overpowering the others. Folk-inspired patterns – and even colours – are reinterpreted in modernist designs emphasizing spatial relations. In time she would reduce her zigzag patterns, particularly in her

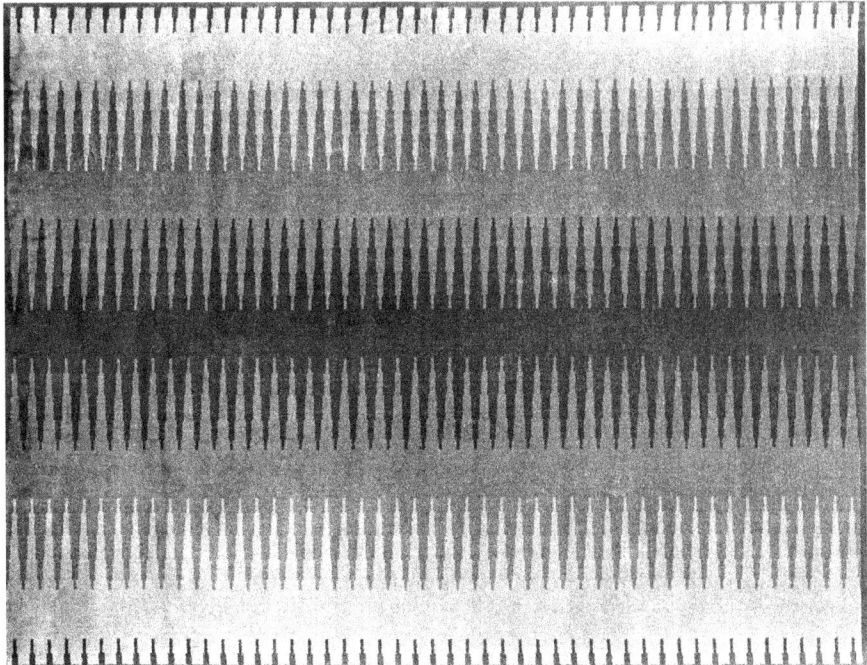

Fig. 5.2 Klint's Axminster carpet in a pattern of elongated diamonds, originally in two shades of blue, for the Cotil Collection (1957). Courtesy of Designmuseum Danmark/The Library

flat-woven Norwegian-wool rugs, to nothing but monochromatic rectangles with thin geometric lines on solid backgrounds; with no border and no recognizable reference to cultural precedents, the effect is similar to Frank Stella's monochromatic canvases in the late 1950s and early 1960s and their use of thin geometric lines to focus attention on surfaces (as in 'Six Mile Bottom', 1960, Tate Gallery). Watercolour sketches of Klint's rug designs offer a clear example of her geometric focus and subtle design strategy.[20] Klint felt, from the beginning, that her work fell under the aegis of utilitarian design. If any element pervades, it is an overall sense of balance imparting lucidity through a single weaving technique, a quality particularly evident in her thin repp (or ribbed) rugs. The simplification most modernists espoused in their ongoing rhetoric found elegant expression in Klint's thoughtful woven designs.

Lis Ahlmann

Like Vibeke Klint, Lis Ahlmann (1894–1979) also trained with Gerda Henning; the weaving master's first student, she completed her apprenticeship to Henning in 1929 and opened her own workshop in 1934. Before that she had worked as a painter in a ceramics factory and studied with the Danish modernist painter Harald Giersing. Kaare Klint had prompted her to travel for inspiration, and so she studied in Holland, Germany, Belgium, France and England. Ahlmann is often lauded for her ability to transfer her informed and technically proficient weaving experience into industrially produced textiles. In the 1930s, Ahlmann worked with Kaare Klint on some of his early furniture designs, thus instituting the collaboration between architect/furniture designers and textile artists – one that would help to create the 'look' of Danish Modern design. Karlsen and Tiedemann claim that, like Klint, Ahlmann 'relied on tradition' in these early textiles to accompany architect-designed furniture. In 1938, she began to exhibit her textiles – including rya rug weaving – at the Cabinetmakers Guild Exhibitions. That same year, Klint premiered his *Kugleseng* (Circle Bed), a bed with curved sections on its sides and ends corresponding to sections of a complete circle and rendered in African mahogany (Juhl would later ridicule this design as impractical). Ahlmann designed the textiles for the imposing bed: blue and white cotton bed linens in a surprisingly simple pattern of stripes in alternating thickness. According to different sources, the design took its inspiration either from Navajo patterns or from the covers for down comforters used in old Danish farmhouses. The effect against the highly polished wood of Klint's curvaceous design is one of juxtaposition, rather than the 'appropriateness' often ascribed to it: the bedding looks like a peasant design – and this marks the inception of Ahlmann abstracting these peasant designs, with an emphasis on stripes and checks, into textile designs that are unpretentious, but geometric and bold (Fig. 5.3). She was also a self-contained weaver: Ahlmann not only designed the patterns and chose the colours, but she also sorted materials and spun her own wool.

In 1942, Børge Mogensen, then chairman of the Danish cooperative FDB's department of furniture design, designed a line of mass-produced furniture, inspired

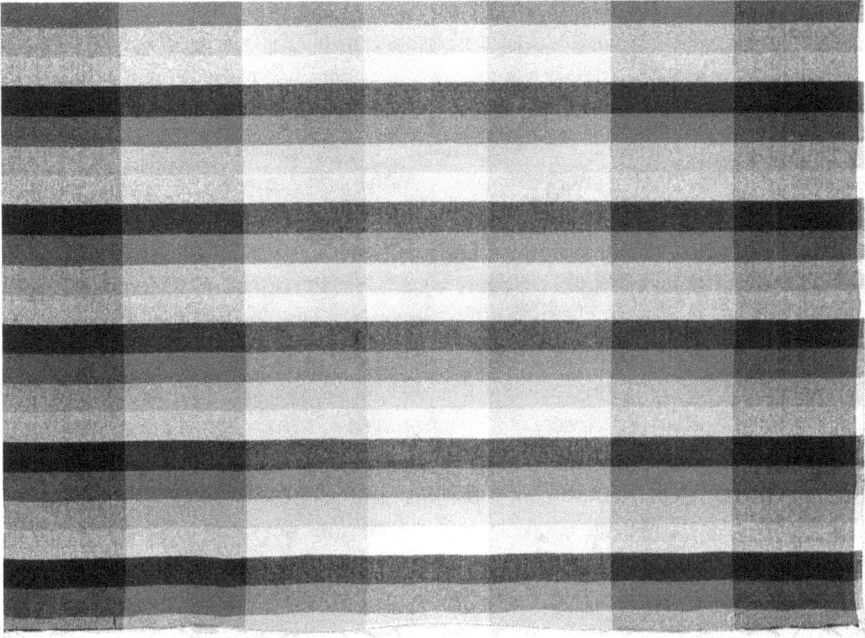

Fig. 5.3 Lis Ahlmann relied heavily on peasant patterns, especially checks and stripes, as an inspiration for her everyday, utilitarian fabrics. Courtesy of Designmuseum Danmark/ The Library

by Shaker and other populist designs, intended to be more affordable and therefore marketed as accessible to the average Dane. These were also individual coordinated pieces that could be chosen, mixed, and matched at the consumer's discretion.[21] Mogensen turned to Ahlmann to design the fabrics for his FDB designs. Because of material shortages during the Second World War, much of this furniture was manufactured in beech, a hard, blonde wood imparting a more casual appearance. This collaboration also spurred on the move from hand-woven textiles, which would be too expensive for these more mass-produced designs, to industrial variants of Ahlmann's designs. Her fabrics, simple striped and checked designs, suited the chroma of the wood pieces: warm colour combinations, often relying on a sand, tan, golden yellow, or orange ground, echoed the light wood tones. Mogensen said of the combination: 'Lis's textiles were a meeting of the stringent and the painterly. My furniture had gotten its clothes – and it seems that clothes do make the man-furniture.'[22] Ahlmann's strong reliance on peasant patterns offered a textile parallel to the Klint School's employment of previous historical styles in furniture designs, and on this front she and Mogensen shared an ideological approach. Her geometric crisscross patterns, reminding the viewer of the basic warp and weft construction of weaving, also illustrate Albers' insistence on remaining focused on the principles of construction in weaving as 'the intricate interlocking of two sets of threads at right angles.'[23]

Even in textiles, this careful visual coordination also gives rise to the rhetoric of bifurcation between enduring Modern design and temporal style. In 1960, Ulf Hård af Segerstad wrote: 'The result of this collaboration [between Ahlmann and Mogensen] has been ageless fabrics which transcend fashion changes.'[24] In his introduction for the catalogue of the 1974 retrospective exhibition, 'Børge Mogensen møbler = Lis Ahlmann tekstiler' ('Børge Mogensen Furniture = Lis Ahlmann Textiles'), at Designmuseum Danmark, Mogens Koch stresses that finished work results in harmonic, clarified designs. He notes that the work of both designers indicates systematic study, a containment of 'experimentation to the workshop' and the creation of 'common types' rather than singular designs, an echo of the aspirations of the early European modernists. Koch sees Ahlmann's textiles as fitting into the modernist technical insight that enabled consumers to surround themselves with industrial design.[25] As late as 1996, on the occasion of the fiftieth anniversary of the Danish Weavers Guild, Arne Karlsen continued to draw a dichotomy between Modern textiles and sheer fashion. Commenting on Ahlmann's later work, he observed: 'Lis Ahlmann was of the old school, but even her recent work has a wonderful tinge of youth. Which does not mean that they follow the time's *trend*.'[26] Writing in Danish, Karlsen chose the English word for trend, another rhetorical move stressing the difference between what is Danish and what is disposable fashion.

In 1953, when the textile manufacturer C. Olesen decided to institute a line (Cotil) of industrially produced fabrics, he turned to Ahlmann and Mogensen to form an artistic advisory committee. Their collaborative designs for Cotil reveal a wealth of striped fabrics in both natural tones and bolder colours. Some of Mogensen's most famous furniture designs became aligned visually with Ahlmann's grid-driven patterns. In its second incarnation in beech (it was originally produced in mahogany but only sold fifty copies), his *Tremmesofa* – designed in 1945 but not put into full production until 1961 – featured cushions covered in a checked pattern created by black and red stripes on a sand-coloured ground[27] (Fig. 5.4). Karlsen and Tiedemann refer to Ahlmann's work for Cotil as 'the moral backbone of the modern textile industry,'[28] and Karlsen notes that 'her sober choice of patterns has given the textiles the calmness they require to fit in with the needs of the many homes.'[29] Comments such as these disclose the ethical and normative veneer superimposed on modernist design decisions – even in textiles. In 1959, Ahlmann and Mogensen's participation in another exhibition 'Ler, Træ og Væv' ('Clay, Wood and Weave'), at Designmuseum Danmark, emphasized the significance of weavers to broader concepts of Modern design; the combination of artists also reinforced the mid-twentieth-century articulation of design and art as 'one' (especially in the appearance of sculpture by Adam Fischer). A tablecloth designed by Ahlmann looks quite at home in the exhibition's mix, even though it was originally designed in 1928.

Ahlmann reinforced her views on design and the use of natural fibres in a roundtable discussion she had with Mogensen and Wegner; their conversation was published in the Danish daily newspaper *Politiken* in 1964. Although Ahlmann, at seventy, was twenty years older than the two furniture designers at that point, she explained the reason for

Fig. 5.4 Børge Mogensen's *Tremmesofa* (1945, 1961) became associated with Ahlmann's checked peasant patterns. The two designers worked together frequently. Courtesy of Designmuseum Danmark/The Library

her continued interest in her craft: 'I have never been interested in what is fashionable. I've taken my own path, so to speak, limited my tools.'[30] Whereas Wegner argued for an embrace of new materials and experimentation in designing, Mogensen – in line with his mentor Kaare Klint – believed that overstepping one's bounds would only teach one to return to a narrower focus based on a material's limitations (the article is entitled 'On Limiting Oneself'). Throughout the discussion, Ahlmann sides with Mogensen. Unlike Vibeke Klint, who eventually worked also in synthetic materials, Ahlmann rejects the use of any new materials, which she refers to in the article as 'temptations,' and clings instead to working solely in wool and cotton. 'There is no end to all the strange things they want you to weave with,' she laments. 'I say, no.'[31] Ahlmann's and Mogensen's arguments point to the belief of some modernists that only by staying within certain parameters involving materials (wood, natural fibres) can they achieve worthwhile designs. Yet, by 1964, the date of the article, Jacobsen, Panton, and Kjærholm had already abandoned the hierarchy of wood or the sole use of natural fibres.

Further abstractions

A number of trained architects and furniture designers also designed textiles in the post-war years, and their work, for the most part, reflects a strong move into abstraction with numerous designs for industrial production. Arne Jacobsen's shift from the intricate botanicals he developed during his stay in Sweden (during the German occupation of Denmark) into the geometric patterns he designed in the 1950s, including his fabric designs for the SAS Hotel, parallel Leth's evolution from warm botanicals and nature-driven imagery to cooler geometric abstraction. Mogens Koch designed textiles, primarily hand-woven rugs, with his wife Ea Koch, who had been trained by Gerda Henning. Axel Salto (1889–1961), known mostly for his ceramics, designed textiles transferring nature images into small abstracted forms, and the lithographic artists Gunnar Aagaard Andersen (1919–1982) and Rolf Middelboe (1917–1995) also produced mathematically driven, highly graphic textile designs. Both designed textiles for Unika-Væv, the Danish company that would also produce many of Verner Panton's vibrant Pop- and Op-art fabrics in the 1960s. Both chromatically and texturally, textiles functioned as an integral part of the various examples of *Gesamtkunstwerk* designed by both Jacobsen and Panton. Nanna Ditzel, who was trained as a cabinetmaker and studied at the Kunsthåndværkerskole, designed a number of textiles, most notably Hallingdal, the first fabric for the Danish textile company Kvadrat, in 1965. The fabric, executed in two tones of highly textured wool and viscose, and thanks to its resilience employed in numerous public spaces such as doctors' offices and schools, has experienced such success that it was given its own exhibition, 'Hallingdal 65,' in 2012: seven curators from around the world nominated thirty-two artists to create innovative designs using Ditzel's fabric. The results – in what must have been the only time a textile has received its own exhibition – included shoes, benches, toys, tents, and tables.

Abstract art drove the hand-painted tapestries and clothing of Tusta Wefring (1925–2014), who was born in Oslo but trained at the Kunsthåndværkerskole and resided in Denmark. Many of her angular designs in the 1950s recall the strong graphics of Saul Bass. Nostalgia for these 1950s designs, and the mid-century culture and utopian dreams they seem to represent, emerged in a comment by Mana Thorne, the head of Munkeruphus in Drønningmølle, where an exhibition of Wefring's painted fabrics, along with silver and sculpture by her husband Søren Georg Jensen, was shown in 2014: 'It was a period with a blossoming cultural life. Great thoughts were thought . . . Arne Jacobsen built exciting new architecture, and PH gave the Danes faith in a brighter and more open relation to society.'[32] This comment, applied to a textile exhibition, indicates how the work of the Danish textile artists was historicized, aesthetically and socially, into the cultural framework of mid-twentieth-century design.

Perhaps it was easier for the textile artists to fulfil Albers' modernist requirements, spelled out in 'Design: Anonymous and Timeless,' not to stand in the way of their materials and to recognize that construction is affected by material choices. Weavers remain relatively anonymous by the very nature of what they do; even more so than wood or stainless steel, their materials and practical considerations often dictate usage, and popular culture is much less inclined to learn or even recognize the names and work of weavers and textile printers. Albers' admonishments to textile designers to take a less subjective approach and to cooperate with materials seem apparent in both the minimalism of a designer like Vibeke Klint and the geometric reductions of Lis Ahlmann. Still, the Danish textile designers' work came to define, as much as any piece of silver, glass, or ceramic, what was considered both Danish and Scandinavian Modern. Although their names do not come up as frequently as those of the Danish furniture designers, the textile artists are mentioned by name, and their work reproduced, in almost every history of Danish Modern design – from Mogens Koch's *Moderne dansk kunsthaandværk* (1948) to Erik Zahle's *Hjemmets Brugskunst* (1961) to Thomas Dickson's *Dansk Design* (2006).

Notes

1. Anni Albers, 'Designing as Visual Organization,' in *On Weaving* (Middletown, CT: Wesleyan University Press, 1965), 75.
2. Ibid., 73.
3. Idid., 71.
4. T'ai Smith, *Bauhaus Weaving Theory: From Feminine Craft to Mode of Design* (Minneapolis, MN: University of Minnesota Press, 2014), loc. 360.
5. Ibid., loc. 1122.
6. Albers, 'Design: Anonymous and Timeless,' in *On Weaving*, 7.
7. See Bent Salicath, 'The Development of Danish Textiles for the Home,' in *Modern Danish Textiles*, ed. Salicath and Arne Karlsen (Copenhagen: Danish Society of Arts and Crafts and Industrial Design, 1959), 5–10.
8. Storey also commented on the relationship between furniture and textiles: 'How naturally rough-textured, hand-woven blue fabrics combine with Danish cabinet work is evident in a sofa that achieves a hospitable air from its rounded lines.' The American businessman Louis Bonnard organized the exhibition with participation from Den Permanente. See 'Home Decoration: Danish Crafts Rank High as Art,' *The New York Times* (8 October 1939), 63.
9. Harry Booth, 'A Travel Report on Design in Scandinavia,' *Journal of the Royal Society of Arts*, (96)4767 (1948), 311–16.
10. Like Leth, Day also won a Gold Medal at the Milan Triennale in 1951 for this design.
11. Erik Zahle, ed., *Hjemmets Brugskunst, Kunsthåndværk og Kunstindustri i Norden* (Copenhagen: Hassings Forlag, 1961), 152.
12. Quoted in Charlotte Paludan, *Stoftrykkeren Marie Gudme Leth* (Copenhagen: Rhodos, 1995), 28.
13. Annual Report 2011/2012 (Herning, Denmark: BoConcept Holding A/S, 2012), 12.
14. See Patricia McFate, 'The Art of Simplicity: An Interview with Vibeke Klint,' *Scandinavian Review*, 71(3) (1983), 31.
15. 'Now you have to plow your way through this thick book on binding techniques, just to find out that the simplest way is the most beautiful.' Quoted in Inge Alifrangis, *Vibeke Klint: The Weaver,* trans. Hanne Ejsing Jørgensen (Copenhagen: Rhodos, 1997), 15.
16. Ibid., 24.

17. McFate, 'The Art of Simplicity,' 40.

18. Picture of part of rug reproduced in Charlotte and Peter Fiell, *Scandinavian Design* (Cologne: Taschen, 2002), 356.

19. Diane Waldman, *Kenneth Noland: A Retrospective* (New York: Solomon R. Guggenheim Museum, 1977), 28.

20. See Alfrangis, *Vibeke Klint: The Weaver*, 23.

21. In cooperation with Kvist Møbler, Coop re-introduced a number of FDB's models in 2013 (FDB closed its doors in 1980). Among the renovated designs is Mogensen's J52, a variant on the English Windsor chair, which was also sold in the United States.

22. Quoted in Thomas Mogensen, *Et fuldt møbleret liv. En bog om Børge Mogensen* (Copenhagen: Gyldendal, 2004), 70.

23. Albers, 'Constructing Textiles,' *On Weaving*, 13.

24. Segerstad, *Scandinavian Design,* trans. Nancy and Edward Maze (Stockholm: Nordisk Rotogravyr, 1961), 71.

25. See Mogens Koch, ed., *Børge Mogensen møbler = Lis Ahlmann textiler.* Catalogue (Copenhagen: Det danske Kunstindustrimuseum, 1974), 3.

26. Arne Karlsen, 'Tre Pionerer. Dansk tekstilkunst i midten af det 20. århundrede,' in *I tråd med tiden. Stoftrykker- og Væverlaugets 50 års jubilæumsudstilling* (Copenhagen: SKANDIA-Grafik, 1996), 15.

27. For the original mahogany version shown at the Cabinetmakers Guild Exhibition, Ahlmann used a dark checked fabric with light stripes.

28. Karlsen and Anker Tiedemann, 'Danmark,' *Hjemmets Brugskunst*, 20.

29. See Karlsen, 'Lis Ahlmann,' in *Modern Danish Textiles*, 12.

30. Jørgen Hartmann-Petersen, 'Om at begrænse sig. Rullebords-samtale mellem tre af pionererne i dansk kunst håndværk,' *Politiken* (29 March 1964), 29.

31. Ibid.

32. Quoted in Andreas Hansen, 'Scener fra et ægteskab,' *Kunstavisen* (2014) [http://www.kunstavisen.dk/viewnews.jsp?id=d305c0e8274a6a440127f65c2a430292; accessed 16 February 2015].

6 Hegelian Reading: Designing Community in the SAS Royal Hotel

Aage Strüwing's black and white photograph captures an attractive blonde woman – her hair pulled up à la Inger Stevens in *The Farmer's Daughter* – standing in a tailored suit, holding a drink in an elegantly curved glass, and smoking by a bar (Fig. 6.1). The tilt of her head reflects the angle of an orchid suspended between glass walls to the left. The L-shape of the bar, with panels of backlit bronze on its surface, repeats in the muted glow of two banks of rectangular smoked Plexiglas lights hanging above it. A handsome blonde bartender focuses on mixing a drink, while two men in suits are drinking and sharing a conversation at the end of the bar. Blocks of rosewood panelling serve as a backdrop, their verticality echoing both the Plexiglas boxes that comprise the lights and the bronze panels on the front of the bar. The year

Fig. 6.1 The Orchid Bar in the SAS Hotel: staged mid-twentieth-century Nordic noir. Photo: The Aage Strüwing Collection

is 1960, and the entire scene, obviously staged, exudes an understated mid-twentieth-century sophistication: Nordic noir via *Mad Men*. The scene is the Orchid Bar in what was once the SAS Royal Hotel in Copenhagen. The entire hotel, including a two-storey passenger hall that served as the terminal for SAS Airlines, was designed by the architect Arne Jacobsen (1902–1971) between 1956 and 1960. Jacobsen is the most recognized name in modern Danish design from the last century, due in great part to the continuing popularity and appearance of his chair designs, including the machine-manufactured Ant and Seven Chairs (some of the most manufactured in the history of chair design) and, especially, the Egg and Swan Chairs, designed specifically for the hotel.

When the SAS Royal Hotel opened its doors in 1960, visitors were able to step into one of the last modernist attempts at a *Gesamtkunstwerk:* a total work of art in which every aspect of the structure, from its sheath-like exterior to the organic furniture to the minimalist door handles in the rooms, is supposed to work together to form a whole and to express a unified vision. In *Art and Industry: The Principles of Industrial Design* (1934), the British theorist Herbert Read addressed the issue of the constructive planning of modes of living: '. . .an artist must plan the interiors of such buildings – the shapes of the rooms and their lighting and color . . . the furniture of those rooms, down to the smallest detail, the knives and forks, the cups and saucers, and the door handles.'[1] His words reflect the modernists' attraction to creating a *Gesamtkunstwerk*, an effort that would stretch their normative aesthetic sensibility across every aspect of designed space and an approach that Jacobsen embraced wholeheartedly. The composer Richard Wagner first used the word in an 1849 essay bemoaning the fragmentation of the arts; he is often cited as the progenitor of this artistic approach, an encompassing vision in which he synthesized music, literature, and art (Thomas Mann found Wagner's efforts to be dilettantism raised to the level of genius).

In modernist design, late-nineteenth-century and early-twentieth-century architects built on the notion of uniting all physical elements in approach and style. In Germany, the idea of the *Gesamtkunstwerk* is often associated with the work of Peter Behrens (as in the designer's house at Darmstadt) and in Austria with Josef Hoffmann (for example, in his Palais Stoclet). The progressive artists of the Vienna Secession, founded in 1897 and led by Gustav Klimt, took a holistic approach to their anti-academic designs, also applying a unified visual style to their journal, *Ver Sacrum* (1898). Even the Secessionists' building (1898, by Josef Maria Olbrich) presented a unified design front to the Neoclassical architecture prominent in Vienna at that time. Meanwhile, the French Symbolists saw something more spiritual, even mystical, in the total work of art. In a speech to Bauhaus students in 1919, Gropius predicted that 'out of individual groups a universally great enduring, spiritual-religious idea takes shape, which finally must find its crystalline expression in a great *Gesamtkunstwerk*.'[2] The notion of a total artwork and interplay among various genres of the arts also occupied the German Expressionists, such as Otto Dix, Ernst Ludwig Kirchner, and filmmaker Robert Wiene. In Nordic design, the architect most associated with the

Gesamtkunstwerk is Alvar Aalto, whose individually enduring designs such as the Paimio Armchair (1931) and the Savoy Vase (designed with his wife Aino Marsio in 1937) were actually part of larger projects, the Paimio Sanitarium and the Savoy Restaurant, respectively.[3]

In Europe and North America, markedly diverse examples of *Gesamtkunstwerk* emerged, from Victor Horta's elaborate Art Nouveau masterpiece the Hotel Tassel in Brussels (1893–94) to Frank Lloyd Wright's desert-driven designs for Taliesin West in Scottsdale, Arizona (1937). The overwhelming curvilinear tendrils of Horta's designs throughout the Hotel Tassel – in columns, door handles, panels, and windows – bring botanicals into the artifice of architectural design in an all-determining style. In these Art Nouveau efforts, one searches in vain for an ideological force behind the often purely decorative elements. Wright's angular filigree and rough-hewn locally culled rocks throughout Taliesin West draw the desert landscape, its flora and fauna, into all aspects of the painstakingly designed complex. On this front, one begins to discern a split in effect among the varying holistic visions of the *Gesamtkunstwerk*. Wright's Taliesin West hunkers down into its hilly desert surroundings, its buildings and interconnected Southwestern design elements struggling to become a natural part of their rugged environment. George Nelson said of Taliesin West that it 'has its structure on the outside . . . a jagged outline as sharp and as savage as the cactus that surrounds it.'[4] Just as Heidegger once noted the ancient Greek temples' ability to draw viewers back to the mountains in the surrounding landscape, Wright's domestic and educational structures at Taliesin West interact with the natural surroundings in a reflective manner that draws viewers into a consideration of living in this specific desert environment. Rather than intruding upon it, Wright's architectural artifice reinforces the natural sense of place.

The architectural *Gesamtkunstwerk* reflects a striving for totality, for an absolute vision that not only drives all elements of the designed environment but also imparts a specific way of looking not only at objects but also at living. From a more philosophical perspective, one might say even a Hegelian one, a *Gesamtkunstwerk* should erase any sense of estrangement between perceivers and the world around them. The architect Folke Nyberg has defined the concept of *Gesamtkunst* as 'the expression of community life based on common myths and materialized through artisanal activity.'[5] Nyberg cites *Baukunst* – the art of construction – as the platform on which certain modernist artists struggled 'to meet Hegel's challenge for art in architectural terms by seeking to develop a dialectical process of building and dwelling.'[6] Nyberg delineates the Marxist, materialist reading of Hegel (the Left-Hegelian point of view), which aligns architecture with economic determinism, from the Right-Hegelian reading, which emphasizes the spiritual function of art, a growth towards the liberation of consciousness. In the latter, the link between people and place serves as an advancement towards spirit. In a speech given in 1958, 'Function and *Gestalt*,' the Swiss designer and theorist Max Bill observed: 'The environment . . . has a decisive impact on people's well-being, from which we can conclude that art occupies a key position within our mental and spiritual world, in the sense formulated by Hegel in his aesthetics, namely that art is the form of human expression that speaks highest of the interests of the spirit.'[7] The early modernist movement towards a *Gesamtkunstwerk* was also the movement away from *Stilarchitektur*, because in its eclectic nature the latter, particularly in its neoclassical efforts, no longer represented the spirit of the times. Thus, when Nyberg turns his attention to *Gesamtkunst*, he defines it as 'the artistic expression of everyday life and of values held in common.'[8]

The *Gesamtkunstwerk*, from this viewpoint, should embody those shared values in an environment planned, visually, to reflect the spirit of a time and especially its people (the *Volksgeist*). Nyberg also frames this notion as a conflict in Germany between Muthesius, who wanted to return to the *Baukunst* of the medieval craft tradition, and Gropius, who viewed *Gesamtkunst* as a 'total architecture' but one driven by the imperatives of industry and struggling towards place-less universals. '*Baukunst* accepts the importance of technology,' writes Nyberg, 'but considers building an ontological activity that directs construction to serve dwelling by being place-specific.'[9] A sense of community emerges as a necessity from this approach towards building and dwelling, whereas Bauhaus efforts lean on industry for the construction of art. More than this, in the Hegelian sense, an edifying quality should emerge from every aspect of the successful *Gesamtkunstwerk*. In 'Hegel and Architecture,' John Whiteman defines Hegel's view as 'the articulation of architecture as a device of and for human sensibility – a device that has a higher purpose than itself.'[10]

The conflict between machine-driven, universalist approaches to architecture (and design) and more place-specific and communal efforts echoes many of the Danish modernists' tension between International Modernism and some form of tradition, between Bauhaus-inspired industrialism and craft-driven aesthetics (*Baukunst*). Jacobsen's hotel represented another step in the development of the *Gesamtkunstwerk,* but its coordinated designs also proffered something more than simply a physical environment. The sculptural quality of Jacobsen's designs inside the hotel is not an extension of the universalist, geometric efforts of the Bauhaus; instead, Jacobsen's emphasis lies in forms and in the interplay of forms, often organic against the rectilinear. In 1912, Muthesius had argued that 'far higher than the material is the spiritual, far higher than function, material, and technique, stands Form.'[11] Jacobsen pulls viewers in with his organic yet sculptural and often abstract designs, and in them one senses a yearning for the best possible forms for human interaction. Curvilinear shapes and colour abet this effect to diminish any sense of estrangement between viewer/experiencer and environment. Jacobsen attempted to inscribe the spirit of the times into every aspect of the hotel, a synthesis between the boxy International Style (an outgrowth of the Bauhaus) that drives the building's architectural shape and the more organic designs that in both their forms and elegance impart a hopeful image of a better and more unified way of living. Even in his approach to materials, Jacobsen reveals a meld of using new industrial materials (like Styropor foam to mould certain chairs and sofas) and the handcrafted sculpting of their forms (emphasized by the hand-stitching tracing their outline). At every turn, a synthesis surfaces in this overall approach.

A number of syntheses drove much of Jacobsen's oeuvre, especially as time progressed. Architecturally, he was influenced by Asplund and by the Bauhaus, as evidenced in early projects such as his House of the Future (*Fremtidens Hus*, 1929, designed with Flemming Lassen) and the 'White Modernism' of his Bellevue complex (1930), but he was also proficient at constructing low, two-storey row homes in brick, like the diagonally stacked Søholm I (1946–50), where he had his own residence. He was not social in the programmatic sense, like Henningsen and the Danish avant-garde in the 1920s and 1930s, yet the botanist in him was painfully aware of environmental effect and the use of nature in and around his buildings (Henningsen had argued for garden homes in urban planning). Jacobsen could blend his training from the Architect School of the Royal Danish Academy with a strong regional sensibility that reflects the Danish striving (which appeared even in some of Henningsen's rhetoric) to find a place-specific reading of modernist currents. In 'A Whole Other World: Jacobsen and the Idea of the *Gesamtkunstwerk*' (2002), Thau and Vindum note the double influence of both the Bauhaus and the Wiener Werkstätte on Jacobsen. The latter allusion is particularly telling: Loos had been quite negative about the Ruskin- and Morris-influenced efforts of the Werkstätte but, more importantly, Hoffman and Moser, the founders of the Werkstätte, had derided the 'boundless evil' of 'mass-produced goods' in their 1905 manifesto. Jacobsen produced a synthesis of the Loos-driven distaste for ornament that had helped to give birth to the machine aesthetics of the Bauhaus *and* the distaste for shoddy industrial goods and the respect for exquisite craftsmanship in the Werkstätte. Presaging some of Henningsen's contentions in 'Tradition and Modernism,' Hoffman and Moser insisted: 'As long as our towns, houses, rooms, cupboards, utensils, clothes, jewelry, language and feelings fail to express the spirit of the times in a clear, simple, and artistic manner, we shall remain infinitely far behind our ancestors and no pretense will conceal our lack.'[12]

In all of his syntheses, Jacobsen endeavoured to produce designs that reflected the spirit of their times by combining technological advancements – in creating the thinnest possible surfaces, in bending plywood, in using moulds made of new materials – with an increasingly minimalist vision of sculpted forms.[13] In Jacobsen's specific approach, his synthesis becomes paradoxical: the more his designs reflect their time's 'spirit,' particularly in the mid-twentieth century, the more they transcend their specific time. The *Gesamtkunstwerk* that was the SAS Royal Hotel in its original form offered the very avatar of this paradox: many of its place and time specific designs remain in production.

When Henningsen suggested in 1928 that the Danes should let go of their affection for brick, he could have not have foreseen that in 1956 that predilection would still hold sway. Discovering that year that Arne Jacobsen would be the architect behind the new SAS Hotel and terminal, Poul Erik Skriver, writing in *Arkitekten*, sighed with relief: 'Just think if it had been an architect with no background in red brick.'[14] However, red brick was the farthest thing from Jacobsen's mind for the SAS project. Inspired by the Lever House (1950–52) in New York, Jacobsen designed Copenhagen's first high-rise consisting of two rectangular boxes, a horizontal one lying on its side and following the line of the streets on two of its sides, and a vertical box towering over the horizontal one (Fig. 6.2). The two forms have sometimes been derided as looking like two cigarette boxes placed perpendicular to each other. The ground floor of the hotel's darker clad horizontal section is also recessed, further diminishing the immediate sense of intrusion and resulting in a cantilevered second storey. In an article that appeared on 28 February 1971, shortly before his death, Jacobsen told *Politiken*: 'When the SAS building was inaugurated, a paper ran a competition to select the ugliest building in the city – I won first prize.'[15] Like the Lever House – designed by Gordon Bunshaft for Skidmore, Owings & Merrill – the SAS Hotel also features a recessed third floor, enhancing not only the vertical nature of the high rise but imparting a floating effect, particularly when seen from a distance. Built in the International Style established in North America by Henry-Russell Hitchcock and Phillip Johnson – heavily influenced by the geometric abstraction of Le Corbusier, Gropius, Mies, and the De Stijl architect, J.J.P. Oud – the Lever House was New York's second curtain-wall high rise (after the UN Secretariat Building).

Another synthesis emerges in the way Jacobsen enhanced the reflective quality of the Lever House's curtain wall on the SAS Hotel: he sheathed the hotel's tower in a grey-green glass and thin aluminium mullions reflecting Copenhagen's shifting sky and the immediate environment around the hotel. In this sense, the rectilinear hotel is always mirroring its surroundings and always a part of its cityscape, constantly defying those who feared its visual intrusion among Copenhagen's historical towers and spires.[16] Like Wright's Taliesin West, but using the images of its sky and surroundings as the locally 'culled' element, the boxy 'un-Danish' SAS Hotel draws viewers back to the city that already existed. This effect also reveals another Hegelian approach: the building mirrors the community surrounding it, helping to erase any sense of estrangement. In this reflective coming to awareness in material culture, culture has an autonomy similar to spirit but not as abstract. Jacobsen took a Bauhaus-inspired format – the International Style – and through *Baukunst* (the building's art of construction, particularly its reflective sheath) brought community and place back into a modernist structure (one cannot deny the Miesian aesthetic in either the Lever House or the SAS Hotel). Tradition, which would be all but abandoned in a Left-Hegelian approach, has been brought back into the picture in what can best be described as a Right-Hegelian reading of modernist architecture (sans conservatism). In this endeavour, Jacobsen parallels Klint and Henningsen in their rejection of any superimposed modernist aesthetic for its own sake. The hotel offers yet another example of a Danish designer mitigating the impersonal effect of modernist design without yielding to historical or national forms.

Perhaps this was also Jacobsen's way of appeasing architectural critics and the various members of the press who had feared the Americanization of the Danish capital and the appearance of 'New York in Copenhagen.' This fear may well stem from Henningsen's admonishment of Le Corbusier for his admiration of the skyscraper, which PH viewed as an unhealthy solution to urban living. In his article

Fig. 6.2 In his use of a reflective glass-and-aluminium sheath on the hotel's exterior, Jacobsen was influenced by the design of the Lever House in New York. Photo: The Aage Strüwing Collection

'Fremtidsperspektiver' ('Perspectives on the Future'), which appeared in *Politiken* on 22 July 1930, he took issue with Le Corbusier's affection for the American skyscraper. Henningsen, who favoured lower row houses because he felt they were more conducive environments for the working class, viewed the skyscraper as an unhealthy solution to condensed development in city centres: 'Naturally, the result has been that hygienic conditions with respect to daylight and traffic have deteriorated extraordinarily.'[17] Nor was Henningsen particularly fond of Jacobsen's hotel design: while he praised the architecture for exhibiting 'the harmony, beauty and fatal balance the modern city wants to display,' he viewed all of it 'in the service of conformity . . . industrialism in bloom, a pillar in glass and steel and reinforced concrete, hovering over those who govern us all, including our politicians.'[18]

Still, one senses a cultural resistance to luxury for its own sake in the response of the Danish press at the time of the SAS Hotel's premiere. Although Skriver was relieved that the hotel was not too 'ascetic,' as in some of Jacobsen's other minimal interiors, he was also glad to find 'no abundant luxury, no intimidating symbols of exclusive high-life.'[19] Writing in *Politiken*, Svend Erik Møller also lauded Jacobsen for avoiding 'luxury's innumerable pitfalls.'[20] In addition to the minimalist nature of many of his designs, Jacobsen managed to impart this avoidance of parvenu excess mostly through his use of space. Pictures reveal, for example, that the lobby was surprisingly uncluttered by today's standards. Groupings of Egg Chairs (and a pair of rare Egg sofas), their curves echoing the spiral staircase, are spaced out on rectangular rugs, leaving large sections of the light-grey marble floor exposed. There isn't a chandelier in sight; instead, rows of smaller recessed spots in the dark green ceiling imparted a soft glow to the lobby's space. Even in the restaurant on the second floor, chandeliers consisting of rings of smoked glass bells were recessed into circular skylights, adding to the soft diffusion of light. For comparison, one might consider Morris Lapidus's Fontainebleau Hotel lobby in Miami (1954). 'I wanted people to walk in and drop dead,' Lapidus once deadpanned about the hotel's lobby, an effusive 27-colour mix of Italian Renaissance and French Provincial design featuring illuminated ribbed columns, faux-attic statues and busts, and three-million-dollar chandeliers.[21] An elaborate staircase to 'nowhere' (actually a cloak room, allowing guests to then descend the stairs in grand entrance) wrapped around a photomural of a Piraniesi street scene. If one were to bring a purely stylistic barometer to the two lobbies, Jacobsen's design depicts an exercise in restraint, emphasizing a resistance towards visual overstatement. Also, other than an affinity for excess, no philosophical concept drove the creation of the Fontainebleau's lobby.

Photographs of Jacobsen's original understated lobby disclose a quietude enhanced by the open spatial sense.[22] Over the reception area, a chain of backlit planes hangs on barely visible strings, creating the illusion of a line of suspended light. The lobby's spiral staircase, a 'floating' design that Jacobsen had employed before in such projects as the A. Jespersen & Søn office building (1952–55), adds a sense of upward movement. In the Jespersen project, Jacobsen designed a large glass tube encasing a spiral staircase for the fire escape passing through the open ground floor and connecting the second storey with the basement. The space-age looking structure is a minimalist's dream of 'floating steps' emancipated from bearing structures or bannisters, the wedges of steps emanating from a central column. In 'The Dynamics of Shape' (1966), Rudolf Arnheim, using the Jespersen building's stairs as an illustration, describes the spiral staircase as 'a forerunner of the visual reversal . . . The pressure from above has been reduced to a minor force.'[23] For the SAS Hotel, Jacobsen maintained the floating sense by suspending the steps with thin metal supports hanging down through the circular opening in the lobby's ceiling but added a red-painted railing and a grey glass panel curving with the stairs, imparting a more refined visual element necessary in a hotel lobby than a fire escape. Still, the curve swings heavenward; no support rises from the floor to meet the stairs – they are first and foremost suspended, their vertical supports echoing the lobby's columns. Once inside the lobby, the visitor has truly stepped into Jacobsen's designed world; in this sense, the *Gesamtkunstwerk* removes those who experience it from the inconsistencies of everyday living by constructing a visually harmonious environment. To return to Nyberg's Hegelian reading, in its consistency the *Gesamtkunstwerk* strives to erase any sense of estrangement. Subtle visual clues aid in that endeavour: the Egg and Swan Chairs' sinuous curves, for example, recall that of the spiral staircase.

That rising sense was surely abetted by the verticality of the two-storey winter garden, consisting of two glass walls housing hanging orchids, translucent curtains, and white painted columns rising between the two walls (all separating that part of the lobby from the snack bar). Curiously, the motif of the staggered hanging orchids was repeated in the window and lobby displays of manufactured *objets* in the Art Royal boutique, on the corner of Hammerichsgade and Vesterbrogade, which faced both the streets and the inside of the lobby. High-end wares from Georg Jensen silversmiths and the Royal Copenhagen porcelain factory were displayed on hanging, staggered glass shelves; translucent curtains were also used in the shop window displays. In the repetition of these motifs, Jacobsen again attempted to unite nature and industry aesthetically. In the winter garden, the simplistic organic cupping shape of the Pot Chair (1959), rendered in a chartreuse fabric, emphasizes the botanical effect of the hanging orchids. Rosewood tabletops bring yet another natural element into the space, as do rectangles of thick brown rya rugs.

The winter garden's carefully coordinated construction, along with its meld of glass, steel, contemporary forms, and natural textures, recalls the German *Raumkunst* (in Danish, *rumkunst*), which Nyberg employs as another aspect of a Right-Hegelian reading of Modernism, moving architectural expression away from a dependency on style.[24] With its hanging orchids and green and brown colour scheme, the winter garden proffers an organic expression giving form to the spirit of place. Its nature-driven aspects offer a contrast to the cold universal notions of space dependent on a more Cartesian sense of rationality; the winter garden's entire spatial design, including soft translucent curtains, seems worlds removed from the works of Le Corbusier or Mies.[25] The botanical element also reinforces the Danish resistance to banishing nature in a geometric world of glass and chrome. Yet, even more than this, its effect must have surely been ethereal and restful, an effect abetted by designs emphasizing verticality, translucence, and floating. The orchid wall, for example, functioned as a three-dimensional incarnation of Jacobsen's intricate botanical textile and wallpaper patterns, with names such as 'Heather' and 'Forest Floor,' many of them designed while he was in exile in Sweden during the Second World War. Destroyed in 1991, the winter garden presented myriad elements of Jacobsen's specific vision of modern design.

The dominance of certain colours throughout the hotel's original interior design was another way for Jacobsen to draw community into the totality of his project. Chromatically, he chose colours throughout the hotel's spaces that would reinforce the green-grey-blue effects of the tower's sheath. In *Room 606* (2008), Michael Sheridan notes that 'by the early 1950s, Jacobsen had evolved his own vocabulary of color, which was dominated by subtle shades of gray, green, and blue . . .'[26] He designed a line of upholstery fabric, Royal, specifically for the hotel in a subdued palette of blues and greens. While there has been a tendency to define the use of these colours as botanical, they are also aqueous in nature. In the lobby, the light grey marble floor served as a contrast to the ceiling, which was painted a deep green. In 'On Color and Affect,' Ernest G. Schachtel observes that the preference for green – and possibly also for blue – is closely related to the romantic and sentimental view of landscape.[27] Goethe referred to green as the most restful of colours, and that colour also dominates in the original design of the guest rooms. Soft green walls, rendered in a textured fabric and offset by rich wenge-wood panelling, serve as a muted backdrop for blue curtains and bed linens. Chromatically, there are no complements in fabrics, no bright orange or red furnishings to contrast with the soft greens and blues. Sheridan indicates that the Egg Chairs in the hotel rooms were originally covered in a wavy blue-green fabric called Turkis (1959), although one of Jacobsen's own photos reveals the Egg and Drop Chairs in what appears to be a much paler fabric. Even the woven wool carpets Jacobsen designed for some of the hotel's spaces reveal abstract patterns in blues and greens (a more neutral grey carpet with dots of pale colour was used in the guest rooms). The close relationship between green and blue on the spectrum served as another way for Jacobsen to achieve a sense of unity – but even more so a sense of peace and refuge. As he did in most elements of his designs, Jacobsen was, chromatically, humanizing Modernism in a palette far removed from the bold primary colours of the De Stijl designers.

On forms: a process of becoming

When discussing modernist designs, critics and scholars have often alluded to a Platonic sensibility among designers – the sense that they are driven by achieving an ultimate or final form, one that already exists within the material. Commenting on the sense of completeness in Jacobsen's forms, Thau and Vindum, for example, claim: 'In his work with the material, Jacobsen was undoubtedly driven by such a Platonic assumption: that the chair's ideal form drove him to find its conclusive realization.'[28] Yet, Jacobsen's endeavours are actually more of a process of becoming rather than a discovery of any pre-existing form, in the sense of a Platonic reading. His forms emerge from his working with materials: they do not already exist platonically, either somehow in the materials or, at even more of a stretch, somewhere a priori, outside of his efforts – ideal forms floating around and waiting to be discovered. Some of these Neo-Platonist concepts in modernist readings stem from the lingering effects of Purism after the First World War and the striving to establish a universal aesthetic. In 1934, when MoMA held its 'Machine Art' exhibition, the catalogue opened with a quote from Plato, a paean to geometric abstraction: 'By beauty of shapes . . . I mean straight lines and circles, and shapes, plane or solid, made for them by lathe, ruler, and square. These are not, like other things, beautiful relatively, but always and absolutely.'

Aalto's edict that 'objects are made to be completed by the human mind' undercuts the conventional notion that all modernists were trying to design perfect or ultimate forms. The forms are never completed until they are perceived or, even more importantly with designed objects, until they are used and humans interact with them. Users may embrace, reject, or alter the concepts often inscribed in designs. Aalto, in his lecture 'Rationalism and Man,' observed:

> Nature, biology, is formally rich and luxuriant. It can with the same structure, the same intermeshing, and the same principles in its cells' inner structure, achieve a billion combinations, each of which represents a high level of form. Man's life belongs to the same family. The things surrounding him are hardly fetishes and allegories with a mystical eternal value.[29]

It seems much more productive to look at Jacobsen's designs, especially some of his more inventive ones for the SAS Hotel, as part of his process, as his Baukunst. In this more Hegelian than Platonic reading, forms emerge not only out of the process of working with materials but also out of the desire to erase any sense of estrangement between form and user in this specific environment. The Gesamtkunswerk of the SAS Hotel was an attempt by Jacobsen to create a modernist synthesis of people, society, nature, and industrial crafts. Miller, commenting on Aalto's specific reading of industrial technique, emphasizes the natural: 'Industrial processes were to be subordinated to humanistic values in Aalto's mind, and such values were defined through the individual's harmonious interaction with the totality of nature . . . a conception of nature as a continuous organic system that included both society and the individual.'[30] Just as Aalto was heavily influenced by his appreciation of landscape painting, Jacobsen's work was often infused with his deft skills with watercolour and his botanical interests. Also, whereas Aalto depended predominantly on wood to impart his natural synthesis, Jacobsen found a way so do so in moulded synthetic forms, plywood, and fabrics. By employing noticeably organic shapes, Jacobsen also helped the minds perceiving those forms to complete them; visual analogies are easier to make with recognizable shapes, whether they are eggs, petals, or animals.

Jacobsen's forms – from furniture to light fixtures to cutlery – aided the harmonious interaction necessary to bring the viewer/user into the *Gesamtkunstwerk* as another part, the essential part, of that totality.

A number of Jacobsen's designs for the furnishings of the SAS Hotel have helped to establish his long-lasting international reputation – and none more so than his chairs, the Egg and the Swan (1958). Both chairs are referred to in Denmark as 'shell chairs' because of their moulded shell forms, each of which possesses an enveloping quality. The sculptor Gord Peteran has observed: 'Furniture is our first sculptural encounter, after the body of the mother and slightly before the interior spatial volumes of architecture.'[31] In his highly organic shapes, Jacobsen designed links between those two forces, the nurturing and the rational. This approach was especially useful in the context of the SAS Hotel: the two chairs' blatantly organic shapes, obviously manufactured design, and hand-stitched upholstery present yet another synthesis of industry and nature. The care given to their overall form also spoke well to the time of their inception; just as picture windows in many homes – especially suburban ones – were becoming increasingly larger, thus revealing more of home furnishings from all sides, so Jacobsen designed two chairs that would impress from every angle and even swivelled to do so.

In his Ant (1952) and Seven (1955) Chairs, Jacobsen had already pushed plywood to its limits by bending it in more than one direction. Chair designs for a hotel room or lobby would require providing more comfort than bent plywood, however curved, could supply. In 1957, the American designer George Nelson was still defining the standard chair as a more traditional structure: 'The chair, for instance, is traditionally a four-legged structure of wood sticks held together with nails, glue, pegs, dowels, screws, or joints in the sticks themselves.' Like the contemporary chair designs of Eero Saarinen and Charles and Ray Eames, the softly rounded, biomorphic Egg and Swan bear no resemblance to this description, due in great part to the specifically sculptural approach Jacobsen applied to creating the chair. Technological advancements in production aided his forms. For example, the increased use of foam in producing moulds – as in the aeroplane industry – enabled him to take his cue from the biomorphic shapes of sculptors such as Jean (Hans) Arp and Barbara Hepworth. He was not alone. In 1948, Charles and Ray Eames based the design of their *La Chaise* chair on Gaston Lachaise's bronze sculpture *Floating Figure* (1927), partly because advancements in plastics enabled them to mould the chair's undulating form in an unprecedented manner.[32] The sculptor Sandor Perjesi, who worked with Jacobsen on the plaster models for both the Egg and the Swan, has described how the two men 'spent the whole weekend adding and removing plaster. Back and forth, like a classical sculptor.'[33] The resultant forms are playful and optimistic, soft and organic – all traits enabled by the technical possibilities in the original moulded form and then rendered in fibreglass shells and foam padding, enhanced by the addition of fabric or leather.

Like the rest of the hotel's designs, the Egg and Swan chairs were at their time forward-looking, another part of the effort to create a total environment that would reflect the spirit of a society in a given place (Fig. 6.3). Placing them on an aluminium pedestal base (although the Swan was once also available with a cross-form wooden frame) added yet another sense of verticality to the hotel's many designs: the chairs not only appear more weightless but the absence of intruding legs draws the eye up to the singular form of each chair. Jacobsen's overall approach often appeared to be an effort at designing the fewest possible divisions to achieve the best possible form. The stainless steel cutlery (originally plated in silver) he designed for the hotel's restaurant epitomizes this goal: the utensils have been stripped of every possible division between handle and blade, tongs, and bowl. Thau and Vindum note a blend of primitivism in the simplified form, combined with a radically 'modern' design for its time. This paradox certainly surfaced when director Stanley Kubrick chose the AJ cutlery for use by astronauts in his film *2001: A Space Odyssey* (1968): the cutlery appears briefly – held by the actor Keir Dullea – while the Jupiter Mission crew eats dinner and watches the news. One cannot miss the irony of a movie made in 1968 using a design from 1959 to convey the appearance of an artefact some thirty years into the future. The AJ cutlery was not an immediate hit; in fact, when the hotel opened, the Danish news sent a reporter to try to eat peas with it in an attempt to prove that it was more design than function. In time, the hotel even replaced the AJ cutlery with more traditional utensils – but it remains in production.

Fig. 6.3 The original interior of one of the hotel rooms includes a trio of Egg chairs, a Shaker-base table, the SAS floor lamp, and a Swan sofa. The original chroma was an array of blues and greens playing against the Wenge-wood panelling. Photo: The Aage Strüwing Collection

The Egg and Swan continue to appear frequently in designer magazines, films, television shows, and advertisements. Over the years, the two designs have appeared in steampunk reproductions, special editions for cancer awareness designed by Karim Rashid and Alexandra von Furstenberg, reupholstering by Jonathan Adler and Missoni, and rendered in cowhide, metal, and patchwork quilt. They are examples of Danish Modern long detached from the environment in which they were created, reinterpreted and rearticulated in ways Jacobsen could never have foreseen or desired. Like a number of Jacobsen's designs for the SAS Hotel, the two chair designs are paradoxical: they reflect a space-age sensibility in their time and, simultaneously, are embraced as an example of nostalgia. In 2014, the simplistic Drop Chair (1959), originally designed for the hotel's guest rooms and snack bar, was finally put into mass production by Fritz Hansen. It was one of the few chairs Jacobsen designed with four legs that intersected the base of the chair (in the stacking Ant and Seven Chairs, Jacobsen had used a chrome frame that curved back in beneath the seat to avoid the appearance of lines bisecting the seat).

Another of the hotel's minimalist designs, the door handles, are also still in production (by Carl F. Pedersen, who first produced them in 1956). As in most of Jacobsen's other designs for the hotel, the levered door handle consists of one organic form, combining both the axle and the grasp. The handle looks as if Jacobsen made a mould of the inside of one's hand when grasping a door handle and then sculpted the resultant shape into a sleek, highly ergonomic form based on palm and thumb prints. In emphasizing the human element, Jacobsen once again erases any sense of estrangement between user and object. Visually, the handle's minimalist shape recalls Romanian sculptor Constantin Brâncusi's *Bird in Flight* (1923), a sinuous bronze sculpture depicting flight in abstract form (so abstract that in 1926, US Customs officials refused to believe the sculpture was art and tried to charge a tariff on Brancusi's work as a kitchen utensil). In *What is Modern Design*, his 1950 pamphlet for the Museum of Modern Art, Edgar Kaufmann, Jr. included a photograph of Brancusi's sculpture with a carving knife and propeller blade to illustrate his contention that design is 'related to engineering and art.'[34] In many ways, Jacobsen's door handle fulfils Kaufmann's normative demands even better than Brancusi's sculpture, because the engineering aspect is much more applicable to a utilitarian piece of hardware. Satisfying other modernist demands, the lever – while an elegant design – is so minimal that it is void of any ornament in even the slightest degree. Thau and Vindum (2001) point out that Gio Ponti designed a metal door handle in the same year but that it is less organic. This assessment stems from the fact that Ponti's handle, designed for the Pirelli Tower, is straight, possessing none of the sculptural about it. The 'calculated efficiency' that Kaufmann lauds seems much more evident in Jacobsen's lever.

In retrospect, it would be easy to dismiss the entire project as an exercise in mid-twentieth-century 'style.' As Fred Rush, commenting on Eero Saarinen's TWA Terminal (1956–62) in New York, observes in *On Architecture* (2009): 'No one would want to reduce Saarinen's great terminal building . . . to a matter of style (architects are allergic to considering their work under fashion categories), but to deny that sleekness is part of the concept of the building as well as what the city sought to project by building the terminal is to beggar history.'[35] The sophistication that oozes from the interior photographs taken during the SAS Hotel's first few years, especially some striking black-and-white photos by Aage Strüwing, are rife with messages after more than a half-century has passed. The fetishizing of many mid-twentieth–century designs, coupled with a nostalgia for the Populuxe[36] era in the United States and the international success of the television series *Mad Men* (2007–15), reinforces the sense of a lost, upper-middle-class Shangri-La of style and sophistication. In his final interview, Jacobsen addressed the issue of taste as a determining factor in evaluating design:

> Now, I can't stand the term *good taste* – as if we were talking about ladies' hats. I would rather say: artistic approach, receptiveness, alertness. In one way, the sense of quality has got better; the status symbol in little things is gone. People will dare to have stainless steel, even though the neighbors have silver. I simply think that prefabrication and industrial design make people more neighborly. I think that's a good thing.[37]

Yet, much more than this, the SAS Hotel represented the apex of a modernist vision of communal living in which designed spaces reflected values held in common and in which a building and the objects designed for it worked together to make people feel that they were part of that design at every turn. In *Objects of Desire*, Adrian Forty defines design as much more than an 'inoffensive artistic activity' and suggests that it can 'cast ideas about who we are and how we should behave into permanent and tangible form.'[38] Many of the hotel's shapes – and especially the colours – reinforced the sense that this society in this place was moving forward; however they were received, the designs for the hotel were Jacobsen's attempt to give form to the future he perceived while insisting that nature and natural shapes remain a part of that manufactured vision.

In the hotel, all that remains of Jacobsen's original interior designs is room 606, which retains the blue-green colour scheme he laid out, along with wenge-wood panelling and cantilevered drawers and dressing tables, his minimalist circular lamp designs, and the Egg, Drop, and the more architectonic series 3300 chairs covered in a blue-green fabric. The room reminds us that for a brief moment in time, an entire building and all of its contents depicted one person's ideal of form, a spirited attempt at a totally harmonious Danish Modern design celebrating, at every turn, the art of construction.

Notes

1. Herbert Read. *Art and Industry: The Principles of Industrial Design* (New York: Horizon Press, 1961), 45.
2. Quoted in *German Expressionism: Documents from the End of the Wilhelmine Empire to the Rise of National Socialism*, ed. Rose-Carol Washton Long (Berkeley, CA: University of California Press, 1993), 251.

3. Writing about Aalto's broad design efforts, William C. Miller states: 'These elements were more than mere accents with a spatial setting or decorative ensemble. The design and crafting of a chair, a light fixture, or a glass bowl was as much an architectural proposition as the making of a building.' Miller, 'Furniture, Painting, and Applied Designs: Alvar Aalto's Search for Architectural Form,' *Journal of Decorative and Propaganda Arts*, 6 (Autumn 1987), 6.

4. George Nelson, 'Wright's Houses,' in *Problems of Design* (New York: Whitney Publications, 1965), 113.

5. Folke Nyberg, 'From *Baukunst* to Bauhaus,' *Journal of Architectural Education* 45(3) (1992): 131.

6. Ibid., 130.

7. Max Bill, 'Function and *Gestalt*,' in *Form, Function, Beauty = Gestalt* (London: AA Publications, 2011), 105.

8. Nyberg, 'From *Baukunst* to Bauhaus,' 131.

9. Ibid.

10. John Whiteman, 'On Hegel's Definition of Architecture,' *Assemblage*, 2 (February 1987), 16.

11. Quoted in Reyner Banham, *Theory and Design in the First Machine Age* (London: MIT Press, 1980): 73.

12. Hoffman and Moser, 'The Work Program of the Wiener Werkstätte,' in *The Industrial Reader*, ed. Carma Gorman (New York: Allworth, 2003), 63.

13. Reviewing the hotel after its opening, Poul Erik Skriver wrote that 'the choices in materials are, despite everything, controlled and harmonious, held together by one man's ideal of form': 'Royal Hotel, København,' *Arkitektur*, 4(6) (1960), 210.

14. 'Our Time's City Builders,' *Arkitekten*, 49/50 (1956), 377. Quoted in Thau and Vindum, *Arne Jacobsen* (Copenhagen: Arkitektens Forlag, 1998).

15. Quoted in Poul Erik Tøjner and Kjeld Vindum, *Arne Jacobsen – Arkitekt & Designer* (Copenhagen: Dansk Design Center, 1999), 128.

16. Jacobsen would take this effect even further in his next project, the HEW (Hamburgische Elektrizitäts-Werke) Building (1962–69) in Hamburg, Germany, with its reflective curtain walls descending all the way to the ground.

17. Henningsen, 'Fremtidsperspektiver,' in Neel Pørn, *PHs Arkitekturkritik* (Copenhagen: Arkitektens Forlag, 1994), 111.

18. Quoted in Hans Hertel, *PH-En biografi* (Copenhagen: Gyldendal, 2012), 21–22.

19. Skriver, 'Royal Hotel, København,' 210.

20. Quoted in Thau and Vindum, *Arne Jacobsen*, 442.

21. See http://www.nytimes.com/1988/05/12/garden/drop-dead-lapidus-look-going-for-the-gorgeous-design.html.

22. Thau and Vindum note that the lobby 'was characterized by a particularly inviting and embracing, but in no way intrusive, intimacy . . . a refuge, a retreat': *Arne Jacobsen*, 432.

23. Arnheim, 'The Dynamics of Shape,' *Design Quarterly*, 64 (1966), 10.

24. Nyberg explains: '*Raumkunst* maintains that all architectural and spatial qualities are place-specific and can be understood through a physiology of space': 'From *Baukunst* to Bauhaus,' 131.

25. Thau and Vindum, *Arne Jacobsen*, 436 refer to the entire 'manifestation' of the winter garden as an expression of modern spatial art.

26. Michael Sheridan, *Room 606. The SAS House and the Work of Arne Jacobsen* (London: Phaidon, 2003), 71.

27. Ernest G. Schachtel, 'On Color and Affect,' *Psychiatry*, 6 (1943), 402.

28. Carsten Thau and Kjeld Vindum, *Arne Jacobsen*, in *Store Danske Designere*, ed. Tøjner and Frovin (Copenhagen: Lindhardt og Ringhof, 2008), 260.

29. Quoted in *Alvar Aalto Furniture*, ed. Juhani Pallasmaa (Cambridge, MA: MIT Press, 1985), 117.

30. Miller, 'Furniture, Painting, and Applied Design,' 18.

31. Quoted in Ken Johnson, 'Close Encounters with Tableness and Chairness,' *New York Times* (11 June 2009).

32. Although produced in 1948 and included in MoMA's permanent collection, the Eames *La Chaise* was not produced commercially until 1990.

33. Quoted in Tøjner and Vindum, 80.

34. Kaufmann, Jr. *What Is Modern Design?* Introductory Series to the Modern Arts – 3 (New York: MoMA, 1950), 6.

35. Rush, *On Architecture* (New York: Routledge 2009), 64–65.

36. 'Populuxe,' an amalgam of populism, popularity, and luxury, was coined by Thomas Hine in his 1986 book of the same name. He defined it as 'an expression of outright vulgar joy in being able to live so well.'

37. Quoted in Tøjner & Vindum, *Arne Jacobsen – Arkitekt & Designer*, 131.

38. Adrian Forty, *Objects of Desire: Design & Society from Wedgwood to IBM* (New York: Pantheon, 1986), 6.

7 The Happening: Making Modern Contemporary (Again)

'I cannot stand entering a room and seeing the sofa, the coffee table and two easy chairs,' Verner Panton (1926–1998) once bemoaned, 'and knowing that we will be trapped there for the rest of the evening.'[1] Panton used his designs to address the restrictive nature of the bourgeois living room; just as the early Danish modernist designers in the 1920s had referred pejoratively to upholstered period furniture as 'butcher's sets,' in the 1960s Panton used form and colour to explode the accepted bourgeois suburban furniture arrangement. His decorative eye went far beyond a room's individual furnishings and encompassed every surface; a designer who valued colour over form, he embraced the 1960s aesthetic and put the final nail in the coffin of austere functional furniture. On a number of fronts, his efforts brought to a close much mid-century Danish Modern design as it had evolved from the functionalism of the 1920s. Panton's use of psychedelic and Pop-, and Op-art elements represents a definitive break from privileging any functional concerns over aesthetics, and his blatant – even joyful – use of bold colours and synthetic materials bears no resemblance to the early modernist cabinetmaker-driven focus on natural wood. Acknowledging the end of normative notions about healthy living through design, Panton used design, paradoxically, at this very point of departure; in time, his designs transferred many normative choices to the user. His bold designs reflect an ultimate break with any sense of design-continuity in favour of both material and aesthetic change. Fallan notes that 'in modernism, the synonymity between modern and contemporary ceases,'[2] but Panton retrieved that synonymity in his extremely time-specific designs. By embracing the materials, colours, and attitudes of the 1960s, he used his designs to bring temporal contemporaneity back into what was considered modern.

Like Arne Jacobsen and Finn Juhl, as a boy Panton wanted a career in art and worked in watercolours, and like his two compatriot designers he was also redirected towards a career in architecture by his parents. From 1944 to 1947, he studied masonry at Odense Tekniske Skole (Odense Technical College) and then pursued a degree in architecture at the Royal Danish Academy's Architecture School (where he studied under Kay Fisker and Erik Christian Sørensen). In 1950, Panton worked for Poul Henningsen with whom he studied light theory and from whom he acquired a systemic approach (and whose stepdaughter he married for one year). One evening,

Panton was invited to Henningsen's home to meet Jacobsen, who then hired him to work in his design studio from 1950 until 1952. His work with Henningsen and Jacobsen indicates how concepts and techniques migrated among the various mid-twentieth-century Danish designers. Commenting on working with the sometimes demanding Jacobsen, who often developed ideas during the process of designing something, Panton said of his own approach: 'I usually start with an idea and then try to find some firm that will produce it.'[3] Mads Nygaard Folkmann notes that designed objects are 'permeated by imaginary meaning . . . a structure that operates as a formative power in the process of designing . . .'[4] For Panton, the standard dichotomy of subject and object is all but erased. Ideas are not hiding behind his designs or simply driving his designs; his designed objects become, instead, blatant manifestations of his imaginative notions. Imagination becomes not, as Folkmann points out about the designing process, an early, internal matter, but instead makes its insistent presence clear in the objects Panton designed.

In Panton, previous design efforts by Jacobsen, Juhl, and Hans Wegner achieved a new level of liberation. Panton was able, mostly through the use of new and experimental materials, to expand on the focus on organic shapes pursued by his predecessors. Like Jacobsen in the Egg and Swan chairs, he defied the predilection for natural wood constructions; also in the mode of his former mentor's work on the SAS Hotel (and St. Catherine's at Oxford), Panton's vision was holistic. He took a *Gesamtkunstwerk* approach to numerous projects – even pulling the ceiling and floors into textural, optical, and chromatic oneness – but his vision was more experiential and experimental than Jacobsen's. The expressiveness that Juhl tried to apply to his designs by articulating them with modern sculptures to emphasize their organic forms found even broader application in Panton's efforts. Panton was able to expand the sculptural approach to furniture into an entire room of interlocking modules or multi-formed abstract shapes for sitting and lounging. Increasingly, his designs erased the dichotomy between what were furnishings and what was sculpture. He also went a number of steps beyond the playfulness of Wegner's late-modernist models, such as the *Flaglinestol* (Flag Halyard Chair, 1950) with its casual sheepskin throw, and into a notion of play sans any conventional object forms: chairs were turned into elements in an upholstered landscape, foam squares and rectangles on the floor, curves in a wall, systemic modules turning the consumer into a co-designer. Whereas Wegner once insisted, 'We must play – but we must play seriously,' Panton moved the 'play' from the designer's realm to that of the consumer/user. He reached a peak in these efforts in the late 1960s, especially in his designs for the German chemical and pharmaceutical company Bayer's floating exhibitions (which he renamed Visiona) for the International Furniture Fair in Cologne.

Like a coda on mid-twentieth-century modern Danish Design, Panton embraced the revolution that was the 1960s: looking at photos of his chromatically charged installations, exhibitions rooms, textiles, and furnishings is evocative, at times recalling sets on the American television series *Laugh-In* (1967–71) and the British television series *The Avengers* (1961–69), or props on science-fiction series such as *Lost in*

Space (1965–68), lava lamps, Op art, and Warhol prints. The innovative nature of his designs may best be embodied in the chair that now simply bears his name, the Panton Chair (1960). The notion of designing a chair in one solid form of plastic occupied Panton's thoughts for years; he once cited seeing a helmet made of fibreglass and a bucket made of plastic as his initial inspirations for a chair made of one piece of synthetic material.[5] He began by designing the *S-stol* (S-Chair) in 1955–56, but that cantilevered chair made of continuous bent plywood was not put into production until 1965 (by Thonet – and it is worth noting that it is not Danish companies manufacturing Panton's designs). By 1962, Panton was ready with the design of a single-form plastic chair, but a long and difficult process for finding the right material – or a willing manufacturer – ensued.[6] Even George Nelson turned down the design when it was first brought to Herman Miller in the United States.

After the production of some ten prototypes in fibreglass-reinforced polyester, the German firm Vitra eventually agreed to produce the chair on its own (thanks to the efforts of furniture manufacturer Willy Fehlbaum), and Panton moved to Basel to assist in the process. In 1967, the use of polyurethane foam enabled the chair to become the world's first injection-moulded, single-form chair (the chair went through a number of other materials as they became available, including polystyrene thermoplastic and polypropylene). The design premiered at the International Furniture Fair in Cologne in 1968 – the chair now made in polyurethane hard foam. Because of problems with the way the chair aged, it was actually discontinued in 1979 for four years and then resurrected in 1983 by the plastic manufacturer Horn. Since 1990, the chair has been manufactured by Vitra and has remained popular ever since. Its involved and somewhat tortuous path reflects design as a process, particularly in the case of the evolution of the use of new materials (the challenge to produce a cantilevered chair in solid plastic would not be picked up again until the German designer Konstantin Grcic did so with his stacking Myto Chair in 2008). The Panton Chair's immediately recognizable silhouette, a cipher for technological advancement and modern organic shape, provides a prime example of the ways in which certain Danish Modern designs have pervaded commercial design imagery (Fig. 7.1). Its image has appeared in numerous advertisements and on the cover of *Vogue* (January 1995) and the French newspaper *Liberation* (May 1993); for years it appeared on both the cover and spine of David Raizman's *History of Modern Design* (2003, 2010), one of the most thorough texts on modern design history.

In the Panton Chair, the organic oneness that Jacobsen had striven to obtain in his myriad designs reached a new height. Not only was a chair no longer an object consisting of joinery and four legs – unlike the Egg and Swan, it did not even necessitate a separate base. Folkman observes that the Panton Chair 'balanced modernist ambitions and swooping organic curves [and] changed the space of cultural possibilities for chairs.'[7] It was plastic *and* organic, a sensuous form with a sleek train that looked like the future while echoing the curve of the human body. Yet more than this, it was a canvas for solid colour without interruption, an excellent vehicle for chromatic oneness. Particularly in its original glossy lacquer finish, the

Fig. 7.1 Two models – Marianne Panton (left) and Christine Fehlbaum – pose on two of Panton's single-mould chairs. Courtesy of Verner Panton Design/Louis Schnakenburg

chair has the surface of nail polish and automobile paint. In advertisements, it frequently appears in a bold red (Panton's favourite colour), a colour well suited to the strength and erotic sensibility of the design. Asked about Panton's predilection for the colour, Marianne Panton, his wife and frequent collaborator (and model) in the staging of his designs, explained: 'Red was important for him because it is a signal color with lots of psychological meaning. After he finished his studies, he took a course in color psychology, a subject that was of great interest for him, especially red's psychological properties.'[8] Panton had merged colour with form in a way no previous Danish modernist designer had achieved. Chromatically, the Panton Chair is another step into the autonomous colours of Op and Pop art and of the hard-edged Color Field paintings.

Panton had shown earlier preferences for red tones in his designs. One of his first major assignments, as both an architect and designer, was an extension, in 1968, on the very traditional *Kom Igen Kro*, an old Danish inn once leased by his father on the island of Fyn (Fünen). Panton employed five different shades of red in the interior design of the glass-and-concrete addition's interior ('Red-orange is welcoming,' he once observed[9]). He also exercised his growing interest in Pop art in one of the chairs designed for the extension: the *Kræmmerhus-stol* (Cone Chair, 1958). The upholstered conical chair, its point pivoting on a cross-shaped base, was first covered in the same red fabric as that worn by Royal Danish Life Guards. Circular shapes dominate in both the seat and curve of the backrest. The geometric chair imparts a humorous, Pop-art image – and Panton reinforced the design's whimsy by hanging a pair of the chairs and matching table from the ceiling at the *Købestævne* furniture fair in Fredericia, Denmark in 1959 (so that visitors in the crowded hall could still look up to see his designs). The Cone then gave birth to the red *Hjerte-stol* (Heart Chair), another cone-shaped chair but with a heart-formed enveloping back, in Panton's next project.

In 1960, Panton was asked to design the interior of the Astoria Hotel in Trondheim, Norway: he redesigned an evening restaurant and dance floor, conference room, self-service cafeteria, café with a winter garden, and a cloakroom. Although he did not design the building, Panton had been given a task similar to Jacobsen's with the SAS Hotel and free reign to apply a broad systemic and chromatic approach. He designed the textile series Geometri I–V for Danish textile manufacturer Unika Væv for the project (Unika Væv had started a furniture line, Plus-linje, specifically to market Panton's designs). Geometri's Op-art patterns appeared on the hotel's floors, ceilings, and walls. Geometri I, for example, featured red and orange squares filled with circles of varying sizes; the bold geometric pattern, red and orange shifting places, even covered the support columns in the restaurant. In the café, Geometri II employed patterns of blocks of squares and diamonds in varying sizes. In all these designs, Panton played with the visual effect of both light forms against dark backgrounds and dark forms against lighter ones. Yet, it is the chroma that must have been arresting to the hotel's visitors.[10] Fortunately, the majority of the hotel's spaces were dark, and this may actually explain why Panton designed such vibrant, even jittery, patterns – patterns that he softened with his own Topan lighting (1959), spheres in aluminium or lacquered colours (opened only at the bottom to diffuse light softly).

The Astoria was a way for Panton to submerge visitors in his geometric, chromatic world: it hints at what is to come when he merges colours with forms sans the conventional space of rooms and furniture in later projects. The Astoria's designs proffer an explosion of sensory experience without objective reference beyond geometry. Henningsen reviewed the designs for the hotel in *Nyt* (*New*), the magazine of the lighting manufacturer Louis Poulsen. Although PH lauded the totality of Panton's designs, he felt that the orange and red circles and squares made one want to cover his or her ears at the blaring two-tone effect: 'I don't think that Astoria in Trondheim is the final solution to anything, but I do very much think it is the first solution to the great question that has plagued us since functionalism emerged: How do we make being in a restaurant feel right for the public?'[11] For Panton, like a fauve, that feeling was conveyed through chroma, a move towards imparting colour sans objective reference. As Ida Engholm observes about the experience of visiting the hotel in her 2006 monograph on Panton: 'visitors did not need to be under the influence of alcohol or anything else to take a visual trip.'[12]

Panton's sense of colour is direct; that is, to paraphrase the American painter Frank Stella, it is colour as good as it exists in the can – not muted or diluted – but industrial, the kind of colours intended for covering large surfaces.[13] Panton's approach to chromaticism parallels the artists in the 1960s who let colour function as the prime bearer of content. Pure chroma stimulates the eye of the beholder, and Panton increasingly used colours in his designed spaces to eradicate the distance between his objects and the observer. In his designs for the Astoria Hotel, Panton had saturated spaces with colour to bring colour's force back to its original state; in its strength and mass, chroma – ironically, for a designer – mutes the effect of shape. In *Chromophobia* (2000), David Batchelor notes that attitudes towards colour changed profoundly in the early 1960s as artists took a characteristic step away from oil paints as their primary medium. Batchelor observes that paint, once associated primarily with tubes of oil paints for shading and lightening, now looked blatantly as if it came from a can, and he cites the silk-screens of Warhol and the permeating sponge-work of Yves Klein as examples. Batchelor views this as a new perception of chromaticism: 'an entirely distinct and unrelated use of color occurs in the work of those artists who were identified, for the most part, with the emergence of Pop art and Minimalism.'[14] Batchelor also cites the use of industrial paints as the driving force in this movement: 'the possibility of painting becoming all but indistinguishable from a paint-job.'[15]

In 1964, Panton introduced the *Flyvende Stol* (Flying Chair), a design referred to often as 'fantasy furniture' and 'flying bananas,' at the International Furniture Fair in Cologne. The chair consisted of a simple curved form, covered in foam rubber and wool, and then strung from the ceiling with cords, not only creating a floating hammock-like environment but allowing for different heights and levels of relaxation and communication. Arousing much attention at the fair, Panton's whimsical design also surfaced in a published conversation among his fellow furniture designers Børge Mogensen and Hans Wegner, and textile designer Lis Ahlmann, which appeared in *Politiken* in 1964. The discussion made apparent the fact that Panton was operating on the periphery of the then-diminishing traditionalist legacy of the Klint School. Whereas Wegner was arguing for experimentation and the freedom to work in 'steel, plastic or whatever the hell,' Mogensen (one of Klint's acolytes) and even Ahlmann were less open to mistakes. At one point in the discussion, Wegner observes about the Flying Chair: 'I can also even understand the factory that was so excited about Verner Panton's blimps in hoisting devices shown at the furniture fair in Cologne.'[16] Recalling that Klint had taught him and his fellow students to learn their limitations, Mogensen responds dismissively to Panton's fanciful design: 'That kind of thing is unnecessary. I don't want to be part of that race. There is only one thing that matters – and that is to limit oneself.'[17] A triangulation of design approaches manifests itself in this revealing conversation, and especially in the response to Panton's playful inventions: Panton has blatantly abandoned any connection to the 'sober' tradition of wood-oriented designing that had emanated from the Klint School; Wegner is open to change and experimentation; and Mogensen, still a Klint devotee clinging to the early Danish Modern fealty to wood, will have no part of Panton's synthetic fantasies. Ahlmann also fell in line with Mogensen throughout the conversation.

Colour became another way for Panton to move beyond the limitations of the earlier legacy of Danish Modern design. His encompassing chromaticism, his 'chromophilia' (to borrow Batchelor's word[18]), evinces itself in his designs for the *Hummerbar* (Lobster Bar) for Visiona 0 at the International Furniture Fair (IMM) in Cologne in 1968. From the late 1960s and into the mid-1970s, Bayer commissioned a well-known designer to turn a Rhine excursion steamer into an exhibition showroom for its products. In 1968, the focus was on Bayer's new synthetic textile Dralon, and Panton was commissioned to design the ship's exhibition spaces (he eventually changed the name of the riverboat showroom from the Dralon ship to Visiona). Panton seized the opportunity to design total spaces in which he experimented with colour, light, and texture working in tandem. The Lobster Bar, for example, presented a saturated study in red in which visitors are, characteristically, enveloped in the colour: circular booths – including their seats, tables, and banquettes – are red; the red walls and ceiling are texturized with fringy, hanging carpet (also in circles); the chroma extends to the rug on the floor. Lobster murals line the walls, and Panton's shell lamps, the only non-red element in the design, mimic the dripping textiles as they, too, cascade from the ceiling. A visitor stepping into the space entered the red; as Panton embraced colour without restriction or fear, he surrounded the user with such saturated colour that the only thing remaining is to swoon in surrender. The effect recalls Matisse's *The Red Studio* (1911) in which a single red permeates the walls, floor, and many of the studio's furnishings, to the point that the colour on the canvas trumps depth or perspective, despite various indicators of both. Matisse once explained that the studio's colour was actually a blue-grey colour but that he felt red – and so that is what he painted. 'When looking at red, the pulse beats faster,' Panton wrote in his book *Lidt om Farver* (*Notes on Colour*, 1991). 'Under the influence of red the passage of time is over-estimated . . . Red is inspiring and provides an atmosphere for good ideas.'[19]

In a room filled with furry ball seats covered in bright red-orange Dralon, their shape and colour echoed by the use of the designer's Flowerpot Lamps (1968, introduced at the Visiona Exhibition) in their half-globular form, hanging in various lengths from the red ceiling, Panton employs geometric form to emphasize chromatic effect. His approach recalls Bridget Riley's explanation for her reliance on geometrics in her Op-art endeavours, in which form and colour take precedence: 'I couldn't get near what I wanted through seeing, recognizing and recreating, so I stood the problem on its head. I started studying squares, rectangles, triangles and the sensations they give rise to.'[20] In the enamelled Flowerpot's design, Panton's work with Henningsen's involved studies of light diffusion becomes apparent: the lamps

Fig. 7.2 Panton's employment of Op-art patterns finds full expression in the dining room of the Astoria Hotel in Trondheim, Norway. His Heart Cone Chair (1959) and Topan Lamp (1960) fit right into the geometric setting. Courtesy of Verner Panton Design/Louis Schnakenburg

consist of two hemispherical bowls, the upper bowl twice the size of the lower, painted in the same colour. However, while the interior of the upper bowl is painted white, the bottom bowl features a pink interior to help diffuse light more softly (Henningsen had employed reddish diffusers in a number of PH-lamps). Panton also reintroduced the geometric aesthetic that many in the Bauhaus had embraced and that was then banished for the most part from the Danish designers' more organic, handcrafted, wood-driven approach. Panton's approach functions, instead, as a transition from Pop art to Op art in its sometimes reliance on geometric abstraction (Fig. 7.2). It is softened, however, and swallowed up in colour, diminishing the logical effect of geometry and replacing it with soft chroma, a move from the conventionally masculine to the feminine.

Pop art imagery appears on many of the fabrics Panton designed for the furnishings in Visiona 0. One series, *Anatomi*, designed in 1968 for the exhibition but not put into production publicly until 1978, features large photo images of eyes, hands, lips, feet, and ears printed on solid colour fabric. The effect is paradoxical: Panton has placed readily identifiable images of body parts on fabrics in bold, overpowering colours (usually in two shades). The isolated parts appear eerie, perhaps a nod to Surrealism and to Magritte's disembodied sense of flotation, and are enveloped in swaths of colour; in one circular area of Visiona 0, feet are printed on individual circles of rug and all over the curtains surrounding the space, all in shades of purple. In 'Sixties Art:

Some Philosophical Perspectives,' Sheldon Nodelman points to the intangible nature of colour as purely optical: 'The interspace between picture-plane and spectator is chroma's proper field of action.'[21] Enveloping users in one hue erases any sense of space between them and the materials around them. Panton's designs for the Anatomi series still privilege colour over image, uniting them with some of Warhol's silkscreens in which colour creates a bridge between the recognizable reproducible self and an erasable anonymity acquired in the use of saturated 'unreal' colours. In his line of Anatomi fabrics, Panton has blended the readily identifiably imagery of Pop art with the chromatic interplay of Op art.

In another room for the first Visiona Exhibition, large Dralon balls are covered in a golden yellow, as is a thick circular rug, reflecting the hanging metallic Topan lamps. Promotional photos reveal models (including Marianne Panton) in various stages of repose on piles of the monochromatic Dralon balls. Another room served partially as a paean to Henningsen, four of whose PH-5 lamps encircle one of his large metallic Artichokes in the centre. Panton repeats the bowl shape that had inspired PH's multiple curved diffusers in four hanging 'bowls' for sitting, each bowl filled with round cushions repeating each element's circular forms. A red curtain encircles the round room. In all of these spaces, Panton has elevated casualness to the level of a visual art in defiance of bourgeois living spaces. As Sabine Epple comments: 'the balls and spherical Topan lamps lent the room the quality of an abstract landscape [whereas] the soft lighting and fleecy quality of the textiles generated an atmosphere of well-being and ease, which nevertheless evaded the habitual attributes of "coziness."'[22] The allusion to 'coziness' is pointed, as the Danish proclivity for *hygge* (loosely translated as coziness) has often been romanticized and mocked – and in Panton's case deconstructed for the Pepsi generation. If the elderly Danish couple felt uncomfortable in that 1943 satirical cartoon depicting their living room 'modernized' by an architect/designer, they would have been thrown to the floor trying to relax on Panton's fuzzy round modules.

In Collection Décor, a series of fabrics designed in 1969 for the Swiss company Mira-X, and printed by Pausa and Taunus Textildruk in Germany, Panton stepped full-force into Op-art chromatic effects in brightly coloured textiles for use on wall fabrics, curtains, rugs, and pillows. While teaching at the Bauhaus, the colour theorist Josef Albers noted that he had turned especially to the square because it did not come from science or nature but was, instead, a mathematical creation. More than this, he saw the geometric form as a tool for chromatic inquiry: 'The arrangement of squares in my *Homage to the Square* paintings and prints has become a convenient carrier of what I consider my color interaction . . . It is a container for and a dish to serve my color cooking in.'[23] Albers' employment of contiguous colours because of their rhythmic effect also resonates in many of Panton's fabric designs with their reliance on both geometrics and serial colours. In the *Geometri* line for fabrics, for example, lilac sits next to blue, or gold next to sun yellow, or red next to carmine in circles and squares, the close proximity of colours creating vibrating visuals. Albers claimed he used the square specifically for the 'cultivation of color pulsation and vibration as a color motion from within,'[24] all of which he viewed as a form of serial organization for chromaticism. These descriptions are apt for Panton's fabrics in which he moves a certain element of Modernism – chromatic study – back to the Bauhaus's more geometric experimentation and away from the purely organic design often associated with Danish Modern.

In his brilliant geometric line of fabric designs for Mira-X, Panton also employed the distinct lines of post-painterly abstraction. Colours appear systemically as circles, squares, stripes, checkerboards, and curves, recalling the chromatic chevrons of Kenneth Noland and the hard-edged canvases of Frank Stella. In all his fabrics for Mira-X, Panton employed either a spectrum of eight colours or eight shades of the same colour in myriad shapes. These designs disclose Panton's optical embrace of Stella's dictum that 'What you see is what you see.' The chromatic design for Square, for example, resembles Stella's canvas *Gran Cairo* (1962), and the multi-coloured circles in Panton's Spectrum fabric is redolent of Stella's *Hurrah II* (1967). In this way, Panton was moving 1960s art forms into the home – not simply as individual canvases or prints but as recurring motifs that could appear on pillows, rugs, wall hangings, and throws. This approach became popular throughout that decade: on 12 September 1967, the singing group the Fifth Dimension appeared on the television variety series *The Hollywood Palace* wearing coordinated outfits featuring Noland's multi-coloured chevrons running across them. Design in the 1960s tended to draw art from the walls and into everyday use. Instead of designing normatively, like the earlier modernists preaching functionalism and narrowing user options to what they believed constituted good taste, Panton turned a great deal of the designing process, particularly in his fabrics, over to the user while simultaneously smuggling in the aesthetics of Pop and Op art. Bärbel Birkelbach notes: 'The colors and forms used by Panton for Mira-X gave rise for the first time to a distinct formal vocabulary.'[25]

In 1970, this formal vocabulary became more encompassing in Panton's designs for the second exhibition, Visiona II, for Bayer at the Cologne furniture fair. In these designs he pushed spaces from biomorphic shapes to the limits of designed spaces bordering at times on the amorphous. Many of the exhibition areas consisted of curvilinear landscapes in which multi-coloured walls, floor, seating, and lounge areas merged into one another in a synaesthetic 'experience' involving music and aromas. The exhibition provided yet another variant on the *Gesamtkunstwerk*, but Panton's approach, unlike his mentor Jacobsen's in the SAS Hotel, is open-ended; people can figure out what to do with these environments on their own. That opportunity also held true for the furnishings designed for the exhibition. The Amoeba line of seating, in which a plastic shell enveloped foam seating in the same colour, employed a curved shape, like a punctuation mark, that enabled one person to sit inside the crook of the chair and another to stand behind it and read or rest on its integrated shelf (a photograph for the exhibition shows Marianne in the chair and Panton leaning on the shelf). In the Ilumesa series, Panton combined a lamp and a seat in a cylindrical shape consisting of two circular forms, one placed on top of the other, with the lighting fixture installed in the bottom half, creating luminescence in seating. In one exhibition area, the shaggy texture of a rug gave rise to a mountain range of peaks and valleys for various forms of lounging and relaxing, all rendered in the same deep red colour. Lacquered Pop-art colours come into play in a rectangular green seating area with plastic globular wall- and ceiling-elements and padded furniture, all in two shades of green. Even more than the surroundings being all green or red in some of these spaces, they enable users to 'become' the chroma they are experiencing. Panton enhanced this effect by using analogous colour schemes and by mostly avoiding complementary shades in the same setting. 'I myself work normally with parallel colors whose tones follow consecutively according to the order of the spectrum,' he explained in 1966. 'In this way, I can control the character of the room in terms of warmth and coolness and thereby create the desired atmosphere.'[26]

In addition to finally erasing any dichotomy between furniture and architecture, the more cave-like spaces allowed chroma to step even further to the forefront, as users lounged in various positions on multiple fabric-covered foam forms – thus creating an experiential advertisement for Dralon while offering visitors a new environment in which to reassess conventional notions of living. Referred to as the Fantasy Landscape, these enveloping, womb-like spaces with their piped-in sounds and pleasant aromas created a happening in the 1960s sense of that word (*The Happening* was also the name of a film starring Anthony Quinn and its bouncy title song by the Supremes in 1967). As designed spaces, Visiona II's landscapes turned the imagination inside out, constructing mental spaces, environments in which form bears no resemblance to the distinctly designed furniture of Panton's mid-century Danish Modern predecessors. Visitors found themselves literally inside colours – not simply sitting on them. Referring to Visiona II, Folkmann observes that 'design with this kind of intensified ambience seeks to attract attention and thus both engages the users or the audience in the process of creating ambience and reflectively points to itself as a place of meaning making.'[27] Panton had taken the branding of a synthetic product as an opportunity for consciousness-raising (or at least aesthetic prodding) about domestic spaces and how we use them. 'No design works,' Adrian Forty has written, 'unless it embodies ideas that are held in common by the people for whom the object is intended.'[28] Panton's innovative designs embraced the strong visual changes occurring all around people in the cultures of some societies in the 1960s. Just as Henningsen claimed to have seen the influence of Cubism everywhere he turned in the 1920s, Panton employed the saturated out-of-the-can colours of the Pop and Op art that surrounded him in synesthetic designs testing the very boundaries of Modernism.

Design-wise, much of Panton's chromatically charged work represented an attack on the conventional suburban living room; it is telling to contemplate his designs in light of the burgeoning Levittown housing developments in the United States in the late 1950s and early 1960s. One cannot picture transferring the padded wombs of the psychedelic Visiona landscapes into the repetitive Populuxe homes of post-war suburban America (often viewed as the standard setting of mid-twentieth-century modernist design). For Panton, modern design was not simply a kidney-shaped sofa table in the centre of the living room or a biomorphic pattern on a Formica tabletop; instead, it was an entire living space turned into an organic reverie – a dreamscape of playful shapes and charged chromaticism. What it means to be 'modern' had transmogrified from attempts at classic design or timelessness outside of style, the goal of myriad modernists, and back to now.

Notes

1. Quoted in Ida Engholm, *Verner Panton* in *Store danske desingere* (Copenhagen: Lindhardt og Ringhof, 2008), 662.
2. Kjetil Fallan, *Design History: Understanding Theory and Method* (Oxford: Berg, 2010), loc. 2199.
3. Panton, 'Talent, energi, penge og held,' in Poul Erik Tøjner and Kjeld Vindum, *Arne Jacobsen: Arkitekt & Designer* (Copenhagen: Dansk Design Center, 199), 50–51.
4. Mads Nygaard Folkmann, *The Aesthetics of Imagination in Design* (Cambridge, MA: MIT Press, 2013), 5.
5. See Mathias Remmele, 'All of a Piece: The Story of the Panton Chair,' in *Verner Panton: The Collected Works*, ed. Alexander von Vegesack and Remmele (Weil am Rhein: Vitra Design Museum, 2000), 74–99.
6. Earlier chair designs by both Gunnar Aagaard Andersen and Poul Kjærholm were created as prototypes but never put into production. Kjærholm's steel-thread and papier-mâché models from 1953 sharply resemble Panton's ultimate design. A publicized argument about plagiarism even ensued in the Danish journal *Mobilia*.
7. Folkmann, *The Aesthetics of Imagination in Design*, 1.
8. 'Pantonudstilling i Berlin: Interview med Marianne Panton' (4 February 2011) [http://www.smow.com/blog/2011/02/pantonudstilling-i-berlin-interview-med-marianne-panton/; accessed 6 January 2015].
9. Panton, *Lidt om Farver/Notes on Color* (Copenhagen: Dansk Design Centre, 1997), 15.
10. Perhaps too arresting, as three years later (in 1963) the hotel owner ripped out all of Panton's multi-coloured designs and replaced them with grey furnishings.
11. Henningsen, 'Nyt nordligt lunt mødested,' *Nyt* (28 January 1961), 1858.
12. Engholm, *Verner Panton* in *Store danske desingere*, 654.
13. 'I knew a wise-guy who used to make fun of my painting, but he didn't like the Abstract Expressionists either. He said they would be good painters if they could only keep the paint as good as it is in the can. And that's what I tried to do. I tried to keep the paint as good as it is in the can.' From 'Frank Stella and Donald Judd: Questions to Stella and Judd by Bruce Glaser (1966)' in *Theories and Documents of Contemporary Art: A Sourcebook of Artists' Writings*, ed. by Kristine Stiles and Peter Selz (Berkeley: University of California Press, 1996), 120.
14. David Batchelor, *Chromophobia* (London: Reaktion Books, 2000), 98.
15. Ibid., 101.
16. Jørgen Hartmann-Petersen, 'Om at begrænse sig. Rullebords-samtale mellem tre af pionererne i dansk kunst håndværk,' *Politiken* (29 March 1964), 29.

17. Ibid.

18. Batchelor, *Chromophobia*, 71 associates this term with Roland Barthes and the notion of colour as a kind of bliss: 'chromophobia recognizes the otherness of color but seeks to play it down, while chromophilia recognizes the otherness of color and plays it up.'

19. Panton, *Lidt om Farver/Notes on Color*, 14.

20. Quoted in Dani Cavallaro, *Synesthesia and the Arts* (Jefferson, NC: McFarland, 2013), 85.

21. Sheldon Nodelman, 'Sixties Art: Some Philosophical Perspectives,' *Perspecta*, 2 (1967), 73–89.

22. Sabine Epple, 'Verner Panton as an Interior Designer,' in *Verner Panton: The Collected Works*, ed. von Vegesack and Remmele, 173.

23. Quoted in Edward Strickland, *Minimalism: Origins* (Bloomington, IN: Indiana University Press, 1993), 29.

24. Ibid.

25. Barbel Birkelbach, 'Verner Panton's Textiles,' in *Verner Panton: The Collected Works*, ed. von Vegesack and Remmele, 132–55.

26. Taken from a press statement, 'On the Treatment of Colors' (12 October 1996), and quoted in Epple, 'Verner Panton as an Interior Designer,' 159.

27. Folkmann, *The Aesthetics of Imagination in Design*, 41.

28. Adrian Forty, *Objects of Desire* (New York: Pantheon Books), 245.

8 Minimal Connections: Design as Art/Art as Design

'A shape, a volume, a color, a surface is something itself,' the American artist Donald Judd (1928–1994) once observed. 'It shouldn't be concealed as part of a fairly different whole.'[1] One of the central artists of what came to be called Minimal Art, Judd was also a prolific writer and speaker about the specific objects that compromised much of his three-dimensional work. Richard Wollheim coined the term Minimal Art in 1965, although he used it initially to describe the works of the Neo-Dadaists, the ready-mades of Marcel Duchamp, and the abstract paintings of Ad Reinhardt. Minimalism, therefore, came to be applied to Judd and his fellow practitioners of art – Carl Andre, Robert Morris, Dan Flavin, and Sol LeWitt, all of whom relied on materials such as cubes, metal plates, fluorescent tubes, and plywood, arranged only to be themselves. In their works, space became actual and not illusionary, and materials referred only to themselves, yet, the term 'Minimal Art' was not one these artists embraced or even used.[2] In *Minimalism: Art & Polemics in the Sixties,* James Meyer notes: 'All of the artists identified with minimalism distanced themselves from this label, at first because it was insulting and eventually because it implied a stylistic and theoretical coherence to which none of them subscribed.'[3] Instead, the broader term 'minimalism' has been used stylistically to describe pared-down tendencies in such diverse genres as literature, music, design, painting, and sculpture since the early 1950s.

Looking at images of Judd's various untitled works known generally as 'stacks,' begun in 1965, one could easily perceive shelves (Figure 8.1). His stacked installations usually consist of ten units, boxes of copper and/or Plexiglas, stacked at even intervals up to 15 feet high. They are attached to the wall invisibly; that is, there is no apparent bracket or guide holding the forms to the wall, thus reinforcing their individuality. The stacks have also appeared horizontally, with a varied number of forms, up to ten units. Without fail, they consist of either unified colour or a metal and Plexiglas combination. One could look at any of these installations and ponder placing books or other objects on them, but their relentlessly polished surface – not to mention the sheer height of many of the vertical stacks – seems ill suited to any functional use. The interaction between open and closed space is striking in Judd's stacked constructions, as it is in all his works, but it is not an open space calling to be inhabited or filled in any way by humans. It is simply a visual juxtaposition between the often highly polished rectangular boxy forms and empty space. The forms are blatantly manufactured in appearance (Judd employed Bernstein Brothers to make

Fig. 8.1 An installation of Donald Judd's Stacks. The artist poses by his work in the Leo Castelli Gallery in New York in 1966. Photo by Fred W. McDarrah/Getty Images

works for him, thus further exorcising the appearance of any artist's hand in his objects' creation). The repeating segments of Judd's stacks do not comprise, *in toto*, anything: they are not a set of shelves, they are not steps, they are not a metaphor for ascendance or anything else, and they are, above all else, not furniture. They depict nothing but themselves.

In Poul Erik Tøjner's monograph on Poul Kjærholm (1929–1980) for the *Store danske desginere* (Great Danish Designers) series, published in the 2000s, Tøjner spends a solid chunk of his book comparing the design approach of Kjærholm with that of Donald Judd's structures. Kjærholm trained as a carpenter before attending the Kunsthåndværkerskole, where he studied cabinetmaking under Hans Wegner and industrial design under the tutelage of architect Jørn Utzon. An admirer of Mondrian and Gerrit Reiveld, Kjærholm turned to steel as his main material – though he did not let the use of an industrial material negate any sense of craftsmanship inherited from his training. He made this aspect clear in a 1963 interview about his choice of material: 'Steel's constructive principles is not the only thing that interests me; for me, light's refraction on its surface is an important link in the artistic work. I view steel as a material with the same artistic merit as wood or leather.'[4] As a lecturer in furniture design at the Royal Danish Academy of Fine Arts, Kjærholm also indicated that, however artistic his furniture might look, he was not in any way rejecting the idea of functionalism. While constructing a dichotomy of intention, he connected that focus with the Furniture School's origins in Kaare Klint's teachings. 'It is Klint's method of working we carry on,' Kjærholm explained, 'not his personal, aesthetic formulas.'[5] In the course of this rare interview, the usually laconic designer also emphasizes a rationalist approach resting on metrics and the 'language of material' as the source of his designs, and he lauds the Bauhaus's efforts while rejecting its social and ideological programme. Most interestingly, in 1963, Kjærholm compares his own designs to those that appear in the Cabinetmakers Guild Exhibitions as consisting of 50 per cent handwork and 50 per cent industry.

Tøjner sees similarities in Kjærholm's and Judd's use of industrial precision and in their conscious choice of materials, and he asserts that Judd viewed the object as establishing space through its physical presence. Tøjner feels that both Kjærholm and Judd, in an avoidance of anything pictorial in their work, serve as spokesmen for a certain ethic administered by creating a 'minimalist tradition' that involves no narrative, accident, associations, references, decoration, ornament, or signature.[6] Yet, how can a piece of furniture, no matter how minimal its individual parts, ever be void of all of these traits? Any chair or table, unless it is intentionally made to look so much like something else that it no longer resembles itself, immediately presents a picture of a chair or table, no matter how pared down in design; it provides an automatic reference to other chairs and tables in the immediate recognition of its use-function. Even in decisions pertaining solely to construction, Kjærhlom insisted on references: 'it is necessary to have a reference. When evaluating furniture, you need a truth to refer to.'[7] Also, Tøjner proceeds to discuss 'the human (anthropomorphizing) nature of furniture as a replacement for bodies in our rooms. . . . Because they remind us of beings.'[8] That reminder is dependent, again, on familiarity of usage, a human experience with furniture, and the way we dwell with objects we use. On that front, a chair will always recall the human body because it is designed specifically for sitting; paring down the structure or frame of a chair cannot negate this usage without turning the chair into something else.

In the evolution of Danish Modern chair design, for example, this paring down towards minimalist design follows, at least for a few decades, a natural progression. In his Chair No. 45 (1945), Juhl, with help from his cabinetmaker Niels Vodder, reduced the frame of a chair into challengingly slender, sinuous wooden lines separate from yet supporting the upholstered seat and back. In his Round Chair (1949), Wegner decreased the joinery even further into four straight legs while reducing the top-rail to an abstract form, and by CH88 (prototype, 1955), he too was working in a thin steel frame and had banished the apron. In Chair PK11 (1957), a chair designed specifically to accompany Table PK55, Kjærholm reduced the legs of a chair to three thin steel lines, a half circle connected by a steel diameter and radius beneath a thin, barely elevated leather seat, with a half circle of ash-wood as a backrest, crowned with a thin horizontal layer of ash intimating a top-rail. Yet, no amount of paring down or reductionism can exorcise any of these chairs' shared function as a piece of furniture for sitting on or, thereby, the human association necessitated by the very notion of chair design. Use-function remains apparent: knowledge of the use of furniture – even the mere visual intention of use – creates instant interaction with it. In the case of Judd and his fellow artists, nothing in their specific objects and primary structures in the 1960s looks human or in any way anthropomorphic, nor does any of it imply any form of usage (though one may walk on Andre's floor tiles). There is undeniable presence about the large plywood installations of Robert Morris (1931–), who called his installations unitary forms, but no sense of anything redolent of a 'human being.'

That Kjærholm's designs are minimalist in appearance is a given: in their thin, metallic frames they look like the last stop on the train of Danish Modern that began its journey in the 1920s and 1930s at the intersection of rationalism, objectivity, and functionalism before Panton's colourful, insouciant designs in the 1960s (Fig. 8.2). Kjærholm's designs consist of lines of steel, reductive shapes, flat layers of material for padding, and an insistent tension, in almost every designed object, between two surfaces: steel against leather; steel against woven cane; steel against marble; steel against wood. Their forms are often ciphers, best represented in the PK24 (1965), a chaise lounge consisting of an elongated curve of woven cane resting on a thin steel frame, a chair reduced to a dramatic line drawing. Erik Krogh observes: 'The organic, curving plane hovers freely in the room, at the same time that, in a state of equilibrium, it touches precisely, horizontally and vertically.'[9] That all of these works share a minimalist profile is undeniable, and their use of materials is restricted, mathematical, and deceptively simple in hiding the complexity of their construction. Still, their functional nature and interplay of materials make it difficult to place them under the aegis of the Minimal Art movement of the 1960s. Perhaps a visual analogy can be

Fig. 8.2 A selection of Kjærholm's designs, including (left to right) Table PK 61 (1956), Chair PK 22 (1956), Folding Stool PK 41 (1961), and Lounge PK 80 (1957). Courtesy of Republic of Fritz-Hansen/fritzhansen.com

made between Kjærholm's set of three small stacking tables, PK71 (1957), in close diminishing sizes, and Sol LeWitt's numerous installations of open cube forms. The PK71 tables consist of the outline of a cube in brushed stainless steel, with a flat removable acrylic top in black or white. If one were to remove the top, the tables would resemble the three-dimensional frames of LeWitt's cubes. Yet, the analogy falls apart the minute the tabletop is removed, because the tables can no longer function as tables without a solid top surface to support anything. The immateriality LeWitt wanted to convey in the open space in and around his cubic outlines can serve no useful purpose as furniture, and LeWitt insisted that beauty had nothing to do with his constructions. In addition, a conceptual element influences the serial design of LeWitt's cubes, as the idea of laying them out on a grid drives their varied placement.

A similar tension surfaces in Tøjner's description of the structure in Kjærholm's Chair PK22: 'All his chairs are composites; that is, they can be disassembled into the parts that they not only clearly but also visually consist of. As for PK22, it is created quite simply of three elements, covered in pulled leather or canvas – or covered in cane, the grandest version, as you can see all of the connections.'[10] In his seminal essay 'Specific Objects' (1965), Judd rejects the notion of parts in his structures and emphasizes the whole as a single entity, not a collection of parts. 'The main things are alone and are more intense, clear and powerful,' he writes. 'They are not diluted by an inherited format, variations of a form, mild contrasts, and connecting parts and areas.'[11] Furniture design is, for the most part – and quite intriguingly in the case of Kjærholm – an inherited format reliant on connections and transitional areas: tabletop to table frame, padding to seat frame, additional leaves to tabletop, leather rings to connect padding, etc. Just as the joinery in some of the earlier modernist Danish designers' wooden frames offered a design's most inventive solutions, Kjærholm's points of contact, sometimes almost indeterminably elevated, still present, *contra* Judd, noticeable points of connection between two surfaces (not a single whole as in one of Judd's isolated boxes). Kjærholm is reductive, architectonic, simple – minimalist in almost every way in the genre meaning of the word – but he still plays openly with connections. The slightly elevated points where the woven cane touches the slender steel frame in PK24 is one of the design's most careful elements. Like a true mid-twentieth-century modernist, Kjærholm was resistant to the word style. Asked in that 1963 interview if his mode of expression constituted a 'style,' he replied: 'No, of course not. But the same materials and tools will naturally lead to the same solutions to problems.'[12] Yet, while deflecting the dreaded sobriquet of style, he admits that his goal is a 'complete synthesis in a time when it is common to view things that are professional as exclusive in an unpleasant meaning of the word.'[13] That synthesis appears, from his designs, to rely on a meeting of parts, surfaces, and ideas – none of which, to him, is ever removed from function.

Fortunately, Judd also designed furniture in his lifetime, offering yet another point of reference in the discussion of minimalist art and design. In his essay 'It's Hard to Find a Good Lamp' (1993), Judd insists that the configuration and scale of art cannot be transposed to furniture and that function alone necessitates that the intent of furniture must be different from that of art. Judd calls a chair that lacks function ridiculous. 'The art of a chair is not its resemblance to art,' Judd claims, 'but is partly its reasonableness, usefulness, and scale as a chair.'[14] Proportion, to Judd, constitutes a discernible reasonableness in furniture design. In his most definite assertion in the essay, Judd writes: 'A work of art exists as itself; a chair exists as a chair itself. And the idea of a chair isn't a chair.' At the beginning of his monograph on Kjærholm, Tøjner quotes Judd (from 'On Furniture'): 'A good chair is a good chair.' When Judd makes this claim, though, he implies that a chair is not art by its very nature of being a chair. Judd's own furniture designs, rendered in all wood or metal and never the two materials together, consist totally of flat planes and right angles. One searches in vain for any curvilinear elements; in the wood line, a few of the chairs or stools feature the outline of a boxed frame, an homage to LeWitt's open box forms, but that is as close to any intersection with 'art' that Judd's furniture gets, at least by his own rhetorical standards.

In 'It's Hard to Find a Good Lamp,' Judd sounds like Henningsen in his praise of Thonet's bentwood furniture, his derision of period-style furniture (he particularly berates Victorian for its invocation of a higher class), and especially in his rejection of a machine aesthetic when he describes Breuer's Wassily Chair and Le Corbusier's lounge as 'almost forgivable sentimentalizing of the machine.'[15] Meyer feels that Judd, in his furniture lines, erased the line between the art of primary structures and the minimal look or 'dress' of primary structures: 'For once Judd began to make furniture, he unwittingly closed the chasm that he believed existed between art and design . . .' Yet, one could argue that, instead, Judd abandoned transforming forms from his art when he designed his furniture, which has parts and connections and in its planar appearance recalls Reitveld's designs (as in Reitveld's Zig-zag Chair, 1932). Ironically, a number of Danish design historians have pointed out Kjærholm's indebtedness to Reitveld's structural sensibilities. Christoffer Harlang, for example, indicates that Kjærholm's approach is 'akin to Gerrit Reitveld's in the way the confrontation between each piece of furniture's individual parts is formed.'[16] There are also pictures of Kjærholm teaching from Reitveld's De-Stijl-inspired Red-Blue Chair (1918–23), and yet there are no flat, hard quadratic planes in any of the surfaces of Kjærholm's own chair designs.

Reitveld spoke about Kjærholm's designs at an exhibition of the Dane's work in Amsterdam, at 'op het dak' Gallery in the Metz & Co. building, in 1963. In his inaugural talk opening the gallery, Reitveld contextualized Kjærholm's designs in the conflict between what he referred to as popular Modernism and decadent Modernism, framing the latter as a consequence of yearning for perfectionism resulting from technical possibilities. Reitveld feared that this desire for perfectionism was making it difficult for designers not to fall into the trap of designing things lacking any possibility for development: 'because they indicate a kind of completed stage and thus foster the impression that modern architecture has already developed into a perfect style.'[17] In Kjærholm's furniture, Reitveld saw technical elemental forms and materials taken into account and accepted, along with a 'modern functionalist approach that keeps every excessive tendency toward luxury in check.'[18] Reitveld also commented on the sense that, in Denmark, industry seemed tied to applied arts, and he lauded the treatment of wood and fine finishing, reinforcing the thread of craftsmanship running throughout the history of Danish industrial design. At one point in his talk, Reitveld compared Kjærholm to Jacobsen, whom he viewed as pushing too close to ultimate form, thereby limiting further development. 'Regarding Kjærholm,' he closed, 'I believe I can see a searching for undiscovered possibilities.'[19]

Articulations

In 1965, 'Strukturer' ('Structures'), an exhibition of Kjærholm's furniture, was held in Ole Palsby's showroom in Copenhagen: in this provocative exhibition, the disassembled parts of Kjærholm's designs were displayed in highly organized groupings. Even the exhibition's poster, designed by Bo Bonfils (1941–), depicted the profile of one leg from Kjærholm's PK9, a chair with a tripod base of three bent steel forms gathering beneath the seat, as a disembodied abstract shape (Fig. 8.3). In carefully arranged pieces, Kjærholm's designs were deconstructed, literally and figuratively, emphasizing manufactured forms in and of themselves (most of Kjærholm's furniture was manufactured by E. Kold Christensen), while simultaneously dismantling the human interaction of usage. Thus, the exhibition represented an attempt to privilege the aesthetics of shape over the function of furniture as part of domestic living in the only way possible – by dismantling the designs to negate their usage and to dehumanize them into the predominantly abstract forms of dissociated shapes. The architect Nils Fagerholt, who designed the exhibition, has observed: 'In contrast to use-intended furniture parts, what appears here – free and independent of every context – is the capacity for beauty in the simplest uniform parts.'[20] For example, the PK71 table frames were stacked horizontally, in alternating placements, visually erasing their purpose as table components and emphasizing, instead, their open cubic forms (à la LeWitt). Blown-up Photostats by Keld Helmer-Petersen, a Danish photographer who frequently photographed Kjærholm's work, appeared as backdrops emphasizing natural patterns also reduced to abstraction to complement the blatantly manufactured, isolated shapes. In fact, Helmer-Petersen's name appears above Kjærholm's on Bonfils's poster.

As was evident in Finn Juhl's employment of sculptures by Erik Thommesen and Sigurjón Ólafsson in his exhibitions in the 1940s, design articulation, especially of furniture, has often involved art, presented design as art, or stressed an association between the two. Both Juhl and Kjærholm designed exhibitions for the international exposure of Danish arts and crafts – both winning the Grand Prix at the Milan Triennale (Juhl in 1957 and Kjærholm in 1958). As in the backdrops for the 'Strukturer' exhibit, Kjærholm worked for years (1954–80) with Helmer-Petersen, who pioneered an abstract approach to depicting everyday objects by isolating them, or a part of them, and filming them in black and white, almost completely devoid of background or narrative. As Malene Breunig explains in 'Exhibitable Furniture: Interpreting Images of Design,' Helmer-Petersen's pictures of Kjærholm's furniture function 'as a gestalt for meaningful space around them, which forcefully contributes to defining the furniture hermeneutically.'[21] Breunig views this articulation as a way of using exclusion to remove, if not at least to diminish, any sense of domestic life lived with furniture and an excising of function in visually empty and abstract configurations. She contends

Strukturer
Keld Helmer-Petersen
Poul Kjærholm
4. Dec. 1965-4. Febr. 1966

Ole Palsby   Hovedvagtsgade nr. 8   København

Fig. 8.3 The poster for the *Strukturer* exhibition (1965) uses one leg from Kjærholm's Chair PK 9 (1961) as a motif. Courtesy of Designmuseum Danmark/The Library

that Kjærholm and Helmer-Petersen achieved this construction of emptiness for its own sake through a visual and spatial use of minimalism surrounding the furniture designs, an approach reflecting similar effects in the highly ordered and open modern gallery or museum space. Isolation was a way of elevating aestheticism over usage by flattening out the images of three-dimensional objects into exhibition portraits (the way Helmer-Petersen had flattened out the ripples in water into a large, rectangular, high-contrast, abstract pattern; see Fig. 8.4). Still, there are angles in some photographs of the furniture that in no way diminish the three-dimensionality of the designs.

With no human models sitting or resting on the furniture, with no tableaux recalling a living room or involving a single prop from residential living, the photographs serve

Fig. 8.4 Enlarged Photostats by Keld Helmer-Petersen serve as abstract backdrops to Kjærholm's disassembled designs in the *Strukturer* exhibition in 1965. Photo courtesy of Jan Helmer-Petersen

up images of Kjærholm's designs as outside the realm of mere comfort or everyday living. Considered in conjunction with the 'Strukturer' exhibition, Helmer-Petersen's photographs, like the clever display of disassembled parts, serve the modernist effort to create a-temporal designs, to defy the fickle and vapid style Kjærholm's rhetoric rejected, by removing the visual trappings and any evidence of use-function that must be located in time and place. To return to that 1943 cartoon, 'An Architect Went through the Room' by Carl Jensen, of the elderly Danish couple uncomfortable in their new architect-designed living room: in Helmer-Petersen's photographic constructions, they would no longer have a living room but would reside, instead, in a limbonic state in which furniture exists in the only abstracted way it can – without any social context.

At one point in her discussion, Breunig makes this comment: 'Helmer-Petersen's images of Kjærholm's design evoke . . . intellectual distance, which additionally accords with the furniture's own assertion.'[22] She also emphasizes that the impression of 'calmness' conveyed in the photographs is not created but is, instead, accentuated. Both of these comments return focus to Kjærholm's actual designs – not merely the articulation of them. How would Helmer-Petersen's mediation work with, for example, a Barcalounger? Could the isolation of parts of that heavily padded, suburban-American lounge chair, either in an exhibition of them or in empty photographs emphasizing the solitary chair's isolation, convey the same articulation of cold aestheticism? The mathematical nature of Kjærholm's designs resting on exposed thin steel frames and reduced shapes – not heavily padded invisible wood frames, springs, stuffing, and bunched vinyl as in the Barcalounger – enable their disassembly, enable their association with abstraction, in ways that other designs cannot. Mediation is, therefore, a dance: unless one is after juxtaposition or humour, not every design allows for mediation in the same way. To borrow Breunig's phrase, the design's 'own assertion' is always at play and dependent on its recognizable qualities of thickness, thinness, softness, hardness, volume, elevation, complexity, etc. Even disassembled and arranged on platforms and hung from the ceiling, the mechanical parts of Kjærholm's designs still do not constitute Minimal Art in the sense explained by Judd, because they point to something other than themselves – to their former or intended wholeness, which is a compilation of parts.

The Austrian artist Franz West (1947–2012) found a provocative intersection between art and design in many of his installations, and especially in his plaster and polyester *Passstücke* (Adaptives), intended for viewer usage. During the course of his career, West began to replicate chairs, tables, and other objects already developed by other designers; furniture and abstract sculpture became the two main thrusts of his work after the 1980s. Viewers are urged to touch West's objects, to sit in his brightly painted chairs, and to lie on his divans. His Uncle Chairs (2001–10) offer a prime example of an artist blurring the distinction between art and design: with their minimalist steel frame and vivid woven fabrics, they appear to be functional designer furniture – as well as art. Yet, would they even be considered art outside the setting of a museum? Reviewing West's furniture at an exhibit at the Baltimore Museum of Art in 2008, Ken Johnson observed that the artist's welded-metal chairs and divans 'flout the usual rules of good furniture design. Yet they are comfortable to sit on, and they grow on you visually too; they begin to seem decidedly elegant.'[23] Johnson also views West's creations as conflating furniture and art. In addition, in their usability, they erase the distinction between what constitutes art and what functions in design while playfully addressing the conflict between object of art and utilitarian object. Still, even West's chairs, with their alluring textiles and colours, function primarily as chairs, forcing us to question not only why they are art but what constitutes art, particularly to an artist who focused so much on use.

The line between art and furniture continues to be explored by artists such as the American Social Practice sculptor Andrea Zittel (1965–), whose 'hard carpets' and 'aggregated stacks' recall the efforts of Andre and Judd transferred to both used and usable objects. Zittel also includes a label with her art explaining how people could use her artful systems and objects to change their lives. Thus, she has turned the effort to remove exhibited designs from everyday living on its head and brought designed objects back to use-function. Zittel's work is often compared with early twentieth-century modernist design, a comparison she finds ironic: 'things like white walls, functionalism – things that could be mass-produced – all these things represented poverty. And all of a sudden they were reinterpreted [in Modernism] . . . all of a sudden became the moral elite.'[24] Zittel applies the aesthetic code of modern design to the austerity of her designed spaces, many of which make the most of small spaces. Her 'A–Z Cellular Compartment Units' (2001), in which multi-coloured, multi-level box shapes with holes are divided according to separate domestic usage, bear a striking resemblance to Verner Panton's prototypes for multi-functional, bi-level living units (1966). Zittel maintains an ambiguity in the usage of many of her designs – an ambiguity that would have no place in furniture design from the mid-twentieth century; she cites the influence of Judd on the forms of her white aggregate stacks but insists that the comparison works only if they are not used as shelves. All the conceptual notions informing Zittel's installations point to the dichotomy between the intentional uselessness of 1960s Minimal Art, such as Judd's, and the intrusion of function on design that is read as 'art,' as in exhibitions and re-readings of Kjærholm's minimalist furniture.[25]

The chasm between minimalist art and design was put to the test in an exhibition at the Cooper-Hewitt, Smithsonian Design Museum in 2004: 'Design ≠ Art: Functional Objects from Donald Judd to Rachel Whiteread.' The exhibition featured sculptural furniture by eighteen Minimalists, Post-Minimalists, and post-Post-Minimalists, with an emphasis on Judd's furniture. Reviewing the exhibition in the *New York Times*, Roberta Smith – who found Judd's chairs 'flawed' – observed: 'Artists can do whatever they want in their art; such liberty is the point of the activity. Design involves a kind of selflessness and a complex awareness of the givens: the human body and its needs, social space, the laws of gravity, the means of production and the demands of the marketplace.'[26] Her collection of givens reads like a checklist for most furniture designers, even the Danish Modern ones. Despite the myriad ways that Danish mid-twentieth-century designers – and their promoters – articulated their works as or with art, uselessness or the ambiguity of art was never an element of their endeavours; instead, process of construction and relevance to the human form characterized the majority of enduring Danish Modern designs.

Notes

1. Quoted in Daniel Marzona, *Minimal Art* (Cologne: Taschen, 2004), 60.
2. LeWitt once opined that the term minimal art 'is a part of a secret language that art critics use when communicating with each other through the medium of art magazines.' Quoted in Marzona, *Minimal Art*, 20.
3. James Meyer, *Minimalism: Art & Polemics in the Sixties* (New Haven, CT: Yale University Press, 2004), 30.

4. Quoted in Axel Thygesen and Arne Karlsen, 'En samtale med Poul Kjærholm,' in *Poul Kjærholm*, ed. Christoffer Harlang, Keld Helmer-Petersen and Krestine Kjærholm (Copenhagen: Arkitektens Forlag, 1999), 163.

5. Ibid.

6. Tøjner, *Poul Kjærholm*, in *Store Danske Designere* (Copenhagen: Lindhardt og Ringhof, 2008), 741.

7. Thygesen and Karlsen, 'En samtale med Poul Kjærholm,' 162.

8. Tøjner, *Poul Kjærholm*, 776.

9. Krogh, 'Det skulpturelle og det arkitektoniske,' in *Poul Kjærholm*, ed. Harlang, Helmer-Petersen and Kjærholm (1999), 28.

10. Ibid.

11. Judd, 'Specific Objects,' Judd Foundation [http://www.juddfoundation.org/generalin formation; accessed 26 February 2015].

12. Thygesen and Karlsen, 'En samtale med Poul Kjærholm,' 167.

13. Ibid.

14. Judd, 'It's Hard to Find a Good Lamp,' Judd Foundation [http://www.juddfoundation. org/furniture/essay.htm; accessed1 March 2015].

15. Ibid.

16. Harlang, 'Lethed og tyngde,' in *Poul Kjærholm*, ed. Harlang, Helmer-Petersen and Kjærholm (1999), 158.

17. Printed in 'Poul Kjærholm-udstillingen i Amsterdam,' *Dansk Kunsthaandværk*, 36(3/4) (1963), 76.

18. Ibid.

19. Ibid.

20. Fagerholt, 'Udstillingerne og de særlige rum,' in *Poul Kjærholm*, ed. Harlang, Helmer-Petersen and Kjærholm (1999), 52.

21. Breunig, 'Exhibitable Furniture: Interpreting Images of Design,' in *Scandinavian Design: Alternative Histories*, ed. Kjetil Fallan (Oxford: Berg, 2012), loc. 3794.

22. Ibid., loc. 3865.

23. Ken Johnson, 'Sculpture that Asks You to Sit a Spell,' *New York Times* (19 December 2008) [www.nytimes.com/2008/12/19/arts/design/19west.html; accessed 19 August 2013].

24. 'Andrea Zittel: Influences,' ART21 [http://www.art21.org/texts/andrea-zittel/interview-andrea-zittel-influences; accessed 8 March 2015].

25. In 1999, Zittel's 'A–Z Pocket Property,' a 44-ton floating fantasy island off the coast of Denmark and commissioned by the Danish government, offered a commentary on the isolation that occurs when a person is removed from society.

26. Roberta Smith, 'Designers for a Day: Sculptors Take a Turn,' *New York Times* (9 October 2004) [http://query.nytimes.com/gst/fullpage.html?res=9404EFDC1430F933A2575AC 0A9629C8B63; accessed 27 February 2015].

Thematizing Danish Modern: The Arts of Denmark Exhibition

As mentioned earlier, international exhibitions helped to advance the worldwide presence of Danish Modern design, particularly in the United States, where the concept of Danish Modern furniture took hold in the marketplace in the 1950s. Exposure for the designs of Hans Wegner and Finn Juhl in magazines such as *Interiors* and *House Beautiful* helped to open the door for a larger export market and the branding of Danish Modern as an organic, less machine-driven aesthetic form of modernist design. The largest and most impressive display of Danish arts and crafts and industrial design shown in North America was the Arts of Denmark: Viking to Modern exhibition, which opened in October 1960 at the Metropolitan Museum of Art in New York and presented artefacts from prehistoric times to what was then considered contemporary Danish design. The exhibition of hundreds of items was sponsored by Landsforeningen dansk kunsthåndværk (the Danish Society of Arts and Crafts and Industrial Design) and coordinated in the USA by Edgar Kaufmann, Jr. As director of the department of industrial design at the Museum of Modern Art, Kaufmann had already worked to bring attention to Nordic design in the United States. In many ways, the Arts of Denmark exhibition represented the second major volley on behalf of Danish design following Denmark's participation in the popular Design in Scandinavia exhibition, which opened in January 1954 at the Virginia Museum of Fine Arts in Richmond, toured North America from 1954 to 1957, and was seen by more than 500,000 visitors.

The Design in Scandinavia exhibition, which included the works of some eighty Danish designers, is worth considering as a precursor abetting the dissemination and marketing of Danish Modern within the larger context of Scandinavian Design in North America. Today, the world is familiar with the concept of Scandinavian Design – although to many consumers the nebulous epithet might include budget furniture from IKEA or high-end crystal from Orrefors – but the pan-Nordic term did not actually come into common usage until the 1950s. At that time worldwide exhibitions, organized predominantly by the Nordic countries' Arts and Crafts Societies, strove to present a unified design front to the international marketplace for selling wares from Denmark, Norway, Sweden and Finland. Iceland, partially because of a lack of financial support, only participated sporadically in these early pan-Nordic exhibitions but did take part in both the 1956 Deutsche Handwerkmesse in Munich and in Formes Scandinaves in Paris in 1958–59.[1] Design historians have, for decades, pointed out the construction of the broad notion of 'Scandinavian Design' first referred to in the Milan Triennale Exhibitions of Decorative Arts and Modern Architecture in 1951 and 1954. In *Norge i form* (*Norway in Form*, 1988), for example, the art historian Fredrik Wildhagen states that Scandinavian design – as a concept – was not a Nordic invention but was introduced in connection with the Milan Triennales and then employed again in the Design in Scandinavia exhibition in 1954. In the marketing sense, this is undeniably true, but as elucidated in Chapter 1, Nordic designers and theoreticians had been exchanging ideas about modern design with one another – in lectures, in journals, in technology (consider Aalto's influential innovations in bent-wood), and in regional exhibitions – since the end of the nineteenth century. Fallan observes: 'the phenomenon that brought Nordic design international reputation in the 1950s was built on old traditions – ideologies, movements, organizations, schools and museums dating back to the late nineteenth and early twentieth century.'[2]

The phenomenologist Don Ihde, using Husserl's concepts of *noema* and *noesis*, has commented extensively on types of observation in human experience, and it is worth considering these concepts as they apply to experiencing designed objects in exhibition catalogues. To reduce Ihde's types of observation to a basic level: noema equals what is experienced, and noesis represents the mode of experiencing – *how* we experience something. A person standing in a museum facing and interacting with objects has actional experience, that is, an involved one of immersion (if she spends any time with the object). In thinking about the experience, the observer enters a state of reflection or, as Ihde observes, of 'thematizing' the straightforward experience (in this case, of being in the museum with the objects): 'Thinking *about* experience presupposes both some form of experience as its subject matter and some kind of distance from that subject matter in order to thematize it.'[3] Museum labels and catalogues help to thematize the experience in a specific and directed way, in the case of the catalogue by adding another layer of distance from the actual experience. Exhibitions end, but catalogues continue to conceptualize what has been exhibited, thus influencing our 'experience' of these objects, especially for the reader who experiences the exhibition only in print. In other words, in an exhibition catalogue, focus moves from the 'what' of the objects to the 'how' of their appearance and to contextualizing them in specific ways that influence our responses.

Design in Scandinavia

Focusing on the Design in Scandinavia exhibition, the Danish semiotician Jørn Guldberg has traced the development of the concept of Scandinavian Design as an exercise in discourse.[4] Addressing the concept of Scandinavian Design as codified in text, Guldberg points to the authorship of the catalogue accompanying the exhibit in 1954 – along with other journalistic efforts to erase the difference among the Nordic countries – to construct a notion of shared Nordic values, emphasizing continuity and contiguity, and diminishing any elements of polarizations (wars among the nations, for example, are euphemistically rewritten into the catalogue copy as

Fig. 9.1 A group of chairs from the Design in Scandinavia Exhibition (1954) at the Brooklyn Museum includes Jacobsen's Ant (on far left), Wegner's CH27 and Cowhorn Chair (in the middle), and Juhl's Egyptian Chair and Chieftain (on far right). Photo: Brooklyn Museum Archives

'fraternal strife'). Guldberg also alludes to the 'semantic choices in relation to various writers' identification of the Scandinavian-ness of Scandinavian things.'[5] To return to Ihde, those choices affect our noetic experience. Reviewing the exhibition in *Interiors* magazine, Kaufmann, Jr. commented on the exhibited objects' traits and characteristics, their perceived physical qualities. Kaufmann – who had already tried in the late 1940s to bring a pan-Scandinavian exhibit to MoMA – lauded 'what is good in American eyes about Northern design generally. Clean, well-finished, unobtrusive, carefully considered, ingenious, sensible and elegant.'[6] Guldberg views Kaufmann's description as a sign of ambivalence and questions whether the traits attributed to the objects in the Design in Scandinavia exhibit 'account for physical and functional qualities of things, or should they more likely be understood as an American projection of desirable social and psychological characteristics.'[7]

While it is undoubtedly true that all of these efforts were constructed to market the goods in these exhibits, especially for Design in Scandinavia, to American consumers, we are left with the question of whether or not the objects in these exhibits share any traits regardless of applied marketing notions. Could the same descriptions be applied to objects rendered in a French provincial style, for example, simply because one wanted to apply them? Guldberg notes that the catalogue copy for Design in Scandinavia, written by Gotthard Johannson, exhibits a promotional strategy for emphasizing 'a unique Scandinavian capacity to bridge opposites, such as shared

Nordic values and national differences, solidarity and individual cause, past and present, living tradition and modernity, home industry and mass production.'[8] Yet, he also points out that Johannson's catalogue copy never addresses Scandinavian things and their qualities 'as concrete, physical entities to be touched, moved around, and used by humans.'[9] This dichotomy is a significant one, for Guldberg indicates that nothing in the catalogue copy approaches the exhibition pieces as designed objects, which is, in an actional sense, what the more than 500,000 North Americans visiting the travelling exhibit saw first: physical entities and their myriad qualities, undeniably articulated as if they were part of a larger, cohesive geographic and cultural whole.

Guldberg asks whether the positive attributes assigned to Nordic design by mavens like Kaufmann concern objects and their objective qualities or apply solely to human beings. He also addresses the question of 'Orientalism' that could be said to be superimposed on these objects from the Scandinavian countries by pointing out that, ironically, it is not American journalists (or anyone else for that matter) constructing the perceived 'otherness' of Scandinavian Design: it is, instead, the Scandinavians themselves creating the term to replace other more nebulous or more country-specific terms, such as Swedish Grace (a term that was popular earlier in the USA but was superseded by Danish Modern as a Scandinavian design phenomenon). In '"Just One of Those Things" – the Design in Scandinavia Exhibition 1954–57,' Harri Kahla illustrates the contextualizing of the exhibition in terms of authenticity, domesticity, and nationalism and regionalism, both in the US and Canadian press, and in Scandinavia.[10] Astrid Skjernen reinforces this point in 'Great Expectations – The Foundation of a Design Concept' when she writes: 'The respective countries' decorative arts were outwardly presented as a whole, or rather, as national parts of a regional whole, which represented a common set of values.'[11] According to Skjernen, Kaufmann and figures like the Italian architect Gio Ponti determined that Scandinavian design offered 'an alternative approach representing a reconciliation of tradition and modernity, intuition and rationality, which to them meant securing human qualities and democracy.'[12] Skjernen's mention of 'tradition and modernity' recalls Henningsen's article of the same name from Kritisk Revy. As discussed in Chapter 2, Henningsen had drawn dividing lines between the adherence to tradition and neo-classicism he loathed and a narrow-minded fealty to Bauhaus demands for machine-driven designs in a forced Modernism, which he believed produced such stylistic failures as chairs that were 'bad to sit in.' In Denmark, Henningsen's arguments from the 1920s represent the inception of a design approach that often involved broader concepts of democracy supposedly achieved by de-classing designs with a task-oriented practicality. The presentation of designed objects in the Design in Scandinavia exhibition feeds well into that overarching narrative. A 1959 House Beautiful article pondering if Scandinavian designed objects will be tomorrow's 'heirlooms' reinforces the narrative that the origins of Nordic Modern design lie in problem-solving in which aesthetics emerge from success (while adding a touch of the 'other' in the use of 'their'): 'Their designing starts with the problem and attempts to solve it in the most direct way. If the solution is inspired enough, it will produce beauty naturally.'[13]

More than likely, it was not talk of democratic societies across the Atlantic that drew so many visitors to the travelling Design in Scandinavia exhibition or that prompted their interest in Scandinavian design. The first draw must have, undoubtedly, been the attraction of what many Americans viewed as 'exotic' designs from an area of the world they surely knew little about at that point. In a 1957 issue of *Print* devoted to Scandinavian graphic design, the editors inform readers that Scandinavia 'is a word like Turkestan or Hind or Zanzibar. It sounds as though it were inhabited by wolves and bears, reindeer and warrior Vikings and, in a romantic sense, it is.'[14] A 1958 *Better Homes and Gardens* article on the Scandinavian 'influence' in home decorating states that Scandinavians 'are just as home-loving as we are' and that 'they buy furniture with state help.'[15] More importantly, what most enhanced Americans' interest in the designs they encountered was probably the aesthetic sensibility already established by the mid-1950s in the United States. Therefore, the argument that what 'they' were offering was something entirely novel is less persuasive than one considering that modernist designs from the Nordic countries fit well into an already familiar mid-century design aesthetic in the US. Organic modern design was not a new concept to most Americans: the first 'Organic Design' exhibition, in which Eero Saarinen and Charles and Ray Eames had shown a series of moulded chairs and settees, had been held in 1940 at MoMA. Biomorphic shapes had already surfaced on myriad surfaces, as in the ceramics of Eva Zeisel and the furniture of George Nelson; streamlining à la Raymond Loewy had introduced a futuristic sense of design; and advances in technology and new materials had already entered the stage of consumer goods. Calder's mobiles were in public spaces, and the sculptural forms of abstract art that so heavily influenced Nordic designers like Juhl and Jacobsen were already in existence. Two immigrants had already been imparting a Danish-trained design aesthetic at American institutions: the cabinetmaker Tage Frid (1915–2004) began teaching woodworking and conservation at the American Crafts Council in 1948, and the silversmith Hans Christensen (1925–1983), who had worked for Georg Jensen, had been teaching at the Rochester Institute of Technology since 1953.

Still, in the rounded silver creations of Henning Koppel, in the curvy glass shapes of Tapio Wirkkala, and in Bruno Matthson's curvilinear steam-bent wood forms, Americans encountered Modernism in what appeared to be a less machine-driven idiom. In other words, this softer, more organic Modernism could not be immediately identified with the German Bauhaus in post-Second World War America. That dichotomy was noticed and employed politically and rhetorically (as will become evident in the next section): by the early 1950s, Elizabeth Gordon, the influential and mercurial editor of *House Beautiful*, had already been on a warpath against Bauhaus Modernism and written paeans to the warm, human designs emanating from Scandinavia. She attacked the Miesian 'less is more' slogan as totalitarian in subtext: 'a social threat of regimentation and total control.'[16] Yet, as Rudolf Arnheim has shown, the affection for curvilinear shapes in mid-century modernist design actually runs across the board from the welded legs of Mies van der Rohe's Barcelona Chair (1929) to Hans Henriksen's concave and convex salt and pepper shakers (1945) to Saarinen's then-futuristic TWA Terminal (1961). Arnheim cites a tension between inner and outer force manifesting itself in designed objects featuring curves, which are ambiguous in their sense of direction, a dynamic physical quality he says 'expresses the continuity of growth.'[17] In other words, the preference for curvilinear shapes is more time- rather than place-specific.

Arts of Denmark

Design in Scandinavia helped to lay the groundwork for a more extensive travelling exhibition of solely Danish arts and crafts, which came to fruition in 1960 in the Arts of Denmark: Viking to Modern exhibition at the Metropolitan Museum of Art. Finn Juhl designed the Arts of Denmark exhibition spaces, and the Danish art historian Erik Lassen curated the exhibition and edited the catalogue – a mix of texts, illustrations, and inventories of objects by time period – that accompanied the exhibition (the graphic and textile artist Rolf Middelboe designed the catalogue's cover). The layout of the catalogue, designed by Søren Sass, provides an excellent example of influencing our mode of experiencing designed objects in the visual articulation of written and two-dimensional representation of designed objects and artefacts. Essays and photographs cover 132 pages, printed on a glossy stock, whereas inventories of objects, divided by time periods, are printed on a thick stock resembling artist's drawing paper. All of that stock is off-white, until the staggered sections in 'Contemporary Fine Arts: Arts and Crafts and Industrial Design,' where the paper is blue. Some 378 contemporary objects are listed not by designer but by studio, factory, or cabinetmaker, followed by a description of the exhibited piece – one of the few times such privileging appeared in print. Three objects from Greenland follow at the end, almost as an afterthought. Throughout the inventory, designers' names appear in a column to the right. For example, stoneware objects are listed as 'Saxbo,' the Danish company's name, whereas the names of ceramic artists such as Nathalie Krebs and Eva Stæhr-Nielsen appear in smaller print to the right. The overall historicizing effect is to unite Viking-age artefacts with contemporary designed objects, the entire narrative framed thematically and visually as a natural and national evolution. In the Contemporary section, a colour photograph of a cubist still life (from 1930) by Vilhelm Lundtsrøm and another of Arne Jacobsen's two-storey Klampenborg row-houses add art and architectural elements that also surface in earlier sections on medieval and renaissance art.

In *Swedish Design: An Ethnography*, Keith M. Murphy discusses the indexicalizing effect of the exhibitionary complex and focuses on object placement to create categories 'with an explicit focus on the national origins of objects . . . [to] provide viewers with a model for identifying what kinds of objects to "flag" as Swedish in everyday life, and which ones, by comparison, are left unmarked.'[18] The same could

Fig. 9.2 Designed by Finn Juhl, the Arts of Denmark: Viking to Modern exhibition (1960–61) presented an array of national artefacts, including Royal Copenhagen porcelain and Georg Jensen silver, along with paintings by Christen Købke (1810–1848). Courtesy of Designmuseum Danmark/The Library

obviously be said for any exhibition with a nationalistic focus privileging selected objects by displaying them but, in the case of the Arts of Denmark's sections on contemporary Danish design, doing so not to relegate them to the museum display case but, rather to suggest their usefulness and application to the viewer as consumer by appealing to assumed aesthetic sensibilities about beauty and function.

In the 'Contemporary Fine Arts' section dealing with arts and crafts and industrial design, the catalogue also offers a time capsule of written statements revealing strong adherence to the standard concepts of Danish Modern design that have manifested themselves in the various texts, statements, and readings discussed throughout this book. In the catalogue's texts, especially an essay by the architect Esbjørn Hiort (1912–1992), who was then director of Den Permanente, and one by Kaufmann, Jr., modern Danish design objects are codified into textual descriptions that both historicize them (not surprising in an historically framed exhibition) and also place them sequentially into the cultural narrative about the development of Danish Modern design. In retrospect, the manner in which each author, in 1960, presents Danish design provides insight into attitudes towards design developments during the previous thirty years in Denmark from both the Danish and the American perspective.

Esbjørn Hiort

In his essay 'Trends in Contemporary Danish Design' (sadly, no translator is provided in the catalogue), Hiort begins by citing Henningsen's journal *Kritisk Revy*, which he calls 'avant-garde,' as formulating the functionalist movement into social and technological contexts. For emphasis, Hiort italicizes modifiers on the major issues presented in the journal, as they appeared on the journal's first cover: *modern* town planning, *social* architecture, *economic* technique, and *honest* industrial design. To Hiort, the move away from historical styles created a 'crisis' that could only be solved by functionalism, which provided an ethical foundation sweeping away prevailing aesthetic standards. Still, he admits that theories of design are in a constant state of flux ('forever changing'), which makes the establishment of fixed standards difficult. Like Wegner and so many others, Hiort reinforces the dilatory nature of industrialism's arrival in Denmark and claims, therefore, that there was more time to transfer the qualities of handcraftsmanship into industrialized production.[19] Klint is then cited as 'the first Danish furniture designer who founded his design on purely rational basis'[20] – once again historicizing Klint as the font of rational design in Denmark (while blithely dismissing his employment of English furniture styles as an aesthetic tool).

Echoing the standard arguments for both the creation of types and the necessity for continuity in change, Hiort describes both Juhl's Chair 45 (1945) and Wegner's Round Chair (1949) as prototypes that have since been recreated and altered, implying that they are serving their modernist purpose adequately. After his opening ode to handicrafts, Hiort then offers a defence of mass production in Denmark specifically because it is based on handicraft traditions, which he believes explains the popularity of Danish design in other countries at this point in time. Despite functionalism's reliance on mass production, Hiort notes that Danish factories are small, resulting in a nebulous borderland between handiwork and industrial methods. Hiort insists that machines can easily produce decorated rubbish because ornamentation hides flaws, whereas modern clean lines hide nothing and must be measured exactly. Thus, he clings to an ideological dichotomy in which aesthetic formalism is preferred over simple functionalism, a dichotomy in which handcraftsmanship remains the barometer by which even factory production should be measured. Rhetorically, employing the notion that it is not solely functionalism driving form once again separates Danish functionalism from *funkis*, an effort that has appeared in the words of Danish designers since Klint first founded the Furniture School at the Royal Danish Academy. Hiort uses Kjærholm's designs as a prime example of this observation because of their mix of materials, handworked woods and woven canes, and industrial steel (the latter of which he ties to Mies van der Rohe and the Bauhaus). Hiort's reference to Kjærholm's 'well-calculated employment of materials'[21] conjures up connotations of mathematical exactitude, returning us to the early modernist concept of appropriate form via measurement. Hiort elevates materials to the primary level in designing, recalling Anni Albers' arguments about the designer taking a passive, secondary role and letting the material dictate the results.

Having probably written his essay in 1959 for publication in the catalogue, Hiort also offers a formula for design in the 1950s: 'to simplify form and at the same time make it more expressive and obtain absolute harmony between form and material.'[22] The use of 'absolute' still implies a longing for an ultimate aesthetic resting on the proper use of material. Hiort proceeds to list a group of contemporary Danish designs that, according to him, have achieved this synthesis: silverware by Magnus Stephensen, Henning Koppel, and Erik Herløw (who had designed the display cases for the Design in Scandinavia exhibition); cooking vessels by Jens Quistgaard (whose designs would help put the home goods store Dansk on the international map); Herbert Krenchel's steel and enamelled 'Krenit' bowls (designed in 1953 and then re-launched in 2014 by Normann-Copenhagen); Jacob E. Bang's glassware for Holmegaard; and, of course, Henningsen's lamps. Hiort unites all of these designs in their lack of ornamentation and indicates that decoration only surfaces in Danish ceramics and textile printing. Henningsen's affection for the influence of Cubism did not transfer, however, to Hiort, who derides early modernist efforts at cubist design as 'today completely without interest (except as style history).'[23] Still, he contextualizes some of these earlier efforts, as in Kay Fisker's bowls and jugs for the silversmith A. Michelsen, as utilitarian stops along the way to subsequent developments. Vibeke Klint, Lis Ahlmann, and Marie Gudme Leth had a number of rugs shown in the Arts of Denmark exhibition, and Hiort observes that it was the textile artists' work in the 1930s that laid the foundation for current collaboration between weavers and factories and their collections of carpets and upholstery and curtain fabrics.

Hiort's 'formula' for a design aesthetic in the 1950s – harmony between simple forms and material sans ornamentation – must have resonated with many of the American design *cognoscenti* at that time. In their book *Tomorrow's House: How to Plan Your Post-War Home* (1945), the designer and theorist George Nelson and Henry Wright, the managing editor at *Architectural Review*, had applauded what they hoped was the fact that 'the Colonial dream is approaching its end . . . A new fashion in homes will be created, and the public will follow.'[24] The American designer T.H. Robsjohn-Gibbings, while still in his modernist phase, reiterated these hopes in his book *Good-bye, Mr. Chippendale* (1944) when he lamented: 'The entire commercial furniture industry had become rotten to the very core by decades of reproducing the antique furniture of Europe and Colonial America . . .'[25] Their arguments were the same: the burgeoning suburban American homes of the 1950s needed modern furnishings to replace these cheap imitations of Colonial furniture. Some of these arguments recall the early European modernists' attempts to convince consumers to abandon their period pieces and embrace the healthiness of living with modern design. Instead of an architect, however, a theorist is now going through the room.

Ultimately, Hiort admits that modern industrial design has started to introduce purism into the arts and crafts: 'Precision and perfection are qualities to be expected in an industrial art product, but the industrial product often lacks the human quality which the individual arts and crafts can have.'[26] In these remarks, Hiort sounds like Herbert Read and his contentions in *Art and Industry* about the value of machine arts to produce works with unfailing precision; yet, whereas Read was willing to abandon handcrafted uniqueness in favour of the aesthetic sensibility he believed was offered by industrial design, Hiort still clings to the 'human quality' of individual craftsmanship. The dichotomy Hiort presents in Denmark concerning the arts is therefore not a simple one between industrially produced goods and handcrafted ones. Instead, he insists that even Danish industrial design preserves a connection to handcrafted traditions in the use of 'right' materials and 'right' construction (more vestiges of appropriateness), whereas the handcraftsmanship of individual artists has become 'freer and more rigorous in design, more intense in its cultivation of textures and more daring in its use of color.'[27] Hiort closes with an apologia for the Danish artists not completely fulfilling the desire for design that would bring objects into 'natural agreement' with the demands of daily life. He also contends that such a goal culturally could never reach any definitive stage, because of the individual artist's yearning to progress to the next stage in artistic development – a comment that actually reveals a break in the notion of ultimate or final form.

Edgar Kaufmann, Jr.

In his catalogue essay 'An American View of the Arts of Denmark and Danish Modern Design,' Kaufmann frames the American reception of the contemporary part of the exhibition. He begins by posing the central question: What is specifically Danish about this design? Kaufmann traces various cultural influences on the Danish arts including the Stone Age, Byzantine arts, Romans, Celts, Vikings, and the Enlightenment. The list adds up to determinist rhetoric that not only frames the Danes' sense of 'values' and their image of 'the good life' but that also unites the various historical arts represented in the exhibition. Thus, to return to Ihde, Kaufmann is thematizing the exhibition by adding the national and cultural distance of an 'American' view of designed objects produced in another country and reflecting that country's history of artifacts. As Ihde points out: 'in some phenomenology, the reflective move is characterized as a move outside or above or distanced from straightforward experience.'[28] When Kaufmann writes that Danes and Americans have 'different practical problems,' he constructs another layer of distance for 'experiencing' the designs in the context of the catalogue. However, his ultimate goal will be to collapse that distance.

Kaufmann defines the period between the two world wars in Denmark as dominated by the theme of pride in craftsmanship shared by both designers and the Danish public. Two illustrations flank this part of the catalogue copy: one of Juhl's settee with Niels Vodder from 1948 (which had appeared in the designer's watercolours for the 1949 Cabinetmakers Guild Exhibition), and Mogens Koch's storage units from 1933. Almost thirty years later, the latter is still presented as a standard of workmanship, but its solid wooden construction also illustrates Kaufmann's next argument: that functionalist Modernism found no resonance in Copenhagen – except with Henningsen. Dragging the agrarian narrative into the discussion, Kaufmann attributes this perceived resistance to functionalism to 'rural' influences trumping industry in a culture where machine art was 'too sensational.' Yet, as we have seen, it was not any outright rejection of functionalist Modernism that drove Danish design after the Stockholm Exhibition of 1930 but, rather, a dialectic with it in which functionalism was not supposed to lapse into a sterile modernist aesthetic (or *funkis*). Kaufmann writes of Henningsen: 'The exception was Poul Henningsen, still today a strong progressive whose famous louvered lamps illuminated that great and short-lived classic of modern interior space, Mies van der Rohe's Tugendhat house in Brno.'[29] Henningsen's lamps may have been designed predominantly with metal diffusers, but they do not represent any embrace of the Bauhaus modernist aesthetic he derided repeatedly in his essays, as in his scathing review of tubular steel furniture in the article, 'Die neue Sachliekeit!' It is a device of guilt-by-association for Kaufmann to mention Mies van der Rohe and his use of PH's lamps in Brno as if both designers were suffering from a bad case of ephemeral styling. Design-wise, no difference exists between Henningsen's countless measurements of the distribution of light in his lamps and, for example, Wegner's detailed studies of sitting before designing a top-rail in wood.

Kaufmann builds on this argument in the next section in which he again constructs a dichotomy between doing something innovative and following the dreaded International Style ('that continued as the accepted Western form of modern design in all the arts'[30]). In a comment reflecting Jacobsen's own split between more organic forms in his furnishings and boxy white Modernism in his buildings, Kaufmann claims Danish furnishing design diverged from the architecture that remained driven by the hyper-rationalism of Le Corbusier's influence. Kaufmann then mentions the same split in Juhl's buildings and furniture designs, and these juxtapositions are undoubtedly evident. These observations lead to Kaufmann's main contention that this dichotomy of interest in modernist styles and adherence to craftsmanship in designed objects explains why Americans are drawn to mid-century Danish design. As his essay progresses, Kaufmann is struggling to erase some of the distance added by experiencing the exhibition via the catalogue; therefore, he begins to thematize the main aims of contemporary Danish design as congruent with American 'values.' In a normative mode, he begins with 'correct' design resting on a notion of quality, proceeds to 'expressive' design involving commercial appeal (one of the few times marketing is mentioned in the entire catalogue), and finishes with 'organic' design blending form, structure, and utility 'into a vivid whole that may be somewhat imperfect but is not frozen in a formula . . .'[31] Kaufmann concludes by suggesting that Americans naturally and traditionally lean towards the latter, an organic design that speaks to both cultures' preference for 'scrupulous craftsmanship.' Kaufmann, who had helped to introduce both Juhl and Wegner to an American audience earlier in the 1950s, had also been a tireless advocate for Nordic design throughout the decade; he used a number of Nordic designs as illustrations in his pamphlets for the Museum of Modern Art. In *What Is Modern Design* (1950), Kaufmann defines design as 'conceiving and giving form to objects used in everyday life' and offers twelve precepts of modern design in a normative list that includes such modernist buzzwords as 'appropriate,' 'a visually satisfactory whole,' and 'avoiding extraneous enrichment.'[32] Along with the designs of Charles and Ray Eames, Mies van der Rohe, and Eero Saarinen, Nordic design appears in Kaufmann's pamphlet in photographs of furniture by Juhl, Aalto, and Bruno Mathsson, along with glass by Aalto, Gunnel Tyvman, and Edvin Öhrström, and lamps by Josef Frank and Henningsen.

Reception

Despite the broad sweep of artefacts from prehistoric times to then-contemporary design in the Arts of Denmark exhibition, modern furnishings garnered the spotlight in the press once the exhibit opened, another indication that Danish Modern as both a concept and a brand had taken hold in North America. Reviewing the show in the *New York Times* (15 October 1960), Sanka Knox commented: 'Spare "Danish Modern," a revolutionary style of furnishings that made its appearance in the Nineteen Twenties, is the star of the long-awaited show . . . To the fervent modernist, the exposition of the short but highly productive reign of "Danish Modern" is reward enough.'[33] Knox proceeds to single out Klint's meticulously measured sideboard as a key piece in the exhibition, and she praises Juhl's designs for the overall installation. In an article in the Metropolitan Museum of Art's own *Bulletin* (December 1960), Rosine Raoul contextualizes the contemporary section of the exhibition as suitable to the overall philosophy of the institution: 'Far from being an innovation in these respects, the Arts of Denmark fits a long and honored tradition at the Museum.'[34] She also places the exhibition's industrial objects into the museum's own efforts to present the 'finest examples' of contemporary industrial design and attaches the contemporary Danish tradition of design to a broader bulwark against poor quality mass production. Her rhetoric presents the entire exhibition, therefore, as public relations for the museum's own design philosophy. Mentioning Juhl, Wegner, Ahlmann, textile weaver Paula Trock, Jacobsen, and glass artist Per Lütken, Raoul insists that the exhibition proves that Danish Modern is 'firmly rooted in a craft tradition of great antiquity.'[35] All of these observations, however self-serving, fit the context for the exhibition established by Denmark's then prime minister, Viggo Kampmann, in his foreword to the Arts of Denmark catalogue: 'in style and intent our work rests on old Danish traditions aiming at the development of a simple and natural vocabulary of form in which the material, whether it is clay, silver, glass or wood, is allowed to retain its intrinsic virtues in the artist's creative hands.'[36]

In 1960, in a nationalist exhibition in which the contemporary objects garnered the most attention, the ideological tension between Modernism and handcraftsmanship that had come to define Danish Modern for the last thirty years remained firmly intact and exploited. Displaying these objects at a venue with such agency as the Metropolitan Museum of Art granted further legitimacy to modernist designs for consumers, and in the United States the results were far-reaching. In Long Beach, California, Frank Brothers' furniture store – an early promoter of many Eames, Nelson, Grossman, Saarinen, and Noguchi designs – held a specifically Danish design exhibition in 1961. Reporting for the *Long Beach Independent* (7 December 1961), Shirley Ray noted: 'the furniture that was displayed on pedestals in the New York Metropolitan Museum one year ago will soon be found in living rooms throughout Southern California.'[37] An intersection had been discovered between the Danish reading of Modernism and the regionalist version that had developed since the 1930s in California, both heavily craft-based if only in origin, a profitable juncture indicative of the wide reach of Danish Modern design by the early 1960s.

Notes

1. See Arndis S. Árnadóttir, 'Iceland towards Scandinavian Design,' in *Scandinavian Design: Beyond the Myth*, ed. W. Halén and K. Wickman (Stockholm: Arvinius Förlag, 2003), 87–92.
2. Kjetil Fallan, 'How an Excavator Got Aesthetic Pretensions – Negotiating Design in 1960s Norway,' *Journal of Design History*, 20(1) (2007), 44.
3. Don Ihde, *Experimental Phenomenology: Multistabilities* (Albany, NY: SUNY Press, 2012), 27.
4. Jørn Guldberg, '"Scandinavian Design" as Discourse: The Exhibition *Design in Scandinavia*, 1954–57,' *Design Issues*, 27(2) (2011), 41–58.
5. Ibid., 41.
6. Kaufmann, Jr., 'Scandinavian Design in the U.S.A.,' *Interiors* (May 1954), 108–14, 182–8.
7. Guldberg, '"Scandinavian Design" as Discourse', 42.
8. Ibid., 49.
9. Ibid., 53.
10. See Harri Kahla, '"Just One of Those Things"' – the Design in Scandinavia Exhibition 1954–57,' in *Scandinavian Design: Beyond the Myth*, ed. W. Halén and K. Wickman (Stockholm: Arvinius Förlag, 2003), 67–76.
11. Astrid Skjernen, 'Great Expectations – the Foundation of a Design Concept,' in *Scandinavian Design: Beyond the Myth*, ed. W. Halén and K. Wickman (Stockholm: Arvinius Förlag, 2003), 27.
12. Ibid., 27–28.
13. 'Why will such things be heirlooms tomorrow,' *House Beautiful* 101 (July 1959), 53. No author listed, but probably editor Elizabeth Gordon.
14. *Print*, ed. by Ellison and Frank Lieberman, 10(6) (December/January, 1957), 15.
15. Florence Byerly, 'Scandinavia,' *Better Homes and Gardens*, 36(5) (1958), 58.
16. Elizabeth Gordon, 'The Threat to the Next America,' *House Beautiful*, 95 (April 1953), 126–29.
17. Rudolf Arnheim, 'The Dynamics of Shape,' *Design Quarterly*, 64 (1966), 18.
18. Keith M. Murphy, *Swedish Design: An Ethnography* (Ithaca, NY: Cornell University Press, 2015), 186.
19. Hiort would face a crisis early in his tenure (1959–68) as leader of Den Permanente, when the permanent exhibition of Danish Arts and Crafts and Industrial Design decided to start showing factory-produced furniture, much to the chagrin of the Cabinetmakers

Guild. In 1963, the majority of the cabinetmakers left Den Permanente in protest and opened their own showroom.

20. Hiort, 'Trends in Contemporary Danish Design,' in *The Arts of Denmark: Viking to Modern*, ed. E. Lassen (Copenhagen: Det Berlingske Bogtrykkeri, 1960), 120.

21. Ibid., 124.

22. Ibid.

23. Ibid., 127.

24. George Nelson and Henry Wright, *Tomorrow's House: How to Plan Your Post-War Home* (New York: Simon & Schuster, 1945), 6.

25. T.H. Robsjohn-Gibbings, *Good-bye, Mr. Chippendale* (New York: Alfred Knopf, 1944), 6.

26. Hiort, 'Trends in Contemporary Danish Design,' 130.

27. Ibid., 132.

28. Ihde, *Experimental Phenomenology: Multistabilities*, 27.

29. Edgar Kaufmann, Jr., 'An American View of the Arts of Denmark and Danish Modern Design,' in *The Arts of Denmark: Viking to Modern*, ed. E. Lassen (Copenhagen: Det Berlingske Bogtrykkeri, 1960), 105.

30. Ibid., 106.

31. Ibid.

32. Edgar Kaufmann, Jr., *What Is Modern Design* (New York: Museum of Modern Art, 1950), 7.

33. Sanka Knox, 'Long-Awaited Museum Show Opens,' *New York Times* (15 October 1960) [http://timesmachine.nytimes.com/timesmachine/1960/10/15/119111867.html?pageNumber=14; accessed 16 March 2015].

34. Rosine Raoul, 'The Danish Tradition in Design,' *The Metropolitan Museum of Art Bulletin*, 19(4) (1960), 119–23.

35. Ibid.

36. Viggo Kampmann, 'Foreword,' in *The Arts of Denmark: Viking to Modern*, ed. E. Lassen (Copenhagen: Det Berlingske Bogtrykkeri, 1960), 7–8.

37. Shirley Ray, 'Danish Furniture Display New Here,' *Long Beach Independent* (7 December 1961), 86.

10 Viking Bracelets and Steampunk Eggs: Invariance or Timelessness?

'If a design is timeless,' the polymath designer Nanna Ditzel (1923–2005) once observed, 'it is never relevant.'[1] At the age of twenty, and after only a year of study as an apprentice cabinetmaker at both Richards Skole and Copenhagen's Tekniske Skole (Technical College), Ditzel became one of the first women (one of her classmates was Grethe Jalk) accepted to Kunsthåndværkerskolens Snedkerdagskole (the Cabinetmakers Day School at the School of Arts and Crafts) in Copenhagen. Among Ditzel's mentors were Aksel Bender Madsen, Peter Koch, Ejner Larsen, the painter Victor Isbrand, and the team of Orla Mølgaard-Nielsen and Peter Hvidt (who were both also educated at the Cabinetmakers Day School). Mølgaard-Nielsen had also studied under Klint at the Furniture School of the Royal Danish Academy. While studying under her subject leaders Mølgaard-Nielsen and Hvidt, Ditzel had to investigate Klint's sideboard from 1929, an object frequently alluded to as emblematic of measuring one's way to the perfect or ultimate form because of its capacity to hold exactly twelve full place settings of dinnerware and silverware. Ditzel's response was to design the same sideboard half as deep. 'That way it would not take up as much space,' she explained, 'and you could find things in it. Klint's sideboard was 56 centimetres deep, so that two stacks of plates could stand, one behind the other, which I thought was impractical.'[2] Ditzel's comment indicates an approach she would apply to many of her designs, eventually pushing the limits of Danish Modern into more innovative territory involving the use of new technologies and materials, such as laminates, fibreglass, and foam. In 1944, after only one year of studying at the Cabinetmakers Day School, she and her first husband Jørgen Ditzel (1921–1961) exhibited living room furniture at that year's Cabinetmakers Guild Exhibition. The following year she would add auditing classes at Klint's Furniture School to her weighty schedule. Hanne Horsfeld comments that Ditzel found Klint's teaching 'very laborious' but also a springboard for 'a break with conventions, and thereby also with the Klintian school.'[3] At this time, Ditzel tended to take inspiration from more international currents, including the Italian magazine *Domus*, which she read in the library of Designmusem Danmark (the location of the School of Arts and Crafts), and the designs of Gió Ponti.

In 1952, the Ditzels designed a range of children's plywood furniture for Knud Willadsen Møbelsnedkeri, and at this time Ditzel also became the first woman to design jewellery for Georg Jensen. A hanging wicker chair designed in 1957 became one of the prime examples of late Danish mid-century Modernism, and another line of solid-wood children's furniture for Kolds Savværk spawned a wooden high chair (1955) that became ubiquitous for decades in Denmark. Ditzel hobnobbed with fellow Danish designers Panton and Gunnar Aagaard Andersen, sharing with them an envelope-pushing approach to design, one moving Modernism back into a contemporary context while not completely abandoning certain approaches towards materials and function. Like Panton, in the 1960s, she embraced Pop-art colours and altered states of repose accomplished through the use of synthetic materials and multi-level seating and lounging arrangements, allowing user involvement in coordination and placement. Ditzel also left Denmark for an extended period and lived in England from 1968 to 1986 before returning to run her own design studio.

Ditzel's remark about design being irrelevant if it is timeless is more than simply provocative. Her statement also offers a pointed commentary on the standard narrative that Danish Modern design is 'classic' or 'timeless,' a claim that has even been applied to Ditzel's own designs. In *Scandinavian Modern Design: 1880–1980*, a book accompanying an exhibition of pan-Nordic design at the Cooper-Hewitt Museum of Design, a picture of a silver bracelet Ditzel designed for Georg Jensen in 1956 is captioned: 'The simplicity of design, merging traditional and contemporary aesthetics, makes this bracelet timeless.'[4] The bracelet's form is undoubtedly arresting: it combines a simple circular interior with an oval exterior ending in two points (Fig. 10.1). According to Horsfeld, the design was inspired by ancient jewellery Ditzel had seen at the National Museum in Helsinki, Finland. Thus, it would seem then that two times – rather than no time or all times – exist in Ditzel's bracelet design: Viking Age artefact and a modern re-reading of that shape. Yet, a shape from a former millennium has surfaced in a design from 1956 and is just as usable in the twenty-first century as it was in the mid-twentieth-century. Chances are it will fit on someone's wrist 100 years from now as well. A tacit third time also

Fig. 10.1 Nanna Ditzel was inspired by both Viking and Modern influences when designing this silver bracelet (1956) for Georg Jensen. Courtesy of Designmuseum Danmark/The Library

exists in Ditzel's bracelet design, a time that exists for any design still in use: the now of its reception.

In 2006, Penny Sparke, the Dean of Faculty of Art, Design and Music at Kingston University in London, gave a talk titled 'Danish Modern Design Revisited' at the Museum of Modern Art in New York. The thrust of Sparke's lecture was the response of contemporary Danish designers to the overarching tradition of modern Danish design from the mid-twentieth century. Sparke separated her talk into sections, and in the first, 'Designs of the Past and Present,' she traced the development of the concept of Danish Modern to help listeners understand what she referred to as the design values of the movement. Along the way, she touched upon the major threads that have run through both the history of Danish Modern design and the articulation of it by both design historians and designers: the emphasis on craftsmanship, the refinement of types, and the fealty to the logic of materials. Sparke cited the government bodies that helped to market and support Danish design. She also alluded to issues of continuity and change, as in Wegner's refinements of existing forms, while she emphasized themes familiar to modern design historians: 'Rooted in the past, Danish Modern design sought, nonetheless, to embrace modern life and to align itself with the principles of rationalism, humanism, and democracy.'[5] Sparke also mentioned the efforts of manufacturers to strategize the survival of their products for longevity, and she reinforced the designs' 'timelessness,' based on aesthetic simplicity and quality of craftsmanship.

Claims of 'timeless designs' and 'timeless classics' have been employed for decades when describing myriad forms of design, but they have found particular traction when applied to mid-twentieth-century designs. As early as 1949, the American manufacturer Modernline (now Modern Line) advertised its line of home furnishings as 'timeless modern.' Yet, as vapid as the use of 'timeless' to describe design may seem, as much of an empty piece of marketing copy as it may sound, dismissing timeless claims as meaningless leaves one with the nagging question of why certain designs endure so long past the time in which they first appeared. Much of this problem rests on a misconception of a sense of invariance resulting from linguistic confusion. Whatever the phrase 'timeless design' may mean, it has nothing to do with metaphysics: one can immediately dismiss the notion that modernist designs, or any other designs from any period, are floating around in some metaphysical Never-Land of beauty making them resistant to the whims of time and taste. Designs of material culture are not like Platonic notions of numbers detached from any reliance on temporality. Designs always exist in time, but some are more resistant to the passing of time or to simply being located in or attached to a specific time. George Nelson has observed: 'There are any number of forms which have persisted virtually unchanged over centuries and even millennia.'[6] Ditzel's bracelet illustrates that point. As forms that continue to pass the horizon of their original reception, designs are bound to varying degrees to the meanings assigned to them at any given time – but they are never completely bound to them because users can continue to interact with each design in another context and another time. The self is always finding new ways to define itself, and objects of material culture can abet that endeavour in different ways at different times.

In the case of modernist design from the twentieth century, while it is contingent on the circumstance of human history and fashion, *some* of it appears less bound to a specific time partially (and maybe even primarily) because the restriction of ornament can de-historicize a designed object (not elevate it to a metaphysical level). A Louis XIV Chair, with its intricate carvings inspired by imagery from mythology, flora, fauna, and architecture, and its ornately patterned upholstery, seems visually to exist in a time far removed from our own – the seventeenth century. On the other hand, the Shaker furniture that inspired so many twentieth-century designers did so specifically for its quietude and ease of adaptability to another time; its visual language was elliptical, bordering on mute. A ladder-back transfers easily to even the most contemporary chair design without anyone looking at it and making associations with an eighteenth-century religious sect. The relentless appearance of Thonet's Chair No. 14 (1859) rests predominantly on its simple bentwood forms imparting a quality of visual transference in which it becomes difficult to project temporal associations. The simple chair, an example of industrial production and organic wood in machine-rendered curves, has become ubiquitous in the 2000s, when it often appears painted in myriad colours. How can one deny the invariance of a design produced in the mid-1800s yet so detached from the time of its inception that designers continue to employ it in variegated settings? Henningsen, Le Corbusier, Kjærholm – numerous modernist designers and architects referred to the chair as a touchstone of craftsmanship. None of these observations imply that the Thonet chair, Shaker designs, Viking bracelets, or any other designs for that matter, will maintain their effect in the distant future. However, their relative invariance indicates that marketing cannot exert complete control over the future or the ongoing reception of designed objects.

The Italian-American designer Massimo Vignelli (1931–2014), whose designs with his wife Lella (1934–) spanned graphic design and corporate identity to furniture and architecture, once defined the difference between design he deemed 'timeless' and passing trends as the presence in the latter of vulgarity and greed in an absence of intellectual elegance: 'you train yourself to be disciplined and you train yourself to stay away from trends. And in a sense you get automatically involved into the notion of timelessness, so it takes a long time.'[7] As numerous manifestos, books, and articles indicate, the striving for timelessness and the use of the same appellation are endemic to theoretic developments in Modernism. One can dismiss marketing rhetoric as empty and superimposed, but the issue of timelessness was not a marketing tool to twentieth-century modernist thinkers determined to draw a line between fashion and design. As Fallan observes, the very inception of modernist ideology constituted an effort to make 'modern' a distinct concept from transient contemporary design; and Vignelli's words offer yet another reflection of that effort, however romantic or normative. In Denmark, when Henningsen insisted that only design bearing the stamp of its own time lives forever, he was struggling, already in the 1920s, to be 'modern' sans ephemeral styling. His early allusion to the Thonet chair in his journal *Kritisk Revy* is another example of that endeavour.

Marketing narratives

In the case of Danish Modern, numerous designs first produced predominantly between 1930 and 1960 have managed to survive, remaining in production for more than half a century; a number of designs went out of production only to be put back into production later – many in the past ten years as Danish manufacturers such as Carl Hansen & Søn and Fritz Hansen find a new audience for old designs by Jalk, Jacobsen, Wegner, and Juhl. That this is a marketing effort to sell a larger line of furniture is undeniable: furniture companies are in the business of making money and wise strategies have kept a number of them in business. Yet, legions of designs from all over the world have been marketed since 1930, and the majority of them have passed into oblivion. In the marketing narratives surrounding twentieth-century Danish design, its development and the claims of quality and endurance that have accompanied those narratives through more than half a century, the notion of furniture design being timeless runs deep. Hansen also locates the source of these notions in the attempt by certain designers to discover the perfect or most appropriate version of a design – an approach that manifests itself throughout the history of modern design. Certain Danish designers then became marketed as brands, according to Hansen, and none of these names comes as any surprise: Jacobsen, Juhl, Wegner, and Mogensen. While this reading accurately dissects the commercial aspect of branding designs as timeless, it rests heavily on an economic reading that never seems to address endurance beyond marketing to the elite (or the would-be elite). Valuations of designed objects, of any commodity, are not solely dependent on economics or marketing but on numerous factors, including need and desire, or else all valuations by all people towards the same object would be the same at any given time.[8] Designs become consonant with users in ways no designer, manufacturer or marketer can predict or control completely.

In 'Markets, Marketing and Design: The Danish furniture industry c. 1947–65,' Kevin Davies sees the designers whose names have become synonymous with Danish Modern as mere tools in the marketing of furniture. While discussing the furniture manufacturer Johannes Hansen, for example, Davies focuses on the firm's pride in the size of its export market, whereas the work that Wegner did for Johannes Hansen is reduced to a remark Wegner once made about keeping up with the demand for new designs at the Cabinetmakers Guild Exhibitions as an indication of nothing but profit interest: 'I drew it and Johannes Hansen made it.'[9] The entire quote, however, contextualizes Wegner's remark not as an admission of purely commercial intent but rather as an observation that neither he nor Johannes Hansen expected any great sales to result from the exhibitions. Wegner proceeds to say: 'We were happy if we could sell the chairs we made for the exhibition. That was as far as our hopes went.'[10] Davies' rhetorical move reflects a pattern of delimiting the act of designing furnishings in an attempt to preference the marketing of designs as the sole explanation for their success. An example occurs in his discussion of Wegner's variants (1944) on the Chinese Chair the designer had studied at the end of his two years at the Kunsthåndværkerskole: Davies points to the bloated copy in a catalogue that accompanied Wegner's designs in which a photograph appeared of five historical Chinese chairs, with mannequins dressed in eighteenth-century costume as Danish merchants, framing Wegner's new designs as having an artistic character resulting from the designer's painstaking research. Accompanying that illustration is a picture of his four versions of the Chinese Chair and one Wishbone, a further distillation of the form (Fig. 10.2). The catalogue's copy reads: 'It is this purposeful search for a form and an expression to match the aesthetic and functional demands of a new time and also to meet the requirements of its productive technique, that when the effort has been successful justifies the designation "classical."'[11] This contorted copy borders on humorous, and Davies aptly frames it as blatant marketing discourse. Yet, the history of Wegner's work on those chairs is not simply a promotional fabrication: the marketing copy, however fatuous, is based on Wegner's actual work, an effort resting heavily on the designer reworking the curved Chinese top-rail into more contemporary forms. Davies also places the 'adaptation of tradition by modernity' under the aegis of 'sales discourse,'[12] but as this book has hopefully illustrated, from Henningsen's to Anni Albers's to Max Bill's arguments, adapting tradition for current times was simply a major ideological effort by modernist thinkers, whether successful or not. It comprises one piece in the development of their design sense, especially in Denmark where, in early modern designs, there was initially less effort to reject the past wholeheartedly. The fact that Carl Hansen & Søn, whose success rests primarily on Wegner's designs, continues to open new showrooms, that the Wishbone has remained in continuous production since 1950, and that two of Wegner's other Chinese variants also remain in production has nothing to do with the bloviating copy in a sales catalogue foisted on the public in the 1950s.

Viewed as a designed object rather than an exploited image in a marketing brochure, Wegner's Y-stolen (the Wishbone, 1949) offers a useful starting point for a discussion of invariance, rather than timelessness, in design. After 2010, the chair began to appear in a wide range of colours: although Wegner embraced certain colours, especially orange and green, one can only imagine how the designer might have reacted to seeing the solid wood frame of his chair painted mint or lavender.[13] Structurally, the object remains as originally designed with its split backrest, turned legs, curved top-rail, and woven seat; that is, it maintains its modernist silhouette. Yet, its colour options address not only changes in fashion but the more contemporary desire for users to involve themselves in design decisions. To return to Bill's arguments about continuity and change, the coloured Wishbone provides consumers with a form redolent of the time in which it was produced while not appearing so retro in design that it becomes impossible to extract it from looking like something nostalgic. Simultaneously, making these designs available in contemporary colours opens the design further to current demands without altering the chair's form beyond recognition,

Fig. 10.2 Particularly in its top-rail, Wegner's Wishbone Chair (1949) was a more abstract variant of its historical antecedent in his family of Chinese chairs. It has remained in production since 1949 and in recent years become his most visible design. The various components of the chair also appear on the wall in this press photo. Photo courtesy of Carl Hansen & Søn

while also exorcising some of the normative quality often projected onto modernist design. Whether rendered in wood or colours, the use of the chair in contemporary settings without reference to the mid-century or even to Danish design in general reinforces its invariance – the only reliable meaning of calling a design 'timeless.' None of these observations indicate that the Wishbone will be a viable design at any point in the future or that it possesses time-resistant, metaphysical qualities. Asked how the designers had created the Danish 'style,' Wegner once dismissed the idea of there even being any specific style: 'it really was nothing of the sort. It was rather a continuous process of purification and for me a simplification, to cut down to the simplest possible elements of four legs, a seat and a combined top-rail and arm rest.'[14]

Modern/retro/contemporary

Danish Modern in whatever way one looks at it – as a historical style, as a philosophical approach, as a design aesthetic – has proven relatively resilient. In a contemporary context, it has been surprisingly agile at fitting into different contexts, regardless of how much they rest on home furnishings as status symbols or how superimposed they are on the designs. When a minimalist-designed tea house in Japan opens and fills its atmospheric spaces with Wegner's Wishbone chairs in oak, it indicates the contemporizing of Danish design from the mid-twentieth century. The chairs serve no nostalgic purpose; they offer no contrast or historical intrusion on the designed space, nor do they convey any messages about social engineering. In Riga, Latvia, i'Bar, a combination Apple product store and functioning café and bar that opened in 2015, used Wegner's Round Chair in a contemporary setting of exposed and white-painted brick, reclaimed wood, and track and industrial lighting. Steampunk versions of Jacobsen's Egg Chair adorn an atrium in the Neiman Marcus department store in Scottsdale, Arizona (Fig. 10.3). These employments of Danish Modern design in contemporary spaces migrate the designs out of the twentieth century and away from the narratives of their beginnings: except for the design-conscious, no one would look at the designs and know they were dated or view them in these planned environments and think of democratic efforts in design, cabinetmaker narratives, or the Klint Furniture School and its legacy of measurement. These contemporary variants also resist the reading of mid-century design as museum artefacts by offering the consumer some new physical quality to further de-historicize them or by placing them in settings reflecting similar finishes and materials, thus weaving historical design into the now, a post-postmodern design strategy. Any narratives about modernist efforts at atemporal design are also exorcised in these contemporary usages of Danish designs from the mid-twentieth century.

On the other hand, Danish Modern has also been embraced as an integral part of the retro design movement clinging to the mid-twentieth-century aesthetic as nostalgia. Much of this approach reflects a mythologizing of mid-twentieth-century design movements in which contradictions – such as the fact that many consumers

Fig. 10.3 Steampunk versions of Jacobsen's Egg Chair adorn the atrium at Neiman Marcus department store in Fashion Square, Scottsdale, Arizona. Photo by the author

in the 1950s and 1960s rejected modernist furnishings while clinging to historical styles, inherited antiques, and inexpensive reproductions – are conveniently ignored or at times derided. In addition, the ethical dimensions of the modernist thinkers' numerous tomes are also banished in this narrative as the focus becomes, instead, purely aesthetic: the look of Modernism, not any of its meanings, is preserved. Cara Greenburg's *Mid-Century Modern: Furniture of the 1950s* appeared in 1984 and helped to solidify not only the term 'mid-century modern' but also the pervasive view of the revived design aesthetic that would begin to take hold within the next decade. Greenberg drew a line between what she deemed the 'screaming kitsch' of the decade and 'the fine good taste of the Danes, the fabulous flamboyance of the Italians, and the technical wizardry of the Americans.'[15] Giò Ponti's Superleggera Chair (1957) is referred to as 'timeless' because of its resemblance to 'another timeless classic, the American Shaker chair,'[16] somehow combining all Shaker chairs into one generic design. Numerous websites and books dealing specifically with Danish Modern historically or contextualizing it into the romanticized framework of mid-century design – as part of the Populuxe era, as part of the 1950s 'space age' aesthetic, or fetishized as emblematic of the 'innocence' of suburban-American mid-century living – sustain these readings of Danish Modern furnishings. Some of this affiliation is surprisingly ironic, as the bourgeois mid-century consumer setting seems ill suited to designs that have become exorbitant luxury items.

Many historians cite the appearance of Wegner's *Runde Stol* (the Round Chair; the Chair) on the cover of the American magazine *Interiors* in 1950 as the inception of international, or at least North American, fame for Danish Modern as a design aesthetic. The Danish immigrant Jens Risom (1916–) had already brought his Kunsthåndværkerskole-educated sensibilities to the American furnishings market when he designed the first line of furniture sold by Knoll in the early 1940s (the company with its Bauhaus-driven aesthetic was founded by Florence and Hans Knoll in 1938). In a discussion of neo-modernist design efforts veering towards nostalgia, Espen Johnson defines retro-Modernism as 'a commercial strategy and a tendentious fad for several semi-talented designers, often resulting in a dry, uncritical repetition of a modernist formal language devoid of any novelty.'[17] Retro readings of Danish Modern involve distance and perception, often contextualizing designs from Denmark within the nostalgia for mid-century American popular consumer culture. Marketing can also abet mid-century designs from being trapped in a retro-modern paradigm: Per Lütken's glass bowl for Holmegaard from 1955 was originally called the Arne Bowl (after Holmegaard's then-director Arne Boas) but today is sold as the Provence Bowl, a name not only separating it from its time of origin but from even being Danish. Retro readings can also be employed for visual juxtaposition: in 2014, two of Juhl's Pelican chairs (1940), a chunky upholstered design that looks anything but contemporary, greeted visitors to the Copenhagen showroom of the Danish flooring company Dinesen, with its subdued palette of greys and muted steely blues.

The modern home furnishings store Hip, located in Portland, Oregon, ran an ad in 2015 showing a half-frontal view of Wegner's two-part Shell Chair (1963): the half smile of its moulded laminated wood seat and two of its three double-laminated legs occupy most of the ad. The copy tells readers: 'Impress yourself. Get Hip.' The ad also mentions 'losing yourself in the simplicity of a sofa' and 'letting a chair take you far away.' What does not appear anywhere in the ad, however, is the name of the chair or its designer or any reference to it being 'Danish.' The ad is emblematic of the way many of the mid-twentieth-century objects of Danish Modern exist for today's consumers, especially millennials: Wegner's chair has been stripped of its designer name, of any national association, and thereby of any of the narrative weight that its historical background might carry. For a generation raised on the global and heightened design aesthetic of Apple, where form basically trumps function and design is first and foremost a statement, allusions to aged design developments are relegated to design history or ironic reworking in new forms. Wegner's Shell Chair, as it appears in Hip's ad, is de-historicized and reduced to the very trait the modernists had struggled ideologically and aesthetically to avoid, a style, a style of chair that can fit into a contemporary idea of what it means to be modern sans the burden of history. Timeless has instead become time-less.

The appellation 'Danish Modern,' as well as the broader 'Danish Design,' has suffered highs and lows since the 1960s – even in Denmark. In 2002, the article 'Dansk design slidt i betrækket' ('Thread-worn Danish Design') appeared in *Politiken* and sounded yet another premature death knell for Danish Design. In the article, the writer

Nina Kragh argued that the term Danish Design had become worn out, diluted, and applied recklessly to anything Danish, regardless of quality, and she noted that certain Danish companies, such as the textile manufacturer Kvadrat and the audio giant Bang & Olufsen, were no longer marketing themselves as specifically Danish. In comments quoted in the article, Jacob Holm, the administrative director of Fritz Hansen, the manufacturer of Arne Jacobsen's designs, also distanced the company (which continues to use designers from Italy, Germany, and elsewhere) from defining itself as Danish: 'We have no special need to focus on the fact that we're Danish. If you go back to the 1970s, it undoubtedly had meaning. But not today.'[18] However, a dichotomy emerges in the commentary between the poorer-quality pine-wood furniture made in Denmark, dismissed as 'rubbish' that cannot compete with other cheaply produced furniture from Russia, and 'designer furniture.' The subhead beneath the article's headline reinforces this bifurcation: 'The style spans from the Egg and the Ant to cheap trash made of pine-wood.' Despite everything else being said about abandoning marketing that relies on promoting 'Danish-ness,' Keld Korsager, an editor for the Danish furniture industry's main journal, *Danske Møbler*, observed that it is, nevertheless, designer furniture from Denmark that will carry them into the next decade, 'because even though it only makes up 15 percent of the collective revenue in the industry, it still provides our identity, along with the largest profits.'[19]

At one point in the article, the design magazine *Wallpaper*, which had recently done an eighty-page spread on Denmark, is faulted for focusing on Danish Design as 'retro,' indicating that this is a thematizing that contemporary Danish designers resist. These laments expose the weight of the terms Danish Modern and Danish Design because of their continued association with mid-twentieth-century Modernism. Hansen has discussed this irony at length, particularly from a business standpoint in which the 'definitiveness' of Danish Modern design from the mid-twentieth century serves as a straightjacket on innovation and progression: 'it is telling that the furniture that a small group of furniture designers created in the years from ca. 1945 to ca. 1960 still represents the finest symbols of Danish furniture design.'[20] For Hansen, the very narrative constructed by those who promoted and marketed Danish Modern as a brand became a hindrance to advancement once the initial heyday of Danish design had passed.

Sparke reinforces this view in her observation that 'the shadow cast by the heroic designers of the 1940s and 1950s . . . made it difficult for the next generation to do anything except maintain the momentum of the status quo . . . in a somewhat diluted form.'[21] While addressing the more contemporary (in 2006) response to the legacy of Danish Modern design, Sparke paraphrases the words of designer Kasper Salto (the grandson of the ceramicist Axel Salto), who believed that 'timelessness' was achieved by expressing the essence of one's time – a thought echoing Henningsen's similar contention almost a century earlier. Salto was trained as a cabinetmaker at the Danish Design School, but his Ice Chair (2002), a combination of synthetic materials and aluminium, is the first chair to be manufactured by Fritz Hansen that is fit for outside use. Salto's Guest Chair (2014), a padded stool designed with Thomas Sigsgaard, has a metal base that detaches and folds up to be stored inside the seat, enabling the entire stool to be stowed in minimal space on a shelf. In these design innovations, modernist notions about functionality and simplicity have transferred to contemporary usage. Salto's neo-modernist designs resist the retro trap by being novel in numerous ways (structure, usage) while still leaning on modernist narratives about materials and design. Thus, the cabinetmaker narrative that, especially in Denmark, has weighed heavily on designers since the 1960s is minimalized in technological innovations erasing the tension between industrial art and applied art.

That tension had already been surfacing when designs began to become factory-produced, as in Grete Jalk's laminated chair (1963), with its ribbon-like folds inspired by the steam-bent wood designs of Aalto and Eames (Fig. 10.4). The initial response

Fig. 10.4 Only 300 copies of Grete Jalk's moulded plywood chair, laminated here in teak, were manufactured when it was introduced in 1963. Despite winning first prize in a competition held by the *Daily Mirror* in London, it was forty years before it went into full production. Photo courtesy Lange Production

towards her now-considered 'classic' laminated wood chair, manufactured by Poul Jeppesen, was not entirely positive. Writing about her laminated wood experiments in the journal *Dansk kunsthaandværk* in 1963, Salicath praised her designs (a set of nesting tables with the same base had also been designed to accompany the chair) in what he referred to as 'twisting wood' as 'not involving twisting the brain to find something new to satisfy the press and the commercial market's continued hunt for new things.'[22] However, addressing what is now known as the GJ Chair – only 300 copies were originally manufactured and it took forty years before going into full production – Salicath adds that the chair 'was not completely convincing . . . but was an extremely interesting experiment.'[23] Finding the chair's form 'unclear and dissonant,' particularly at the riveted points of attachment, Salicath could not refrain from also wryly alluding to the handcraftsmanship narrative while discussing Jalk's origami-like construction: 'it illustrates how important it is that the furniture industry, which has taken so much from handicrafts, proceeds with these experiments, if the same industry will not settle for merely eating the bread of charity from handicraft's generous hand.'[24]

Ditzel had been taking an innovative approach for decades before her death in 2005, a further indication of her resistance, as indicated in her quote, towards the spectral image of timeless design. With its fan-shaped back, her laminated-plywood and steel *Trinidad-stolen* (Trinidad Chair, 1993) recalls the previous metal and wood efforts of Wegner – as in his armchair JH701 (1965) – but she based the close row of slits in the backrest and seat design on fretwork she saw on Victorian homes in Trinidad (Fig. 10.5). The ornament, which bears no use-function, was also made possible in Denmark by the appearance of a computer-controlled, four-axle milling cutter. In a 2005 interview, Ditzel explained: 'we decided to make an industrial chair – one that could be mass produced and one that many people could buy.'[25] Technological advancement and design merged, as they did for Jacobsen's moulded forms in the 1950s, but the use of a Victorian-inspired motif illustrates how far from modernist anti-historicist and anti-ornamentation tenets Danish design had moved by the 1990s – even for a designer trained in the bastions of mid-twentieth-century joinery. Also, any notion of the manufactured Trinidad Chair, which is still in production, being democratic or simply financially accessible is undercut by the fact that in 2015 it cost more than $600.

The long arm of handcraftsmanship from modernist ideology continues to pervade Danish design, even for a contemporary designer such as Louise Campbell (1970–), whose work has included lighting, furniture, and dinnerware. Campbell's stainless-steel cutlery (2014) for Georg Jensen is advertised in terms fairly dripping with modernist narratives: the copy on Campbell's website informs readers that when making the prototypes, 3-D modelling was abandoned for handwork; the website also tells visitors that 'the aim was to create a beautiful set of cutlery, but function has come first, and any unnecessary ornamentation has been avoided.'[26] In this instance, the modernist formula remains the same: aesthetic simplicity emerges from de-ornamentation resulting in beauty. In her chairs for the Danish company Hay, a

Fig. 10.5 Ditzel's Trinidad Chair (1993) returned ornament to the concept of Danish Modern: its fretwork also reflects a technological advancement in the use of a computer-controlled four-axle milling cutter. Photo courtesy of Frederica Furniture A/S

manufacturer that has found a way to ameliorate the burden of mid-century Modernism and exploit the legacy in new products, Campbell illustrates contemporary ways to transfer the strong functional narrative into technologically innovative designs. In her Spider Woman Chair (2004; launched 2009), for example, she has employed a laser-cut deep-pressed steel shell and frame, rubber-coated and rendered in an asymmetrical pattern. Functionally, the chair stacks and is usable both inside and outside, but its ornamental asymmetrical pattern flies in the face of the Danish modernist aesthetic in chair design.

Many of the notions of timelessness ascribed to Danish mid-century designs prove to be anything but national or singular upon closer inspection. One curious example occurs in the evolution of T.H. Robsjohn-Gibbings (1905–1976), the British-American designer whose career paralleled the evolution of Danish modernist design. Robsjohn-Gibbings was a long-time promoter of 'timelessness' in design, and he reinforced these notions in his polemical writings in which he used the French term *sans époque* to describe his own designs. James Buresh has traced the development of that concept in the designer's work and writings, but the basic premise sounds remarkably like many of Klint's contentions.[27] The main difference is that whereas both men embraced the study of, rather than the dismissal of, historical styles and the belief that modern solutions could emerge from that study, Robsjohn-Gibbings also transferred decorative motifs from his historical prototypes. He viewed using ancient Greek styles as an essential element towards defying temporality in design, while lauding the Greek *klismos* chair as exemplary and a prime example of timelessness. As Buresh notes, he 'consistently maintained – and proselytized – that contemporary design should be grounded in an understanding of the past.'[28] Also like Klint, the designer believed such an approach would serve as a bulwark against the fickle nature of fashion, constructing the same dialectic as many of the Danish modernists. Elizabeth Gordon also championed Robsjohn-Gibbings's designs in *House Beautiful*, and her rhetoric sounds strikingly similar to her positive commentary on Nordic design: the words democratic, classics, and even functionalist are applied. By 1951, his designs, especially those for Widdicomb Furniture Company, were articulated as an antidote to what some design mavens believed was ailing modern design. Before long, Robsjohn-Gibbings, still clinging to classical precedents as timeless, also abandoned Modernism as an aesthetic, and in his sardonic book *Home of the Brave* (1954) he conveniently accused the growing international style of 'anonymity and impersonality.'

John Heskett, addressing the way in which designs migrate beyond their designers' intentions, observed that although the designed object is created with specific uses in mind, one must be wary of placing too much emphasis on the designer's intentions: 'These can be undermined or even reversed in the processes of use by people's infinite capacity pragmatically to adapt objects to purposes other than those originally intended.'[29] The same could be said for the intentions of marketers and critics at any given time: they are often projections on and re-readings of designs that can be easily ignored or discarded in one's interaction with or personal valuation of the designed object. Claims of timelessness will probably not abate simply because of changes in taste or economies; however, to paraphrase Keats, some designed objects are, at best, the foster children of time.

Notes

1. Quoted on the Maharam website [http://www.maharam.com/stories/nanna-ditzel-hallingdal-65; accessed 2 April 2015].

2. Quoted in Hanne Horsfeld, *Nanna Ditzel* in *Store danske designere* (Copenhagen: Lindhardt & Ringhof, 2008), 565.

3. Ibid., 566.

4. *Scandinavian Modern Design: 1880–1980*, ed. by David Revere McFadden (New York: Harry Abrams, 1982), 166. No author listed for captions.

5. Penny Sparke, 'Danish Modern Design Revisited' (podcast audio). Podcast Chart [http://www.podcastchart.com/podcasts/moma-talks-conversations/episodes/modern-danish-design-revisited; accessed 30 March 2015].

6. George Nelson, *Problems of Design* (New York: Whitney Publications, 1957), 9.

7. Interview. Massimo Vignelli, 'The Art of Timeless Design,' Big Think [http://bigthink.com/videos/the-art-of-timeless-design; accessed 24 March 2015].

8. See Jerry Palmer, 'Need and Function: The Terms of the Debate,' in *Design and Aesthetics: A Reader*, ed. Palmer and M. Dodson (London: Routledge, 1996), 110–22.

9. Quoted in Jens Bernsen, *Hans J Wegner om Design* (Copenhagen: Dansk Design Center, 1994), 12.

10. Ibid.

11. Quoted in Kevin Davies, 'Markets, Marketing and Design,' *Scandinavian Journal of Design History* 9 (1999), 56–73.

12. Ibid.

13. Thank you to Christian Holmsted Olesen for a conversation about Wegner and colour.

14. Quoted in Bernsen, *Hans J Wegner om Design*, 22.

15. Cara Greenberg, *Mid-Century Modern: Furniture of the 1950s* (New York: Harmony Books, 1995), 12.

16. Ibid., 125.

17. Johnson, 'Form Follows Emotion,' in *Scandinavian Design: Beyond the Myth*, ed. W. Halén and K. Wickman (Stockholm: Arvinius Förlag, 2003), 137.

18. Nina Kragh, 'Dansk Design slidt i betrækket,' *Politiken* (20 January 2002) [http://politiken.dk/oekonomi/ECE24129/dansk-design-slidt-i-betraekket/; accessed 11 March 2015].

19. Ibid.

20. Per H. Hansen, *Da danske møbler blev moderne. Historien om dansk møbeldesigns storhedstid* (Odense: Syddansk Universitetsforlag/Copenhagen: Aschehoug, 2006), 571.

21. Sparke, 'Danish Modern Design Revisited.'

22. Salicath, 'Grete Jalks møbeleksperimenter,' *Dansk Kunsthaandværk*, 36(3/4) (1963), 70.

23. Ibid., 72.

24. Ibid., 72.

25. 'Nanna Ditzel talks about the Trinidad Chair by Fredericia Furniture' (2005) [https://www.youtube.com/watch?v=-mnE5zBd77k; accessed 3: April 2015].

26. See http://www.louisecampbell.com/#cutlery [accessed 31 March 2015].

27. James Buresh, 'T.H. Robsjohn-Gibbings: Timeless Mid-Century Modern Design,' *Archives of American Art Journal*, 48(1/2) (2009), 30–45.

28. Ibid., 32.

29. John Heskett, *Design: A Very Short Introduction* (New York: Oxford University Press, 2002), 50.

11 Conclusion: Danish (Meta)Modern

In the 2015 exhibition 'MetaModern,' which originated at the Krannert Art Museum of the University of Illinois in Champaign, a selection of artists employed elements from mid-century modern designs in original works offering visual commentary on modernist contentions and normative concepts. In the multimedia exhibited objects, furniture designs by such stalwarts as Mies van der Rohe, Charles and Ray Eames, and Verner Panton were reconfigured, repurposed, damaged, severed into parts, enveloped in other materials, and often juxtaposed with less revered examples of designed utilitarian goods. The notion that modern designs are pristine or timeless was upended, for example, in Conrad Bakker's *Untitled Project: eBay [Ding]* (2014), a series of nine oil paintings on wood depicting nicked or damaged designs as close-up photos appearing on eBay. Some pieces seemed trapped in a postmodernist paradigm: Barbra Visser's *Detitled* (2000), which consisted of a group of carousel displays with postcards depicting glossy images of slashed and broken modernist furniture designs, exuded anger at the modernist yearning for purity of form.

Cultures clash in Olga Koumoundouros's *Triumph over Survival* (2010), in which an Eames Lounge chair is separated from its base by a stack of lit Himalayan salt lamps, its ottoman functioning as a kneeler before the god-like chair. Writing about Koumoundouros's reconfiguration in the exhibition catalogue, Ginger Gregg Duggan and Judith Hoos Fox observe: 'Ironically, the ancient lamps are currently a New Age craze, and the Eames furniture is distinctly a relic of the past.'[1] Yet, relics are relegated to museums, memory, and lost belief systems; the Eames Lounge, still in use in people's homes and commercial settings, has never gone out of production since its premiere in 1956. To call it a 'relic of the past' implies that the chair's only meaning is nostalgic: the modernist ideology held by the Eameses at the time of its inception, the 1950s. In this view, all products of Modernism have somehow lost relevance – the mistake of locating the designed object only in the environment of its temporal creation – whereas Koumoundouros's playful totemic structure functions much more as an example of visual engagement between cultures and a commentary on projected beliefs about objects.

In Brian Jungen's *My Decoy* (2010), the shells of two Panton Cone chairs have been repurposed into drum-like shapes with elk hide and tarred twine stretched across them (Fig. 11.1). Such accretions add layers of cultural specificity (Jungen is part Dane-zaa) that resist the modernist yearning for universalist designs; Jungen has executed similar renderings of the Eames moulded chairs and Saarinen's Womb

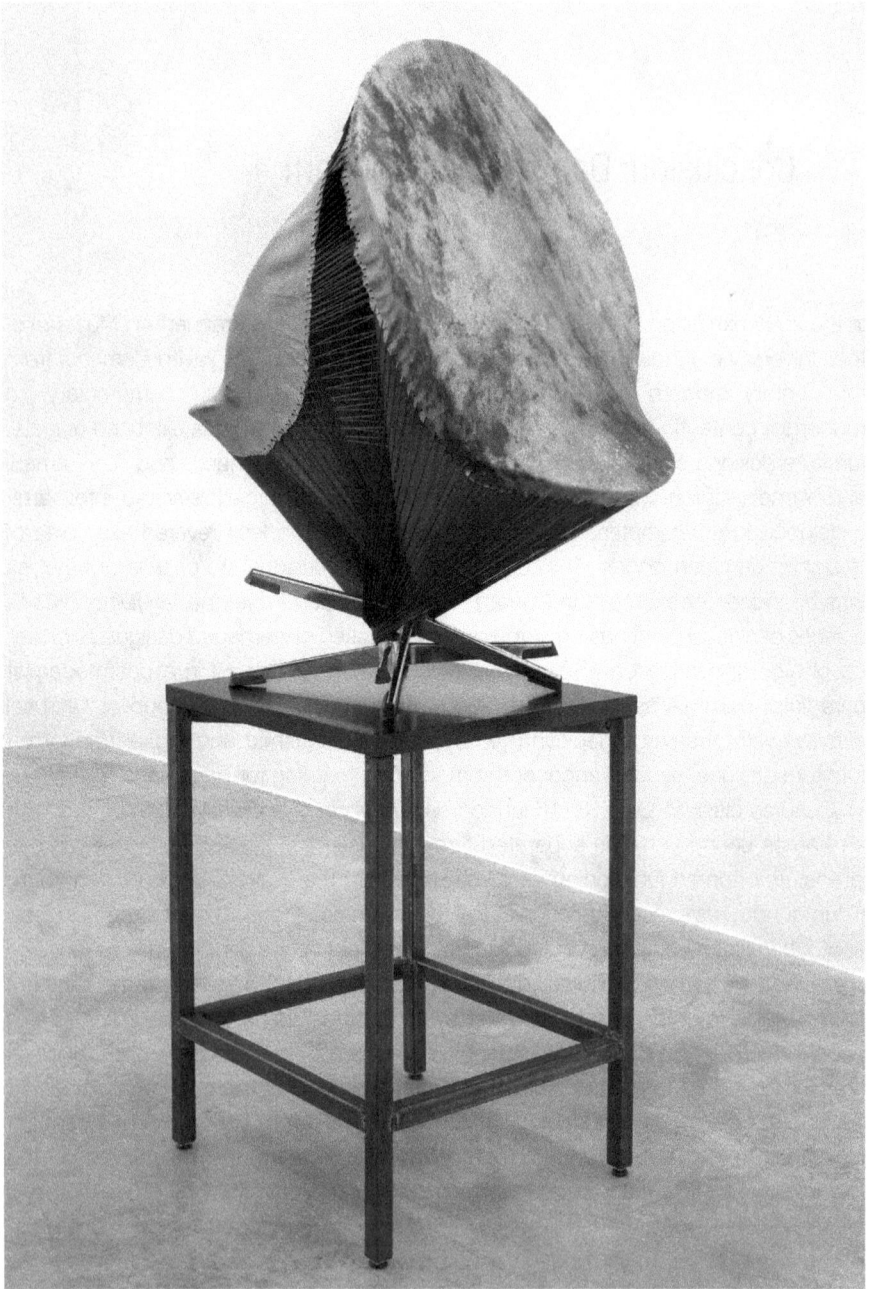

Fig. 11.1 In Brian Jungen's *My Decoy* (2011), included in the MetaModern exhibition of 2015, two of Verner Panton's Cone chairs (1958) serve as the foundation for a reconfiguration as traditional Dane-zaa drums covered in American elk hide and tarred twine. Photo by Cathy Carver, courtesy of the artist; Casey Kaplan, New York; and Sam and Sylvia Ketcham

Chair. The organic nature of these modernist designs serves Jungen well, as in the case of *My Decoy*, in which he employs the conical nature of Panton's design with stretched natural elk skin and, concurrently, reimagines the respected modernist design by undoing any purity of form or resistance to ornamentation while maintaining a utilitarian purpose, albeit a different one than sitting.

In 'Notes on metamodernism,' Timotheus Vermeulen and Robin van den Akker defined the metamodernist approach as one of negotiating between Modern and Postmodern positions, of both commitment and detachment, and one that offers a more productive step beyond Postmodernism than a nebulous notion of post-Postmodernism: 'It oscillates between a modern enthusiasm and a postmodern irony, between hope and melancholy, between naïveté and knowingness, empathy and apathy, unity and plurality, totality and fragmentation, purity and ambiguity.'[2] This quality surfaces frequently in the art on display in the MetaModern exhibition: the unity and purity of many of the original Modern designs have been undercut by cultural plurality and, at times, ironic articulation, but it is not a deconstruction for its own sake or a dystopic articulation. While not embracing or resurrecting the normative claims of Modernism, of pure functionalism or obeisance to reason, Metamodernism still rejects apathy or a cancelling out of any purpose or desire: 'both metamodernism and the postmodern turn to pluralism, irony, and deconstruction in order to counter a modernist fanaticism. However, in metamodernism this pluralism and irony are utilized to counter the modern aspiration, while in postmodernism they are employed to cancel it out.'[3] Vermeulen and van den Akker see this movement towards a metamodernist position as one of pragmatic idealism, of believing in an impossible possibility, a seeking for an irretrievable truth, and a desire for atemporality (the latter a marked trait of various modernist thinkers).

The architects of Danish Modern design were less inclined to an approach anyone might deem 'fanaticism.' This does not imply that their designs, work habits, or ideological tendencies were in any way inherently tentative or intentionally evasive. Henningsen's essays are sardonic, pointed, determined, and persuasive, but many of his arguments are not fanatical: design-wise, this is the very reason he dismissed both an embrace of neoclassicism and an unthinking fealty to any forced modern aesthetic. Oscillation exists in a number of his arguments, evident in the earlier discussion of his essay 'Tradition and Modernism,' and his sense of irony is not only present but at times aggressive. In the 1920s, his response to modernist currents is already variegated, adhering only to a pragmatic sense of addressing the task at hand, even, as delineated in Chapter 2, dismissing what he saw as a fanatical adherence to using a specific material because it is considered 'modern' or 'objective,' such as tubular steel by certain Bauhaus designers. The paradoxicality of his calls for time-stamped solutions that will solve problems beyond their own time also presages the metamodernist yearning. Many of Henningsen's arguments reveal a similar dialectic with and resistance to other modernist contentions, such as the machine aesthetic and *die neue Sachlichkeit*; in addition, the repeated attempt by a number of designers to craft or express a 'Danish' response also indicates a resistance to banishing cultural specificity or accepting universalist tenets. Even in Klint's designs and hyper-mathematical approach, one finds vacillation between retaining some historical style (which would re-emerge in postmodernist executions) and addressing modernist concerns about unity of form and truth to materials. For most of the other Danish mid-twentieth-century designers, no utopian notion hovers over their designs; they were on the whole not bound to purist geometric abstractions (except for those surfacing in modernist textiles). Their demarcation between functionalism and *funkis* illustrates yet another oscillation.

Just as Metamodernism involves a dialogue with modern aspirations rather than, as Vermeulen and van den Akker note, a cancelling out, the early Danish modernists worked in dialogue with the currents of Modernism emanating from Germany while dismissing most of the theoretical weight. For a designer such as Wegner, construction replaced ideology as the driving force of form, a possible reason for his designs remaining in production across decades through stylistic and ideological changes. His embrace and reworking of elements from the historical Windsor Chair offer another example of oscillation between Modernism and Historicism. Juhl preferred abstract sculpture as an inspiration, not utopian dreams, reason, or measurement as ultimate solutions, and Ditzel felt no urge to resist historical precedents or timely expressions. Still, many Danish modern designers struggled against what they viewed as vapid styling, and any precursor of the apathy of the postmodern response is nowhere to be found (although playfulness already rears its head in a number of designs). Also, the paring down of ornament and the striving for one unified form remain modernist endeavours.

In his 1999 essay, 'The Legacy of Modernism,' Adrian Forty, in a defence of certain modernist goals, points out that the most prominent criticism of Modernism is that in the designers' quest for pure form they repressed 'difference' by emphasizing the way an object was produced. This view of Modernism focuses, as Forty notes, on 'Machine Age or International Style design.'[4] As this book has hopefully illustrated, in both their designs and ideological writings, the majority of Danish modernists were less enamoured of Machine Age aesthetics or functionalism for its own sake; the predominance of organic forms also pushes against the rectilinear nature of most of the International Style (a juxtaposition Jacobsen exploited in the SAS Hotel and its curvilinear contents). When Forty illustrates his article with Breuer's tubular-steel and leather-strap Wassily Chair (1925), photographed in Gropius's house in Dessau, he makes the same point that Henningsen had already made some seventy years earlier in *Kritisk Revy* with the same visual example: the chair reflects a self-conscious adherence to an imposed modernist aesthetic instead of addressing its task. 'Once a product is made in large quantities for unknown people,' Forty observes, 'we have to make some judgments about the quality of the object before it reaches the market.'[5] Although Forty also dismisses the broader social efforts of many modernists as mostly an 'illusion,' he admits that 'design can make *some* improvements in our lives.'[6] Many Danish Modern designs have resisted the superimposed weight of any social improvement because their forms offer no allusion to any singular ideological basis or broad social project (or an allusion that has long since been excised or lost in marketing and reception). A number of the designs have survived or been resurrected because, unlike some other modernist designs, they no longer convey any mythical notions about pure form, the 'true' mode, or the ethical advantage of de-ornamentation.

As a concept, the term 'Danish Modern' continues to describe a historical phenomenon, a style with variegated meanings, a broad and sometimes nebulous brand, a nostalgic yearning for the mid-twentieth century, a perceived 'Nordic' sense of taste and craftsmanship, and mostly what it began as and will probably always be: a collection of designed objects bearing the stamp of various designers, ideologies, and approaches while superseding all of them in an ongoing and ever-changing reception.

Notes

1. Ginger Gregg Duggan and Judith Hoos Fox, 'Narrative Composites,' in *MetaModern*, Catalogue (Urbana-Champagne, IL: Krannert Art Museum and Kinkead Pavilion, 2015), 15–24.
2. Timotheus Vermeulen and Robin van den Akker, 'Notes on Metamodernism,' *Journal of Aesthetics & Culture*, 2 (2010) [http://www.aestheticsandculture.net/index.php/jac/article/view/5677/6304; accessed 16 June 2015].
3. Ibid.
4. Adrian Forty, 'The Legacy of Modernism,' *Design Quarterly*, 153 (Autumn 1991), 27–31.
5. Ibid., 27.
6. Ibid., 31.

Select Bibliography

Adams, Nicholas. *Gunnar Asplund's Gothenburg: The Transformation of Public Architecture in Interwar Europe*. University Park, PA: Pennsylvania State University Press, 2014.

Albers, Anni. *On Weaving*. Middletown, CT: Wesleyan University Press, 1965.

Albers, Anni. *On Designing*. Middletown, CT: Wesleyan University Press, 1971.

Alifrangis, Inge. *Vibeke Klint: The Weaver*, trans. Hanne Ejsing Jørgensen. Copenhagen: Rhodos, 1997.

Andersen, Rigmor. *Kaare Klint Møbler*. Copenhagen: Kunstakademiet, 1979.

Andersen, Troels. *Sonja Ferlov Mancoba*. Copenhagen: Borgen, 1979.

Arnheim, Rudolf. 'The Dynamics of Shape,' *Design Quarterly*, 64 (1966), 1–31.

Banham, Reyner. *Theory and Design in the First Machine Age*. London: MIT Press, 1980.

Batchelor, David. *Chromophobia*. London: Reaktion Books, 2000.

Bay, Carl-Erik, and Olav Harsløf, eds. *Kulturkritik I*. Copenhagen: Rhodos, 1973.

Bay, Carl-Erik, and Hans-Christian Jensen, eds. *Tradition og Modernisme: infaldsvinkler til PH*. Odense: Syddansk Universitetsforlag, 2008.

Berger, Barbara. 'Hans J Wegner- Master of Wood,' *Design Directions* (1998), 11–15.

Bernsen, Jens. *Hans J Wegner om Design*. Copenhagen: Dansk Design Center, 1994.

Bill, Max. *Form, Function, Beauty = Gestalt*, trans. Pamela Johnston. London: AA Publications, 2010.

Booth, Harry. 'A Travel Report on Design in Scandinavia,' *Journal of the Royal Society of Arts*, (96)4767 (1948), 311–16.

Bucciarelli, Louis. *Designing Engineers*. Boston, MA: MIT Press, 1994.

Buchanan, Richard. 'Rhetoric, Humanism, and Design,' *Discovering Design: Explorations in Design Studies*. Chicago, IL: University of Chicago Press, 1995, 23–66.

Buresh, James. 'T.H. Robsjohn-Gibbings: Timeless Mid-Century Modern Design,' *Archives of American Art Journal*, 48(1/2) (2009), 30–45.

Byerly, Florence. 'Scandinavia,' *Better Homes and Gardens*, 36(5) (1958), 58–61.

Cavallaro, Dani. *Synesthesia and the Arts*. Jefferson, NC: McFarland, 2013.

Clemens, J. 'Neon Statements. Joseph Kosuth and Conceptual Art,' *The Monthly*, 52 (December 2009/January 2010).

Cohen, Jean-Louis. *Le Corbusier*. Köln: Taschen, 2006.

Cranz, Galen. *The Chair: Rethinking Culture, Body and Design*. New York: W.W. Norton, 1998.

Creagh, Lucy, Helena Kåberg and Barbara Miller Lane, eds. *Modern Swedish Design: Three Founding Texts*. New York: Museum of Modern Art, 2008.

Danto, Arthur C. 'The Seat of the Soul: Three Chairs,' *Philosophizing Art: Selected Essays*. Berkeley, CA: University of California Press, 1999, 144–63.

Davies, Kevin. 'Markets, Marketing and Design: The Danish Furniture Industry,' *Scandinavian Journal of Design History*, 9 (1999), 56–73.

de Gier, Nicholas, and Stine Liv Buur. *Chairs' Tectonics*. Copenhagen: Royal Danish Academy of Fine Arts School of Architecture Publications, 2009.

Dickson, Thomas. *Dansk Design*. Copenhagen: Gyldendal, 2006.

Dilnot, Clive. 'The State of Design History, Part I: Mapping the Field,' *Design Issues*, 1(1) (1984), 4–23.

Dilnot, Clive. 'The State of Design History, Part II: Problems and Possibilities,' *Design Issues*, 1(2) (Autumn 1984), 3–20.

Dormer, Peter. *Design Since 1945*. London: Thames & Hudson, 1993.

Dybdahl, Lars. 'Hele daglivets indhold. PHs design og designkritik,' *Poul Henningsen – dengang og nu. Lysmageren i et nyt lys*, ed. Hans Hertel. Copenhagen: Gyldendal, 2010, 65–84.

Engholm, Ida. *Verner Panton* in *Store danske desingere*. Copenhagen: Lindhardt og Ringhof, 2008.

Eskilson, Stephen J. *Graphic Design: A New History* (2nd edn.). New Haven, CT: Yale University Press, 2012 (first published 2007).

Fallan, Kjetil. 'How an Excavator Got Aesthetic Pretensions – Negotiating Design in 1960s Norway,' *Journal of Design History*, 20(1) (2007), 43–59.

Fallan, Kjetil. *Design History: Understanding Theory and Method*. Oxford: Berg, 2010.

Fallan, Kjetil, ed. *Scandinavian Design: Alternative Histories*. Oxford: Berg, 2012.

Fiell, Charlotte, and Peter Fiell. *Design of the 20th Century*. Köln: Taschen, 1999.

Folkmann, Mads Nygaard. *The Aesthetics of Imagination in Design*. Cambridge, MA: MIT Press, 2013.

Forty, Adrian. *Objects of Desire: Design & Society from Wedgwood to IBM*. New York: Pantheon Books, 1986.

Forty, Adrian. 'The Legacy of Modernism,' *Design Quarterly*, 153 (Autumn 1991), 27–31.

Gage, Mark Foster, ed. *Aesthetic Theory: Essential Texts for Architecture and Design*. New York: W.W. Norton, 2011.

Gordon, Elizabeth. 'The Threat to the Next America,' *House Beautiful*, 95 (April 1953), 126–29.

Gorman, Carma, ed. *The Industrial Design Reader*. New York: Allworth, 2003.

Greenberg, Cara. *Mid-Century Modern: Furniture of the 1950s*. New York: Harmony Books, 1995 (first published 1984).

Greenhalgh, Paul, ed. *Modernism in Design*. London: Reaktion Books, 1990.

Gropius, Walter. *The New Architecture and the Bauhaus*. Cambridge, MA: MIT Press, 1965.

Guldberg, Jørn. 'Den nye tids former: PH om den kunstneriske produktions historiske karakter,' in *Tradition og Modernisme: Indfaldsvinkler til PH*. Odense: Syddansk Universitetsforlag, 2008.

Guldberg, Jørn. '"Scandinavian Design" as Discourse: The Exhibition *Design in Scandinavia*, 1954–57,' *Design Issues*, 27(2) (2011), 41–58.

Halén, Wider, and Kerstin Wickman, eds. *Scandinavian Design Beyond the Myth: Fifty Years of Design from the Nordic Countries*. Stockholm: Arvinius Forlag, 2003.

Hansen, Per H. *Da danske møbler blev moderne. Historien om dansk møbeldesigns storhedstid*. Odense: Syddansk Universitetsforlag/Copenhagen: Aschehoug, 2006.

Hansen, Per H. *Finn Juhl and His House*, trans. Mark Mussari. Copenhagen: Strandberg Publishing, 2014.

Harkær, Goram. *Kaare Klint*, Vols. 1 and 2. Copenhagen: Klintiana, 2010.

Harlang, Christoffer, Keld Helmer-Petersen and Krestine Kjærholm, eds. *Poul Kjærholm*. Copenhagen: Arkitektens Forlag, 1999.

Hartmann-Petersen, Jørgen. 'Om at begrænse sig. Rullebords-samtale mellem tre af pionererne i dansk kunst håndværk,' *Politiken* (29 March 1964), 29.

Henningsen, Poul. *Kulturkritik I–IV*. Copenhagen: Rhodos, 1979 (first published 1973).

Hertel, Hans. *PH-En biografi*. Copenhagen: Gyldendal, 2012.

Heskett, John. *Design: A Very Short Introduction*. New York: Oxford University Press, 2002.

Horsfeld, Hanne. *Nanna Ditzel* in *Store danske designere*. Copenhagen: Lindhardt & Ringhof, 2008.

Ihde, Don. *Experimental Phenomenology: Multistabilities*. Albany, NY: SUNY Press, 2012.

Jacobsen, Egill. 'Salighed og Mystik,' in Per Hovdenakk, *Dansk kunst 1930–50*. Copenhagen: Borgen, 1999, 138–44.

Jespersen, Gunnar. *De abstrakte. Linien. Helhesten. Høstudstillingen. Cobra*. Copenhagen: Berkingske Forlag, 1967.

Johnson, Ken. 'Close Encounters with Tableness and Chairness,' *New York Times* (11 June 2009).

Johnson, Ken. 'Sculpture that Asks You to Sit a Spell,' *New York Times* (19 August 2008).

Judd, Donald. 'It's Hard to Find a Good Lamp,' Judd Foundation [http://www.juddfoundation.org/; accessed 1 March 2015].

Judd, Donald. 'Specific Objects,' Judd Foundation [http://www.juddfoundation.org/; accessed 26 February 2015].

Juhl, Finn. 'Fortid-nutid-fremtid,' *Dansk kunsthaandværk*, 22 (4) (1949), 56–60.

Juhl, Finn. 'Mellem to stole,' *Dansk kunsthaandværk*, 25 (7) (1952), 5–10.

Jürgensen, Andreas, Folke Kjems, Karsten Ohrt, and Lars Kærulf Møller, eds. *Billedhuggeren Erik Thommesen: The Sculptor*, trans. Dan Marmorstein. Holstebro: Holstebro Kunstmuseum, 2001.

Kaplan, Wendy, ed. *Living in a Modern Way: California Design 1930–1965*. Cambridge, MA: MIT Press, 2011.

Karlsen, Arne. 'Tre Pionerer. Dansk tekstilkunst i midten af det 20. århundrede,' in *I tråd med tiden. Stoftrykker- og Væverlaugets 50 års jubilæumsudstilling*. Copenhagen: SKANDIA-Grafik, 1996.

Karlsen, Arne. *Danish Furniture Design in the 20th Century*. Copenhagen: Christian Ejlers Forlag, 2007.

Karlsen, Arne, Bent Salicath and Mogens Utzon-Frank, eds. *Contemporary Danish Design*, trans. Birthe Andersen. Copenhagen: Danish Society of Arts and Crafts and Industrial Design, 1960.

Kaufmann, Jr., Edgar. *What is Modern Design?* Introductory Series to the Modern Arts 3. New York: Museum of Modern Art, 1950.

Kaufmann, Jr., Edgar. *What is Modern Interior Design?* Introductory Series to the Modern Arts 4. New York: Museum of Modern Art, 1953.

Kaufmann, Jr., Edgar. 'Scandinavian Design in the U.S.A.,' *Interiors* (May 1954), 108–14, 182–8.

Klint, Kaare. 'Undervisning i Møbeltegning ved Kunstakadamiet,' *Architektens Maanedshæfte* (October 1930), 193–224.

Knox, Sanka. 'Long-Awaited Museum Show Opens,' *New York Times* (15 October 1960).

Koch, Mogens. *Moderne dansk kunsthaandværk*. Copenhagen: Thanning & Appels, 1948.

Koch, Mogens, ed. *Børge Mogensen møbler = Lis Ahlmann textiler*. Catalogue. Copenhagen: Det danske Kunstindustrimuseum, 1974.

Kragh, Nina. 'Dansk Design slidt i betrækket,' *Politiken* (20 January 2002) [http://politiken. dk/oekonomi/ECE24129/dansk-design-slidt-i-betraekket/; accessed 11 March 2015].

Kristensen, Sven Møller, ed. *Kritisk Revy. En antologi af tekster og illustrationer fra tidsskriftets tre årgange*. Copenhagen: Gyldendal, 1963.

Lassen, Erik, ed. *The Arts of Denmark: Viking to Modern*. Catalogue. Copenhagen: Det Berlingske Bogtrykkeri, 1960.

Le Corbusier. *Towards a New Architecture*. Thousand Oaks, CA: BN Publishing, 2008.

Lees-Maffei, Grace, ed. *Writing Design: Words and Objects*. Oxford: Berg, 2012.

Long, Rose-Carol Washton, ed. *German Expressionism: Documents from the End of the Wilhelmine Empire to the Rise of National Socialism*. Berkeley, CA: University of California Press, 1993.

Marzona, Daniel. *Minimal Art*. Cologne: Taschen, 2004.

McFadden, David Revere, ed. *Scandinavian Modern Design: 1880–1980*. New York: Harry Abrams, 1982.

McFate, Patricia. 'The Art of Simplicity: An Interview with Vibeke Klint,' *Scandinavian Review*, 71(3) (1983), 31.

Meikle, Jeffrey L. 'Writing about Stuff: The Peril and Promise of Design History and Criticism,' *Writing Design: Words and Objects*, ed. Grace Lees-Maffei. Oxford: Berg, 2012.

Meyer, James. *Minimalism: Art & Polemics in the Sixties*. New Haven, CT: Yale University Press, 2004.

Miller, William C. 'Furniture, Painting, and Applied Designs: Alvar Aalto's Search for Architectural Form,' *Journal of Decorative and Propaganda Arts*, 6 (Autumn 1987), 6–25.

Mogensen, Thomas. *Et fuldt møbleret liv. En bog om Børge Mogensen*. Copenhagen: Gyldendal, 2004.

Møller, Viggo Sten. *Funktionalisme og brugskunst siden 1920erne. Danmark. Norge. Sverige*. Copenhagen: Rhodos, 1978.

Mumford, Lewis. *Technics and Civilization* (reprint edition). Chicago, IL: University of Chicago Press, 2010 (first published 1934).

Murphy, Keith M. *Swedish Design: An Ethnography*. Ithaca, NY: Cornell University Press, 2015.

Nelson, George. *Chairs*. Interiors Library 2. New York: Whitney Publications, 1953.

Nelson, George. *Problems of Design*. New York: Whitney Publications, 1965 (first published 1957).

Nelson, George, and Henry Wright. *Tomorrow's House: How to Plan Your Post-War Home*. New York: Simon & Schuster, 1945.

Nodelman, Sheldon. 'Sixties Art: Some Philosophical Perspectives,' *Perspecta*, 2 (1967), 73–89.

Norberg-Schulz, Christian. *Nightlands. Nordic Building*. Cambridge, MA: MIT Press, 1996.

Nørregaard-Nielsen, Hans Edvard. *Dansk Kunst 1*. Copenhagen: Gyldendal, 1983.

Nyberg, Folke. 'From *Baukunst* to Bauhaus,' *Journal of Architectural Education*, 45 (3) (1992), 130–37.

Oda, Noritsuga. *Danish Chairs*, trans. Patricia Yamada. Tokyo: World Photo Press, 1999.

Olesen, Christian Holmsted. *Wegner: Just One Good Chair*, trans. Mark Mussari. Ostfildern, Germany: Hatje Cantz, 2014.

Pallasmaa, Juhani, ed. *Alvar Aalto Furniture*. Cambridge, MA: MIT Press, 1985.

Palmer, Jerry. 'Need and Function: The Terms of the Debate,' *Design and Aesthetics: A Reader*, ed. J. Palmer and M. Dodson. London: Routledge, 1996.

Paludan, Charlotte. *Stoftrykkeren Marie Gudme Leth*. Copenhagen: Rhodos, 1995.

Panton, Verner. *Lid tom Farver/Notes on Color*, trans. Margaret Malone and Dorte Herholdt Silver. Copenhagen: Danish Design Center, 1997.

Paulsson, Gregor. *Vackrare vardagsvara*. Stockholm: Svenska slStockholm: Sve 1919.

Pørn, Neel. *PHs Arkitekturkritik*. Copenhagen: Arkitektens Forlag, 1994.

Rasmussen, Steen Eiler. 'Modern Danish Design,' *Journal of the Royal Society of the Arts*, 96(4761) (1948), 141–42.

Raoul, Rosine. 'The Danish Tradition in Design,' *Metropolitan Museum of Art Bulletin*, 19(4) (1960), 119–23.

Ray, Shirley. 'Danish Furniture Display New Here,' *Long Beach Independent* (7 December 1961), 86.

Read, Herbert. *Art and Industry: The Principles of Industrial Design*. New York: Horizon Press, 1961 (first published 1934).

Reif, Rita. 'Modern Danish Furniture Inspired by a Chinese Copy,' *New York Times* (5 May 1965).

Reitveld, Gerrit. 'Poul Kjærholm-udstillingen i Amsterdam,' *Dansk Kunsthaandværk*, 36(3/4) (1963), 72–76.

Reyburn, Scott. 'European Fine Art Fair Showcases Shaker Furniture,' *New York Times* (12 March 2015).

Robsjohn-Gibbings, T.H. *Home of the Brave*. New York: Alfred A. Knopf, 1954

Robsjohn-Gibbings, T.H. *Good-bye, Mr. Chippendale*. New York: Alfred Knopf, 1944.

Rush, Fred. *On Architecture*. New York: Routledge 2009.

Salicath, Bent. 'Grete Jalks møbeleksperimenter,' *Dansk Kunsthaandværk*, 36(3/4) (1963), 70–72.

Salicath, Bent, and Arne Karlsen, eds. *Modern Danish Textiles*, trans. Birthe Andersen. Copenhagen: Danish Society of Arts and Crafts and Industrial Design, 1959.

Schachtel, Ernest G. 'On Color and Affect,' *Psychiatry*, 6 (1943), 393–409.

Schulz, Sigurd. 'The Jubilee Exhibition of Danish Cabinet-Makers,' *Dansk kunsthaandværk*, 27(10/11) (1954), 150–53.

Segerstad, Ulf Hård af. *Scandinavian Design*, trans. Nancy and Edward Maze. Stockholm: Nordisk Rotogravyr, 1961.

Segerstad, Ulf Hård af. *Scandinavian Design*. New York: Lyle Stuart, 1961.

Sheridan, Michael. *Room 606. The SAS House and the Work of Arne Jacobsen*. London: Phaidon, 2003.

Simon, Herbert. *The Sciences of the Artificial* (3rd edn.). Cambridge, MA: MIT Press, 1996.

Skriver, Poul Erik. 'Royal Hotel, København,' *Arkitektur*, 4(6) (1960), 209–48.

Smith, Roberta. 'Art in Review: Ole Wanscher – "Danish Modern Master Furniture,"' *New York Times* (3 October 2003).

Smith, Roberta. 'Designers for a Day: Sculptors Take a Turn,' *New York Times* (9 October 2004).

Smith, Roberta. 'The Ordinary as Object of Desire,' *New York Times* (4 June 2009).

Smith, T'ai. *Bauhaus Weaving Theory: From Feminine Craft to Mode of Design.* Minneapolis, MN: University of Minnesota Press, 2014.

Sonne, Kristine Irminger. 'Træets kvindelige mester,' *Berlingske Tidende* (12 October 2008).

Sparke, Penny. *The Genius of Design.* London: Quadrille Publishing, 2009.

Sparke, Penny. 'Danish Modern Design Revisited' (podcast audio). Podcast Chart [http://www.podcastchart.com/podcasts/moma-talks-conversations/episodes/modern-danish-design-revisited; accessed 30 March 2015].

Stiles, Kristine, and Peter Selz, eds. *Theories and Documents of Contemporary Art: A Sourcebook of Artists' Writings.* Berkeley, CA: University of California Press, 1996.

Strickland, Edward. *Minimalism: Origins.* Bloomington, IN: Indiana University Press, 1993.

Tesfaye, Mathias. *Kloge hænder – et forsvar for håndværk og faglighed.* Copenhagen: Gyldendal, 2013.

Thau, Carsten, and Kjeld Vindum. *Arne Jacobsen.* Copenhagen: Arkitektens Forlag, 1998.

Tøjner, Poul Erik, and Anne Frovin, eds. *Store Danske Designere.* Copenhagen: Lindhardt og Ringhof, 2008.

Tøjner, Poul Erik, and Kjeld Vindum. *Arne Jacobsen – Arkitekt & Designer.* Copenhagen: Dansk Design Center, 1999.

Tregidden, Katie. 'Inside Scandinavian Design at the Stockholm Furniture Fair,' *Design Milk* (25 February 2015).

Vermeulen, Timotheus, and Robin van den Akker. 'Notes on Metamodernism,' *Journal of Aesthetics & Culture*, 2 (2010).

von Vegesack, Alexander, and Mathias Remmele, eds. *Verner Panton: The Collected Works.* Weil am Rhein: Vitra Design Museum, 2000.

Waldman, Diane. *Kenneth Noland: A Retrospective.* New York: Solomon R. Guggenheim Museum, 1977.

Weston, Richard. *Modernism.* London: Phaidon, 1996.

Whiteman, John. 'On Hegel's Definition of Architecture,' *Assemblage*, 2 (February 1987), 6–17.

Wildhagen, Fredrik. *Norge i form.* Oslo: Stenersen, 1988.

Wittgenstein, Ludwig. *Philosophical Investigations* (3rd edn.), trans. G.E.M. Anscombe. New York: Macmillan, 1992.

Woodham, Jonathan M. *Twentieth-Century Design.* Oxford: Oxford University Press, 1997.

Zahle, Erik, ed. *Hjemmets Brugskunst. Kunsthåndværk og Kunstindustri i Norden.* Copenhagen: Hassings, 1961 (translated as *A Treasury of Scandinavian Design.* New York: Golden Press, 1961).

Index